Scaling Cloud FinOps

Proven Strategies to Accelerate Financial Success

Sasi Kanumuri
Matthew Zeier

Apress®

Scaling Cloud FinOps: Proven Strategies to Accelerate Financial Success

Sasi Kanumuri
Maple Valley, WA, USA

Matthew Zeier
Dublin, CA, USA

ISBN-13 (pbk): 979-8-8688-0387-1
https://doi.org/10.1007/979-8-8688-0388-8

ISBN-13 (electronic): 979-8-8688-0388-8

Managing Director, Apress Media LLC: Welmoed Spahr
Acquisitions Editor: Shaul Elson
Development Editor: Laura Berendson
Coordinating Editor: Gryffin Winkler
Copy Editor: William McManus

Cover designed by eStudioCalamar

Distributed to the book trade worldwide by Apress Media, LLC, 1 New York Plaza, New York, NY 10004, U.S.A. Phone 1-800-SPRINGER, fax (201) 348-4505, e-mail orders-ny@springer-sbm.com, or visit www. springeronline.com. Apress Media, LLC is a California LLC and the sole member (owner) is Springer Science + Business Media Finance Inc (SSBM Finance Inc). SSBM Finance Inc is a **Delaware** corporation.

For information on translations, please e-mail booktranslations@springernature.com; for reprint, paperback, or audio rights, please e-mail bookpermissions@springernature.com.

Apress titles may be purchased in bulk for academic, corporate, or promotional use. eBook versions and licenses are also available for most titles. For more information, reference our Print and eBook Bulk Sales web page at http://www.apress.com/bulk-sales.

Any source code or other supplementary material referenced by the author in this book is available to readers on GitHub (https://github.com/Apress). For more detailed information, please visit https://www.apress.com/gp/services/source-code.

If disposing of this product, please recycle the paper

To Mom, Sujatha, my inspiration.
You taught me to dream big and strive with determination.
Everything I've achieved, I owe to you.
This book is for you.

~Sasi

To my father, Steven, to whom I am eternally grateful
for helping shape who I am today.
Had he stopped me from digging in the neighbor's trash, I'd have never
found my first computer magazine, picked up BASIC programming,
taken programming classes as a 4th grader, or found my way to Silicon
Valley at the Internet's infancy.

~Matthew

Table of Contents

About the Authors

Sasi Kanumuri is a renowned cloud strategy and FinOps/cloud economics expert known for his innovative frameworks and diverse skill set. With a deep understanding of cloud architecture and expertise in cloud infrastructure, Sasi specializes in driving high efficiency and optimization across organizations. He has a proven track record of achieving substantial cost savings and leading successful cloud migrations.

Sasi's thought leadership in FinOps has left a lasting impact on the industry. He has led FinOps teams at large companies like Slack and Lacework and at UC Berkeley, shaping the future of cloud efficiency programs and guiding organizations toward significant cost reductions. His expertise in vendor management and deal strategy has resulted in advantageous agreements and solid, long-lasting partnerships.

As a pioneer in cloud economics, Sasi bridges the gap between finance, procurement, operations, and engineering, setting new standards for efficiency programs and redefining industry norms. He continues to be a sought-after leader in the field, committed to customer success and ongoing innovation, empowering organizations to optimize their cloud investments and drive sustainable growth.

Sasi Kanumuri's unique #Piggy-Bank Framework for cost governance is at the core of his approach. This innovative framework gives organizations insights and knowledge to promote cost awareness and meaningful conversations about cloud expenditure.

Additionally, Kanumuri has trained and mentored numerous individuals in the cloud sector. He has a passion for continuous learning and a commitment to professional education. He's led educational sessions, workshops, and internal meetups, sharing expertise and empowering engineering teams to flourish and succeed.

Matthew Zeier is a veteran of supporting and running at-scale production services across some of the largest high-tech companies, including Mozilla, Apple, VMware, and Lacework. Early in his career, he recognized that managing cloud spend should be part of engineering culture and has worked to advocate for efficient cloud usage across organizations.

ABOUT THE AUTHORS

As a former network engineer turned sysadmin turned SRE leader, Matthew can understand cloud usage and architecture across several discreet system components. Using customer happiness as his North Star, he focuses on platform reliability and efficiency as two foundational elements of a FinOps practice. As an engineering leader, Matthew has supported small and large teams (70+) while supporting infrastructure and services with 12x user growth. He has done this while being hyperaware of the economics behind those services.

As an automation fanatic, Matthew coined #BeachOps as a framing device for automation to build for the lazy rather than the busy and to ensure engineers focus on the important over the urgent.

About the Technical Reviewers

Otieno Ododa is a seasoned senior engineering leader specializing in site reliability engineering (SRE), DevOps, and infrastructure engineering in data centers and the cloud. Over his 20 years in Silicon Valley, his deep-rooted passion for engineering excellence has taken him to companies such as Twitch, Patreon, Zeta Global, and Opendoor, where he has built, nurtured, and scaled high-performing platform and infrastructure engineering teams, both domestically and internationally. Before leading teams, Otieno spent years as a site reliability engineer and cloud infrastructure engineer at various companies, including Friendster, Chomp, and Apple, managing data centers and large distributed systems.

Julie Herd has been a marketing leader for over 25 years, beginning in data storage and moving into cloud technologies. Julie is passionate about startups and has worked with pioneers in the cloud and storage industries, delivering innovative solutions built on the latest technologies. Her career has spanned hardware and software, product management, and product marketing, building and mentoring strong teams. Julie has led product and marketing teams at companies such as Harness, NetApp, and BlueArc (acquired by Hitachi Data Systems).

Julie has recently focused on building strong marketing teams that bridge the communication gap between what a product does and why a customer should care. She is a FinOps Certified Practitioner and is excited to continue her journey of helping build strong, scalable FinOps practices.

Acknowledgments

Special thanks to a few fantastic people who kept me going and helped make this book a reality.

First and foremost, my wife and daughter deserve my deepest thanks. Their love and unwavering belief in me made all the difference during this challenging journey.

I want to thank my uncle, Laxmikanth Malladi, who ignited my passion for cloud solutions architecture. Your inspiration continues to shape my path.

I want to thank my friends and family for their encouragement and belief. Their constant support meant the world to me. I appreciate you acknowledging all my accomplishments and being there to support me during difficult times.

I want to thank Deepanshi Mehrotra, the editor/proofreader of this book. Your expertise ensured clarity and professionalism in every sentence, whether editing or proofreading.

Thank you to Mike Fueller for sharing your valuable insights and guidance on crafting a compelling book. Your input proved invaluable in shaping the overall structure and narrative.

I want to thank my brother, Venkata Kanumuri, and my friend Naveen Koppuravuri for additional support and encouragement.

Thanks to Lewis Cowell for letting me use his content in the book.

Thank you to Apress for trusting in me and bringing this book to reality.

Finally, I am grateful to Christina Wheeler, Julie Herd, and Otieno Ododa, who reviewed and provided feedback. Because of your critique, the content is deep and accurate, making this book an invaluable asset to the reader.

To all of you—thank you for believing in me and this project.

—Sasi

Introduction

Imagine that you are building your dream home and have assumed the role of the general contractor. Your overriding concern is to stay within your allocated budget. Through meticulous planning, you have identified all the building materials required to build the house, purchased them upfront, and delivered them to the construction site. You are on-site daily, tracking every brick and board the subcontractors—analogous to organizational departments—pull from the stored materials. This scenario is analogous to the traditional on-premises IT model, where upfront costs are king, and all IT equipment, such as servers, storage devices, and Networking hardware, is purchased and managed in-house. This model often lacks flexibility, as any changes or additions require additional time, effort, and cost. Unlike cloud computing, which offers scalable and on-demand resources, the traditional on-premises model can be rigid and less adaptable to changing needs.

Now, picture building your dream house with a magic "cloud supply store." Instead of purchasing all the materials upfront, you grab what you need, pay as you go, and can easily adjust your plans as requirements change. In this model, subcontractors—analogous to organizational departments—pull materials from the cloud supply store as needed, representing decentralized procurement. Each department can independently manage its resources, scaling up or down based on real-time needs. This flexibility allows for more dynamic and responsive project management, similar to how cloud computing operates. However, with this great power and flexibility comes great responsibility. Without proper oversight and effective governance, costs can spiral out of control, leading to a potentially hefty bill. Therefore, it is crucial to implement strategies and tools to monitor and optimize cloud usage to reap the benefits while controlling expenses.

Before cloud computing became the de facto standard for new application development, applications were developed using on-premises hardware and software. IT costs were considered capital expenses, and centralized IT departments were responsible for procuring and providing compute, networking, and storage resources. All acquisitions were approved by the procurement department before purchase, which made the cost of goods sold (COGS) and R&D expense reporting relatively straightforward for the finance team.

However, with the advent of cloud computing, engineering teams can now access cloud-based compute, networking, and storage resources on demand, allowing them to provision and deprovision cloud resources quickly with a pay-as-you-go model. While this flexibility has greatly increased application development and deployment agility, it also has decentralized procurement outside traditional IT.

As a result, cloud spending has become fragmented, and cost accountability has suffered as finance departments need help understanding their cloud bills. This has increased the need for better cloud cost management (CCM) processes, with multiple organizations striving to create effective and efficient cost management processes.

As someone who has built Cloud FinOps practices from scratch at several large enterprises, I, Sasi Kanumuri, want to help organizations, regardless of their size, build world-class Cloud FinOps teams and avoid pitfalls that can hinder their Cloud FinOps journey. While building and scaling lean FinOps teams, I created a blueprint and road map, the 6-Factor FinOps Formula (presented in Chapter 1), to navigate the complex world of Cloud FinOps. The 6-Factor FinOps Formula expands on the FinOps Framework, developed by the FinOps Foundation, moving beyond theory into practical application.

This book is your one-stop shop for navigating the world of Cloud FinOps, regardless of your role in the cloud ecosystem. This guide will equip you with the knowledge and tools to achieve sustainable cost efficiency in the cloud era, whether you are in any of the following roles:

- Finance professional roles:
  - Financial analysts
  - Finance managers
  - Business partners
- Technical and tech-adjacent roles:
  - Cloud architects and solutions architects
  - Enterprise architects
  - Cloud engineers, platform engineers, and site reliability engineers (SREs)
  - Software engineers

- Technical program managers (TPMs)

- **Executive and leadership role:**

  - Engineering managers

  - Directors/VPs of engineering/finance

  - CTOs, CIOs, COOs, CFOs (CXOs)

  - Other executives who drive cloud initiatives

This book will help you to navigate the cloud's financial landscape and will introduce you to FinOps. It will equip you with the knowledge and tools to leverage the cloud's agility while controlling your costs, preventing your dream house from becoming a financial nightmare. This book will delve deep into the 6-Factor FinOps Formula concepts, providing practical insights, case studies, and actionable strategies to build and scale FinOps practices from the ground up. It also includes a comprehensive framework, the #Piggy-Bank Framework (in Chapter 5), for creating a culture of cloud cost awareness across engineering, finance, and management teams. Throughout the book, you'll embrace the power of Cloud FinOps and unlock the full potential of your cloud investments, maximizing business value for every dollar spent.

CHAPTER 1

Cloud FinOps

The preceding Introduction presented the hypothetical cloud supply store for obtaining materials to build your dream house. Such a store would offer incredible flexibility, however keeping track of all the resources being pulled from the store by subcontractors on an as-needed basis would be overwhelming. You would want your dream home to be a manageable financial burden, right?

This chapter delves into the world of FinOps, your construction project manager for the cloud. Just as a project manager ensures your house is built efficiently and within budget, FinOps helps you navigate the financial aspects of your cloud journey.

In today's rapidly evolving digital landscape, businesses rely on cloud technologies to drive innovation, agility, and scalability. Cloud services offer enhanced scalability, flexibility, and cost-effectiveness compared to traditional on-premises architecture. As organizations embrace the cloud to unlock its vast potential, they encounter a crucial challenge: managing the costs associated with these robust cloud services.

Cloud FinOps is an emerging discipline that seeks to solve the challenge of cloud cost management by creating a set of practices and principles to optimize costs while maintaining operational excellence. This chapter will explore the definition and basic tenets of Cloud FinOps to provide the foundation for the strategies and best practices for building and scaling FinOps covered in the rest of the book.

This chapter lays the foundation for understanding FinOps and why it matters. So get ready to master the financial aspects of your cloud journey and build a cost-effective and sustainable dream house...in the cloud, of course!

Cloud FinOps Defined

In the context of cloud cost management (CCM), the FinOps Foundation defines Cloud FinOps as a portmanteau of "Finance" and "DevOps," representing the intersection of finance, procurement, DevOps (that is, combining development and operations to

1

S. Kanumuri and M. Zeier, *Scaling Cloud FinOps*, https://doi.org/10.1007/979-8-8688-0388-8_1

increase the efficiency, speed, and security of software development and delivery), and engineering to provide a comprehensive framework for efficient cloud cost management.

While the FinOps Foundation offers a comprehensive definition, here's my take on what FinOps truly encompasses: Cloud FinOps is the practice of maximizing business value for every dollar spent in the cloud and cultivating a culture of cost awareness, accountability, and strong collaboration between finance, procurement, and engineering.

The Cloud FinOps methodology gives teams the framework to establish accountability, visibility, and control over cloud costs. Cloud FinOps is a liaison between finance and engineering teams, enabling them to collaborate effectively on cloud resource spending throughout an application's or project's lifecycle. This includes cultivating a culture of cloud cost awareness, establishing cloud usage policies, and leveraging the right tools to maximize cloud resource usage.

By leveraging people, processes, and technology, Cloud FinOps enables organizations to manage cloud costs effectively, allowing them to visualize costs better and make informed decisions to optimize cloud investments.

In some organizations, Cloud FinOps is also referred to as *Cloud Economics*, and the two terms can be used interchangeably when referring to the practice of ensuring strong financial management of cloud computing resources.

We'll also be using the shortened version "FinOps" interchangeably with "Cloud FinOps" throughout the rest of the book, so make sure that you do not confuse "FinOps" with its alternate meaning of "financial operations," a broader term that encompasses all aspects of managing an organization's finances.

A Glimpse into the Pre-FinOps Era: Traditional Cloud Operations Model

According to the Flexera 2024 State of the Cloud Report, an average of 30% of cloud spend often ends up as waste or idle resources? Almost anyone developing software in the cloud has at least one cautionary tale about out-of-control cloud costs, usually because they didn't see a cost spike as it happened or missed a savings contract expiring. Unused or underutilized resources such as idle instances, dormant storage, or poorly configured services can lead to significant ongoing expenses.

This warrants the need for cloud cost visibility that allows businesses to manage their cloud resources and costs effectively while maintaining optimal performance and security standards. Without cloud visibility, cloud costs often remain uncovered and drain the budget.

Running a business without clear visibility into its costs dramatically limits its decision-making ability. Organizations can make educated decisions regarding resource provisioning, choosing the right pricing models, or identifying cost optimization opportunities only if they fully grasp the costs of various cloud services. Clear cloud visibility can help ensure effective decisions, seized opportunities to optimize costs, and efficient use of cloud resources.

Financial Impacts

We can't overstate this fact enough: a lack of cloud cost visibility directly impacts your bottom line. Multiple experts and research studies state that, on average, 30% of cloud spend is wasted *for any organization*. Every dollar wasted could be better utilized in your cloud to accelerate your business growth. Potential financial impacts from a lack of cloud cost visibility include the following:

- *Overspending and budget overruns*: Cost visibility is necessary for efficient financial planning and budgeting. Operating with limited or no visibility into cloud costs increases the risk of running over budget and spending more than initially planned. If finance teams need proper visibility into cloud computing costs, allocating the right amount of funds among the many departments and projects becomes a monumental task. Unless finance teams dedicate full time to reporting cloud spend, organizations spend beyond their cloud budget and need help managing overall spending.

- *Incapability to make predictions or plans*: Understanding costs is necessary for short-term and long-term financial planning. It's easier for businesses to make accurate future spending projections if they comprehensively understand past data and patterns relating to costs and spending. A lack of cloud cost visibility can make it challenging to effectively budget and manage finances, making it harder to adequately allocate resources, anticipate cost variations, and adjust to changing business needs.

- *Obscure financial reporting*: Cost visibility is vital for meeting financial reporting and compliance criteria. Finance teams require accurate and auditable cost data to report cloud expenses, allocate costs to departments, and ensure compliance with regulatory norms. Providing transparent and accurate financial reports is only possible with apparent awareness of costs, and businesses risk encountering problems during audits and regulatory assessments.

- *Lost prospects for improvement and cost optimization*: Clear visibility into costs lets you keep tabs on your spending and spot areas where you may save money and improve efficiency. For procurement teams, this visibility directly impacts cloud contract purchasing strategies. With visibility into forecasted cloud spend, procurement teams can take advantage of potential cost-saving initiatives, such as strategically using savings plans, negotiating corporate enterprise license agreements, or purchasing the right type and quantity of reserved instances. A lack of cloud cost visibility can result in lost opportunities to cut expenses and optimize cloud computing investments.

Technological Impacts

Operating without cost visibility in cloud computing has repercussions that transcend financial implications, affecting your engineering teams and overall technological development. Engineering teams play an essential role in managing cloud spending as they focus on their primary charter of creating innovations for the organization. Potential technological impacts from a lack of cloud cost visibility include the following:

- *Poor utilization of available resources*: Engineers need visibility into cloud costs and performance to make informed decisions about provisioning the right types and amounts of cloud resources for their application workloads. Facing a trade-off between overprovisioning resources for guaranteed performance and underprovisioning resources to save costs, engineers prioritize customer experience, potentially incurring higher expenses. Moreover, without insights into cloud costs and performance, development teams often use excessive resources or select overly expensive solutions. Unaware of the financial implications, they may unknowingly contribute to overprovisioned resources or miss opportunities for consolidation and optimization. This results in inefficient resource allocation, higher costs, and missed opportunities for savings.

- *The application's layout and optimization*: Cost visibility is essential in directing engineers to create cost-efficient application architectures. Cloud architects risk mistakenly developing cloud resource-intensive and costly solutions because they often lack knowledge of the financial consequences of the many architectural choices available to them. Engineers can discover opportunities for cost optimization, use efficient approaches to resource utilization, and design scalable and cost-effective solutions when they have visibility into the costs involved.

- *Systems performance monitoring*: Engineers require visibility into how resources are utilized and the expenses associated with those uses, whether they are troubleshooting performance issues or optimizing application performance. Poor visibility of cloud resource performance can cause bottlenecks, suboptimal performance, inefficient resource allocation, more downtime, higher costs, and lower customer satisfaction. Proper visibility is crucial for efficient resource utilization.

Organizational Impacts

Lack of cloud cost visibility can have broader impacts on the people and processes of your business. Still, these impacts can often be overlooked because they don't directly affect the bottom line. Potential organizational impacts from a lack of cloud cost visibility include the following

- *Priorities that are not properly aligned*: Various teams can have contradictory priorities regarding cloud resources if they do not have visibility into the costs involved. For instance, engineering teams may prioritize performance and functionality more without considering the associated expenses. In contrast, finance teams may place a higher priority on cost control and budget compliance. This imbalance can lead to friction and difficulty when attempting to balance satisfying corporate objectives and optimizing costs.

- *Lack of collaboration*: Increased cost transparency fosters collaboration between engineering and finance teams. When both groups have access to the same cost data, they can better collaborate to maximize the use of available resources. They can spot opportunities to cut costs and arrive at well-informed judgments that balance functionality, performance, and cost-effectiveness. Running a business without clear visibility into its expenses might make collaborating more challenging and lead to categorized decision-making.

- *Potential for layoffs*: In extreme cases, organizations experiencing financial strain due to uncontrolled cloud spending may resort to layoffs as a cost-cutting measure. This action can negatively impact morale, productivity, and employee trust. Implementing clear cloud cost visibility solutions can help organizations optimize their cloud environment and avoid unnecessary layoffs, allowing them to focus on growth and innovation.

- *Abdication of personal responsibility*: Cost exposure encourages accountability for employees inside the firm. Linking expenses to specific departments, teams, or projects is challenging when cloud spending is invisible. This lack of accountability can lead to disengagement and hamper efforts to encourage responsible resource usage and cost-conscious behavior.

Organizations should prioritize implementing effective cloud cost management procedures and tools to reduce the repercussions of needing more visibility into cloud costs. This involves using native cost management tools supplied by cloud service providers (CSPs), utilizing cost optimization solutions provided by third parties, building transparent governance frameworks, putting chargeback or show-back mechanisms in place, and routinely evaluating cost data to identify cost optimization opportunities. Organizations that embrace cloud cost visibility can reduce their exposure to financial risks, improve resource allocation, improve their ability to make educated decisions, and more effectively manage their costs.

Why Focus on FinOps?

Creating a new FinOps practice in your organization can seem daunting, especially when considering the competing priorities for investments in time and effort of the people needed for a FinOps practice. Just as the switch from on-premises to cloud computing was driven by the need to ensure long-term business growth and agility, implementing FinOps is a strategic investment in your business to reap long-term gains.

Cloud computing provides elasticity and scalability and bypasses traditional procurement processes to procure cloud infrastructure resources, enabling businesses to adapt quickly to shifting customer requirements. FinOps helps to maximize this flexibility by creating a transparent accountability system for cloud spending across engineers and business units. It allows companies to monitor, allocate, and attribute costs granularly to specific projects or applications and stakeholders, developing a culture of fiscal responsibility. FinOps makes it possible to make informed decisions.

The FinOps methodology encourages collaboration between finance, operations, procurement, and engineering departments. The goal is to foster a *culture of cost awareness* and drive cost efficiency, breaking down silos and encouraging collaboration between different functional areas. When teams become more cost aware of their cloud infrastructure, they can use this knowledge to make data-driven decisions to maximize cost savings. This cultural shift can lead to significant cost savings through cost-conscious architectural choices and improved cloud cost efficiency.

FinOps provides the guardrails needed to help businesses optimize their cloud costs by offering insights into resource spend, efficiency and govnernance frameworks at scale. The FinOps frameworks assist in identifying opportunities for cost savings and promoting strategies that can help reduce waste. Organizations can make the most of their investments in the cloud by ensuring their costs align with the business benefit.

Implementing FinOps governance policies and frameworks promotes long-term cloud resource efficiency by implementing rules that govern resource utilization and rightsizing, cloud security, and compliance. The cloud governance procedures developed by the FinOps teams ensure effective risk management in cloud environments.

FinOps is critical in driving cost optimization plans by fostering cost awareness and opportunities for collaboration and oversight. By employing a FinOps approach, a business can efficiently manage and optimize cloud costs, harness data-driven insights for cost optimization, and develop a culture of cost consciousness. The cross-functional collaboration and continuous improvement hallmarks of the FinOps methodology allow businesses to realize the greatest possible return on their cloud investments and conduct cloud operations cost-effectively.

Vision, Mission, and Charter of FinOps Teams

The goal of implementing FinOps is to bring together the technology, operations, and finance teams to manage costs and improve overall efficacy. Achieving cost efficiency and fostering a culture of cost awareness while maintaining or improving the performance and functionality of cloud-based systems should be the primary focus of a FinOps team.

The combined team will need extensive knowledge of CSP pricing methods, resource allocation, and usage patterns to accomplish this. The team analyzes consumption data, identifies cost drivers and cost optimization opportunities, and implements procedures to maximize efficiency while collaborating closely with engineering and operational departments.

The Vision

The *vision* of FinOps teams is to revolutionize how enterprises manage and use cloud resources by incorporating financial accountability into the cloud operating model.

The goal is to establish a culture where everyone involved, from developers to executives, knows the cost implications of their actions. They should collaborate to find ways to minimize costs as much as possible. The vision involves building a framework that allows enterprises to make data-driven decisions, maximize resource allocation, and use cloud computing most cost-effectively while retaining their agility and innovative spirit.

The Mission

The *mission* of FinOps teams is to enhance organizations' CCM capabilities by utilizing procedural frameworks and strategies to maximize business value from efficient cloud and Software as a Service (SaaS) resource usage.

FinOps teams' primary focus is to equip technical and nontechnical staff with the techniques, procedures, and tools to monitor, report, and analyze their cloud expenses. These techniques enable organizations to make informed decisions and accelerate cloud financial success.

The Charter

The FinOps team *charter* within an organization is a set of guiding principles, objectives, and obligations for implementing and practicing FinOps. While the exact charter for an organization should be tailored to its specific requirements, FinOps charters include the following elements:

- *Cost transparency and cost responsibility*: FinOps establishes cost visibility and responsibility within an organization, which is crucial for financial success. FinOps teams create effective cost-monitoring methods that give stakeholders clear insights into cloud costs. By understanding the economic consequences of cloud resource utilization, stakeholders become accountable for their costs and take ownership of their decisions. This culture of cost awareness encourages teams to optimize cloud usage and minimize costs. In short, FinOps is essential for effective cost management and cloud financial success.

- *Collaboration and cross-functional alignment*: Finance, operations, and engineering teams benefit from increased collaboration and cross-functional alignment when implementing FinOps. This allows for more effective communication and a more profound comprehension of cost issues, bridging the gap between technical and financial viewpoints. Facilitating collaboration and ensuring that cost optimization strategies are established and implemented cooperatively with input from all key stakeholders is one of the primary responsibilities of FinOps teams, and it is accomplished through regular meetings, discussions, and shared goals.

- *Strategies and frameworks for cost-effectiveness*: FinOps offers strategies and frameworks to formulate cost governance and optimization plans. It establishes procedures and rules for allocating, using, and rightsizing available resources. FinOps teams work closely with engineering and operations teams to pinpoint areas of cost inefficiency and wasted spending. Using data-driven insights and cost analysis enables FinOps teams to identify and implement cost-cutting initiatives that reduce considerable expenses. These tactics may include rightsizing instances, optimizing storage, or using reserved or savings plans.

- *Continuous improvement and optimization*: The FinOps methodology encourages a culture of continual improvement and optimization. FinOps teams can discover opportunities for optimization and take proactive measures to drive cost efficiency thanks to their vigilant monitoring and analysis of cloud costs. They continually examine the success of cost optimization measures, assess cost trends, analyze the factors contributing to costs, and so on. This iterative strategy allows enterprises to hone their cost optimization efforts and ensure that they align with the shifting requirements of their businesses and advances in technology.

- *Cost governance*: FinOps is a critical component of formulating and enforcing cost governance regulations. FinOps teams ensure that suitable policies and controls are in place to oversee costs by collaborating closely with finance and compliance teams. FinOps teams establish budget thresholds, construct approval processes, and implement methods to track and allocate expenditures effectively. FinOps teams ensure that cloud resources are provided and utilized in line with business policies, compliance standards, and cost optimization goals. In this role, they serve as gatekeepers.

- *Team education and empowerment*: FinOps teams are responsible for educating and empowering teams throughout the enterprise so that they can make informed decisions about cost optimization. They offer training, direction, and recommendations for best practices to teams involved in providing and utilizing cloud resources. FinOps teams encourage and foster a culture of cost awareness, promoting awareness about the influence of cloud charges on the organization's financial health. FinOps enables teams to actively contribute to cost optimization by providing the necessary information and tools.

- *Financial planning and forecasting*: One way that FinOps contributes to accurate financial planning and forecasting is by utilizing historical cost data and current patterns. FinOps teams can reliably anticipate future cloud expenses by examining previous cost information, which enables enterprises to manage budgets effectively and plan for growth or scaling requirements. Because of this financial transparency, stakeholders can better make educated decisions and connect their cloud strategies with their financial needs and business goals.

The preceding charter elements work great to build and scale a FinOps team when the company is big enough to budget for a dedicated FinOps team and/or there's executive buy-in. The next section talks about how you can build a road map to FinOps when there's limited buy-in from execs.

A Road Map to Executive Buy-In

An improperly managed cloud might reduce your organization's return on investment (ROI). Creating a FinOps team can greatly reduce cloud costs, but its success depends on getting executive support.

The following methodical strategy serves as a road map that can help you to get executive support and unleash a FinOps team's potential for cost savings.

1. Collaborate for quick wins—partner with a purpose:

   - *Identify a cross-functional team*: Partner with a team (e.g., engineering or finance) that is already familiar with your cloud environment. This expedites the process and leverages existing expertise.

- *Concentrate on chances with high impact*: Determine the most significant opportunities for cost savings in collaboration with the team. This might include the following:

  - *Rightsizing compute resources*: Analyze current resource utilization and identify opportunities to downsize instances when appropriate.

  - *Optimizing reserved instances*: Explore potential cost savings by using reserved instances for predictable workloads.

- *Quantify the benefits*: Estimate the cost reductions achievable through these initial actions. This tangible data strengthens your case for a dedicated FinOps team.

2. Foster cost awareness—a culture shift:

   - *Implement the #Piggy-Bank Framework*: Introduce this collaborative approach to cultivate cost awareness within the identified team. (This framework is described in Chapter 5.)

   - *Establish shared communication channels*: Create dedicated communication channels (e.g., Slack) for transparent discussions about cloud costs.

   - *Celebrate successes*: Regularly acknowledge and celebrate cost reduction wins within the team and broader organization.

   - *Ensure leadership visibility*: Apprise leadership of these ongoing efforts and their positive impact on cloud costs.

3. Secure executive sponsorship—building on momentum:

   - *Present a compelling narrative*: Leverage the data on achieved cost savings and the established culture of cost awareness to showcase the effectiveness of your collaborative approach.

   - *Outline a scalable plan*: Develop a clear plan for establishing a dedicated FinOps team. Outline the team's mission, vision, and charter, highlighting how it will build upon the initial successes.

   - *Request sponsorship*: Present your plan to executives and request their sponsorship to scale these practices across the organization.

This road map offers a precise and practical strategy for getting executive buy-in. By working with a cross-functional team, concentrating on high-impact possibilities, and encouraging a cost-conscious culture, you can provide a solid basis for a committed FinOps team. With executive sponsorship, you can enhance your organization's cloud ROI and realize the full benefits of cloud cost optimization.

FinOps acts as a catalyst for a transformative shift in cloud resource management within organizations. FinOps teams empower businesses to maximize the value they extract from their cloud investments by fostering collaboration, transparency, and cost consciousness. A structured approach and continuous improvement processes enable organizations to achieve optimal cost efficiency, maintain agility and innovation, and ensure sustainable cloud financial success. As the cloud landscape evolves, embracing the FinOps methodology will equip organizations with the tools and strategies to optimize their cloud expenses and ultimately achieve their business objectives.

Leading the FinOps Charge: Dedicated Teams vs. Shared Responsibilities

While a dedicated FinOps team is pivotal in achieving optimal cloud cost management and optimization, its implementation within an organization can vary. Let's explore different approaches and their advantages and disadvantages.

Cloud Infrastructure/Platform Team Integration

Often, FinOps is treated as cost optimization work, and the workload falls under the purview of the cloud infrastructure/platform team. While integration with this team is necessary, the focus should not be on cost optimization alone but also on cultivating a culture of cost awareness.

Pros:

- Leverages existing technical expertise in cloud operations.

- Promotes ownership and responsibility within the teams directly utilizing the cloud.

- Can be a good starting point for smaller organizations.

Cons:

- Risk of conflicting priorities with core infrastructure/platform duties.

- Requires training and development of FinOps skills within these teams.

- Needs more dedicated focus and a strategic perspective on cost optimization.

Cross-Functional Tiger Team

This team forms when organizations lack the necessary excecutive buy-in or budget to support a dedicated FinOps team. They may choose to form a cross-functional tiger team to address FinOps on an ad hoc basis.

Pros:

- Brings diverse perspectives and expertise from different departments (finance, engineering, operations).

- Encourages broader buy-in and understanding of FinOps principles.

- Can be agile and adaptable to changing needs.

Cons:

- Requires strong coordination and communication across silos.

- Needs more sustained momentum, credit and accountability of cloud economics. Lacks dedicated ownership and may not sustain long term.

- Risk of conflicting priorities among participating teams.

Dedicated FinOps Team

While this is the best-case scenario, organizations need more budget/executive buy-in to build a dedicated FinOps team. This team can bring in FinOps best practices, oversee the entire FinOps program, drive cost optimization, and foster a culture of cost awareness.

Pros:

- Deep expertise in cloud cost management methodologies and tools.

- Centralized visibility and control over cloud spend.

- Fosters cross-functional collaboration and accountability.

- Drives cultural shift toward cost optimization.

Cons:

- Requires additional headcount and investment.

- May initially face resistance from existing teams who feel ownership over cloud costs.

The Benefits of Different Placement Options for FinOps Teams

When considering the placement of FinOps teams within an organization, it's essential to understand how different structures can influence their effectiveness. Proper placement can enhance the integration of financial management practices within existing workflows, leading to improved cost control and resource optimization. Here, we explore the benefits of situating FinOps teams within Cloud Infrastructure/SRE and Finance teams.

Cloud Infrastructure/SRE Teams

Integrating FinOps teams within Cloud Infrastructure or Site Reliability Engineering (SRE) teams can provide significant advantages by embedding financial management practices into the organization's operational framework.

Immediate Insights into Resource Utilization and Optimization Opportunities: Embedding FinOps teams within Cloud Infrastructure/SRE teams provides real-time visibility into resource usage. This allows for quick identification of optimization opportunities and effective cost management.

Proactive Cost Management Embedded Within an Operational Workflow: FinOps teams integrated with SRE teams can embed cost management practices directly into operational workflows. This ensures that financial considerations are integrated into daily operations, leading to more proactive and efficient financial management.

Finance Teams

Placing FinOps teams within Finance teams ensures strong alignment with the organization's broader financial goals, promoting accountability and comprehensive visibility into cloud spending.

Strong Alignment with Financial Planning and Budgeting Processes

Placing FinOps teams within Finance ensures that cloud financial management aligns closely with the organization's financial goals and budgeting cycles. This promotes a unified approach to financial planning and cost control.

Ensures Cost Visibility and Accountability at an Organizational Level

Embedding FinOps within Finance facilitates comprehensive visibility into organizational spending. This placement enhances accountability and ensures that cloud costs are managed rigorously, as other financial metrics do, enabling more accurate forecasting and reporting.

Choosing the Right Placement

Your organizational structure, culture, and priorities will determine your FinOps department's location. By considering each strategy's advantages and disadvantages and the benefits of various placement possibilities, you can choose the model that best meets your demands. Whether embedded within Cloud Infrastructure/SRE teams for operational insights or within Finance teams for strong financial alignment, the strategic placement of FinOps teams is crucial for effective cloud financial management.

Demystifying the Current FinOps Framework

The IT infrastructure has radically changed with the widespread adoption of cloud computing, which offers unparalleled scalability, agility, and innovation. However, this paradigm shift requires a solid structure to oversee cloud finance operations. The FinOps Foundation (https://www.finops.org/) provides such a structure in its

FinOps Framework, which transcends mere cost controlling and assists organizations in modifying their culture by encouraging cooperation and accountability between the business, IT, and finance departments. By working together, this cooperative strategy guarantees cost-effectiveness and effective resource use while enabling enterprises to utilize cloud resources fully. Figure 1-1 presents a succinct overview of the current FinOps Framework.

Note   The FinOps Framework is evolving! Get the latest version from the FinOps Foundation at `https://www.finops.org/framework`.

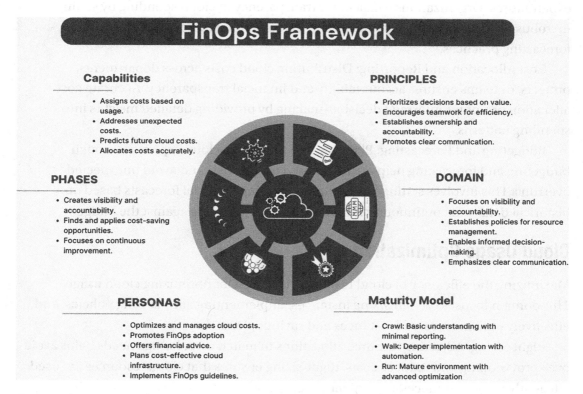

Figure 1-1. *FinOps Framework from the FinOps Foundation*

The following sections describe the FinOps Framework in more detail.

FinOps Domains and Capabilities

Understanding the key domains and capabilities within the FinOps framework is essential for effectively managing cloud financial operations. This structured approach provides a comprehensive strategy for achieving cost efficiency and optimizing resource utilization across the organization.

Cloud Cost Management

Effective cloud cost management is the cornerstone of the FinOps framework. This domain involves various practices for tracking, analyzing, and managing cloud expenditures. Organizations can achieve transparency in cloud spending by setting up robust cost allocation mechanisms and implementing thorough budgeting and forecasting practices.

Cost Allocation and Reporting: Distributing cloud costs across departments, projects, or teams ensures accountability and financial transparency. Accurate cost allocation promotes informed decision-making by providing detailed insights into spending patterns.

Budgeting and Forecasting: Planning and predicting cloud expenses through budgeting and forecasting help organizations control costs and avoid unexpected overruns. This involves setting budget limits, creating financial forecasts based on historical data, and continuously monitoring actual spending against the budget.

Cloud Usage Optimization

Maximizing the efficiency of cloud resources is crucial for optimizing cloud usage. This domain focuses on rightsizing instances, implementing auto-scaling policies, and effectively utilizing reserved instances and savings plans.

Right-Sizing: Adjusting resource allocations to match actual usage needs helps avoid over-provisioning and reduces costs. Right-sizing ensures that cloud resources are used efficiently without unnecessary expenditure.

Automation and Tooling: Automation reduces manual effort and increases efficiency by implementing workflows for provisioning and de-provisioning resources. Utilizing tools for continuous monitoring and optimization streamlines processes improves accuracy, and ensures timely responses to changing cloud usage patterns.

Cloud Governance and Compliance

Ensuring cloud usage aligns with organizational policies and regulatory requirements is vital for maintaining a secure and compliant cloud environment. This domain includes establishing governance frameworks, enforcing compliance policies, and conducting regular audits.

Governance and Compliance Capabilities: Establishing and enforcing policies that align with regulatory requirements helps mitigate risks, avoid fines, and maintain a secure cloud environment. Regular audits ensure ongoing compliance and security.

Benchmarking

Benchmarking provides a reference point to gauge the efficiency and effectiveness of cloud financial management practices by comparing cloud usage and costs against industry standards or internal benchmarks. Industry Benchmarking: Comparing your cloud usage and costs against industry standards helps identify areas for improvement and sets a benchmark for efficiency.

Performance Benchmarking: Evaluating the performance of cloud resources and services against predefined benchmarks ensures optimal utilization and cost-effectiveness.

Education and Training

Continuous education and training for all stakeholders involved in cloud financial management are crucial for staying updated with the latest practices and trends.

Ongoing Education: Providing continuous education on FinOps practices, cloud cost management tools, and emerging trends ensures that all stakeholders are well-informed and capable of managing cloud finances effectively.

Certification and Professional Development: Encouraging team members to pursue FinOps certifications and attend professional development workshops enhances their expertise and keeps them updated with industry best practices.

By understanding and implementing these FinOps domains and capabilities, organizations can build a robust framework for managing cloud financial operations. This ensures cost efficiency, optimized resource utilization, and a secure, compliant cloud environment. Integrating these domains and capabilities provides a comprehensive approach to FinOps, empowering organizations to make informed decisions, foster accountability, and drive continuous improvement in their cloud financial management practices.

FinOps Personas

Successfully implementing FinOps frameworks requires the cooperation and involvement of various stakeholders within an organization. These parties, often known as FinOps Personas from FinOps Foundation Franework, consist of:

- *Cloud Cost Owner*: This individual optimizes and manages cloud costs for their specific sector.

- *FinOps Champion*: This is someone who promotes and encourages the adoption and cooperation of the FinOps methodology inside the company.

- *Money Business Partner*: This person offers financial expertise and advice on cloud cost control choices.

- *Cloud Architect*: A cloud architect plans and executes cloud infrastructure solutions to minimize costs.

- *Cloud Engineer*: This person follows FinOps guidelines while managing and allocating cloud resources.

Comprehending the functions and duties of these FinOps Personas promotes efficient communication and cooperation among diverse organizational divisions, culminating in the triumphant execution of FinOps.

FinOps Phases

The FinOps Framework outlines three iterative phases that guide organizations through the process of establishing a cost-conscious cloud culture:

1. *Inform*: This phase creates visibility and accountability for cloud expenses by implementing cost allocation, chargeback, and showback systems.

2. *Optimize*: This phase uses the knowledge gathered during the Inform phase to find and apply potential cost savings through automation, rightsizing, and resource optimization.

3. *Operate*: This phase focuses on continuous improvement and governance by establishing sustainable practices for cost management, monitoring, and reporting.

FinOps Principles

When implementing the FinOps Framework, organizations can resort to the following guiding principles that serve as its cornerstone. These principles allow companies to establish a cost-conscious cloud culture and maximize their cloud investment strategies.

- *Business Value*: Cloud resource allocation and utilization decisions should be driven by demonstrable business value. Every cloud-related decision should be evaluated based on its contribution to the organization's goals.

- *Collaboration*: Fostering collaboration and shared responsibility for cloud costs across all organizational units is critical for success. This includes fostering communication and teamwork between finance, technology, product, and business teams. Everyone involved should work together to improve efficiency and innovation continuously.

- *Financial Accountability*: Establishing clear ownership and accountability for cloud financial management is essential. This involves pushing accountability to "the edge," empowering individual teams and engineers to manage their usage and costs. Decentralized decision-making encourages teams to consider cost as a new efficiency metric throughout the software development lifecycle.

- *Transparency*: Clear communication channels and cross-organization visibility into cloud expenses are essential for making well-informed decisions. Real-time data access, data-driven decision-making, and uniform visibility at all organizational levels are all part of this transparency.

- *Continuous Improvement*: Long-term success in cloud financial management depends on implementing an iterative strategy that prioritizes ongoing learning and optimization. This entails taking an agile and iterative approach, prioritizing proactive system design, and regularly checking in and making adjustments to ensure effective cloud utilization.

FinOps Maturity Model

The FinOps Maturity Model within the FinOps Framework offers a systematic framework for evaluating FinOps procedures and pinpointing areas for improvement. This iterative "Crawl, Walk, Run" method allows firms to begin small and progressively expand their FinOps capabilities as their knowledge and proficiency increase.

The FinOps Maturity Model outlines three primary maturity levels:

1. *Crawl*: This maturity level represents an organization with a basic understanding of FinOps functionalities. Activities are limited, with minimal reporting and tooling in place. The organization can allocate around 50% of its cloud costs and achieve a basic resource-based commitment discount coverage (around 60%). However, their forecast accuracy compared to actual spending might be low (20% variance).

2. *Walk*: This maturity level signifies a deeper understanding and implementation of FinOps practices in an organization. Automation and processes are established for most capabilities. The organization can identify and address most cost optimization opportunities, even though some complex situations might still need to be addressed. Allocation rates increase (around 80%), discount coverage improves (around 70%), and forecast accuracy gets closer to actual spending (15% variance).

3. *Run*: This maturity level represents a mature and optimized
    FinOps environment. All teams understand and follow
    best practices. Automation is the preferred approach, and
    the organization can address even the most complex cost
    optimization scenarios. They achieve high allocation rates (over
    90%), optimize resource-based commitments (around 80%
    coverage), and have superior forecast accuracy (12% variance).

The following are key points regarding the FinOps Maturity Model:

- *Emphasis on value*: Setting priorities according to company value
  is the aim rather than just hitting the "Run" maturity level in every
  capability. The main goal should be to develop capabilities that yield
  the best return on investment.

- *Continuous improvement*: Iteratively based, this strategy promotes
  continuous improvement by helping firms evaluate their
  performance regularly, spot areas for improvement, and gradually
  advance their FinOps maturity.

- *Customization*: Businesses can adapt the model to meet their specific
  goals and conditions by using it as a flexible framework. Achieving
  the intended results in line with each person's needs should
  be the main priority rather than rigorously pursuing particular
  maturity levels.

By maximizing spending and extracting more value, the FinOps Maturity Model
assists businesses in identifying areas for improvement, creating a road map, and
maximizing the returns on their cloud investment.

By adopting the FinOps Framework, enterprises may fully realize the benefits
of their cloud computing expenditures. This all-encompassing strategy encourages
transparency, cooperation, and ongoing improvement in addition to cost consciousness.
Organizations are given a clear road map for implementing technological optimization,
creating a shared responsibility culture, and establishing best practices through the
six FinOps Domains. Furthermore, using the FinOps Maturity Model, businesses can

evaluate where they are now, pinpoint areas where they can improve, and progress toward their cloud cost optimization objectives. Ultimately, the FinOps Framework allows businesses to maximize their cloud investments, guaranteeing a long-term and economical path through the constantly changing cloud environment. The next section introduces the 6-Factor FinOps Formula I, Sasi Kanumuri coined to build and scale a FinOps practice at your organization.

Introducing the 6-Factor FinOps Formula

The importance of building a FinOps practice today cannot be overstated. As the cloud becomes increasingly prevalent across industries, businesses face the challenge of ensuring cost efficiency without compromising performance and growth. In this era of rapid digital transformation, the need for a FinOps mindset has never been greater.

FinOps distinguishes itself from traditional cost-cutting measures by cutting costs without cutting people. In other words, FinOps focuses on optimizing cloud spending while maintaining a solid foundation for innovation and growth. Organizations can effectively balance financial aspects with business alignment. This is crucial to their ability to adapt and thrive in the ever-changing market.

A dedicated FinOps team plays a pivotal role in achieving these objectives. FinOps spearheads cloud cost management and optimization. The FinOps team's mission revolves around driving cost transparency, enabling data-driven decision-making, and fostering a culture of accountability and collaboration.

I have coined a unique 6-Factor FinOps Formula to navigate through your FinOps journey; whether your organization is in the crawl, walk, or run phase of FinOps, these six factors are designed to help at any phase. The FinOps team's vision and charter revolve around six key factors, illustrated in Figure 1-2, forming the foundation of our blueprint for building and managing FinOps at scale.

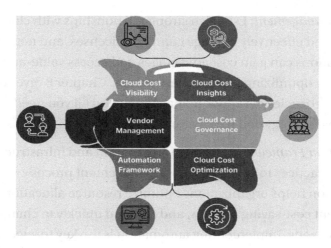

Figure 1-2. *6-Factor FinOps Formula*

The following are the core tenets of the 6-Factor FinOps Formula:

- *Cloud Cost Visibility*: Establish robust processes and tools to gain comprehensive visibility into cloud costs. This ensures accurate tracking and monitoring of spending across various cloud services and resources. Cloud cost visibility is covered in detail in Chapter 2.

- *Cloud Cost Insights*: Extract meaningful insights from cloud cost data to identify trends, patterns, and optimization opportunities. Organizations can make informed decisions and drive continuous improvement by leveraging data analytics and visualization techniques. Cloud cost insights are covered in detail in Chapter 3.

- *Cost Governance*: Implement governance mechanisms to enforce cost controls, establish budgeting frameworks, and allocate costs effectively. This objective ensures costs align with organizational priorities and policies. Cost governance and policies are detailed in Chapter 4.

- *Cloud Cost Optimization*: Develop strategies and tactics to optimize cloud costs without sacrificing performance or scalability. This objective involves identifying areas of overspending, rightsizing resources, and leveraging pricing models and discounts that CSPs offer. Cloud cost optimization techniques are elaborated on in Chapter 6.

- *Vendor Management*: Establish strong relationships with cloud vendors and effectively manage contracts, licenses, and negotiations. Organizations can gain cost advantages and access value-added services by optimizing vendor relationships. Chapter 8 dives deep into the intricacies of vendor management and all you need to know about deal strategy and negotiation.

- *Automation Framework*: Leverage automation and infrastructure-as-code practices to streamline cost management processes. Automation helps organizations optimize resource allocation, implement cost-saving policies, and respond quickly to changing business needs. Implementing automation is the key to successfully scaling FinOps. While this concept is interwoven in every chapter of this book, Chapter 7 details automation in depth.

FinOps KPIs: Measuring Success Across the Framework

Imagine driving blindfolded. Cloud cost management without key performance indicators (KPIs) is akin to that—a perilous venture with an uncertain destination. KPIs act as your headlights, illuminating the path toward financial clarity and cost optimization. They empower you to track progress, identify areas for improvement, and, ultimately, achieve your cloud financial goals.

You may better evaluate how much you spend on the cloud, pinpoint areas for development, and ultimately optimize your cloud financial management for long-term success by making efficient use of these KPIs.

Cloud Visibility KPIs

Cloud visibility is the foundation for effective FinOps practices. Cloud visibility KPIs measure your ability to monitor and understand the money and resources you spend on the cloud. They tell you how well your expenses are being tracked and how efficiently your cloud resources are being used. High resource utilization might indicate a need for rightsizing, while orphaned resources highlight potential cost leaks. Accurate cost allocation empowers teams to be more accountable for their cloud spending.

The following are important cloud visibility KPIs:

- *Resource Utilization*: Proportion of memory, storage, CPU, and network usage. This KPI facilitates the identification of chances for resource rightsizing and possible overprovisioning.

- *Cost Allocation*: Amount of cloud expenses apportioned to departments, projects, and teams. Precise cost distribution promotes responsibility and enables groups to arrive at well-informed conclusions.

- *Tagged Resources*: Percentage of resources tagged for accurate cost allocation and identification. Proper tagging is crucial for granular cost visibility and optimized resource management.

- *Orphaned Resources*: Percentage of unused or unallocated resources identified for potential cleanup. Identifying and eliminating orphaned resources reduces unnecessary spending and optimizes resource utilization.

Cloud Insights KPIs

Cloud insights KPIs go beyond basic visibility and delve deeper into analyzing trends and identifying areas for improvement. These KPIs help you determine where possible hazards or areas for optimization are located and how your cloud spending is changing. They also help you identify areas for cost optimization and potential hazards by examining cost trends, variations, and resource utilization. They also highlight the importance of cloud security in overall cost management. The inclusion of carbon footprint as a potential future KPI reflects the growing focus on environmental responsibility within cloud computing.

The following are important cloud insights KPIs:

- *Cost Trends*: Month-over-month (MoM), week-over-week (WoW), and quarter-over-quarter (QoQ) comparisons of cloud expenses. Tracking cost trends helps identify unexpected spikes and enables proactive cost management.

- *Unforecasted Cost Variance*: Percentage difference between actual and budgeted cloud costs. This KPI highlights discrepancies between planned and actual spending, prompting investigation into root causes.

- *Idle Resources*: Number or percentage of idle resources identified for potential rightsizing or termination. Identifying underutilized resources allows for optimization and cost savings.

- *Security Incidents*: Number or rate of security incidents related to cloud resources. Monitoring security incidents helps ensure the protection of your cloud environment and potentially reduces costs associated with breaches.

Unit economics can help depict a better picture here. When you have one or more Unit metrics, their trend can be a great proxy to determine if your operational expenses have increased or decreased and is a better metric than generic cost trend. If the unit metric trends up, it indicates poor cloud efficiency and opportunity to improve.

Cloud Governance KPIs

Cloud governance KPIs assess the effectiveness of your policies and procedures in managing cloud resources securely and cost-effectively. These KPIs ensure your cloud environment is well controlled and well optimized for financial responsibility. Cloud governance KPIs ensure your cloud environment is configured and managed according to best practices. They track adherence to security and cost optimization policies, the utilization of cost-saving options like reservations, and the effectiveness of access controls. Monitoring service level agreement (SLA) compliance helps maintain optimal service performance and avoid unnecessary costs.

Important cloud governance KPIs include the following:

- *Policy Compliance*: Percentage of cloud resources that are compliant with security and cost optimization policies. Enforcing well-defined policies encourages resource conservation and guarantees adherence to security best practices.

- *Reservation Coverage*: Proportion of workloads that savings plans or cost-saving reservations cover. Leveraging committed-use discounts through reservations or savings plans can significantly reduce cloud costs for predictable workloads.

- *Access Management*: Number of active users with appropriate access controls for cloud resources. Granular access controls reduce security risks and possible cost overruns by preventing illegal access and resource usage.

- *Compliance with Service Level Agreements (SLAs)*: Percentage of time that predetermined performance standards are satisfied by cloud services. Maintaining optimal performance and avoiding any financial penalties linked to service interruptions are ensured by honoring SLA commitments.

Cloud Cost Optimization KPIs

Cloud cost optimization KPIs, which gauge the success of your attempts to cut back on needless cloud spending, are the foundation of finance operations. These KPIs monitor the results of your cost-cutting efforts in real time. Cloud cost optimization KPIs directly measure the financial impact of your FinOps practices. Tracking cost savings, RI utilization, spot instance adoption, and rightsizing efforts helps you identify areas for further improvement and quantify the success of your cost optimization initiatives.

Important cloud cost optimization KPIs include the following:

- *Cost Savings*: Percentage or dollar amount saved through cost optimization efforts. This is the ultimate measure of success in FinOps. It reflects the combined impact of various optimization strategies.

- *Reserved Instance (RI) Utilization*: Percentage of RI hours consumed compared to total running workloads. High RI utilization indicates efficient usage of cost-effective reservations for predictable workloads.

- *Spot Instance Adoption*: Percentage of workloads running on cost-effective spot instances. Successfully migrating suitable workloads to spot instances can lead to significant cost savings.

- *Rightsizing*: The quantity or proportion of resources that are scaled properly for best results and lowest costs. You may be confident that you are only paying for the resources you really need by doing away with overprovisioning and properly scaling resources.

Vendor Management KPIs

Effective vendor management is crucial for optimizing cloud costs. Vendor management KPIs assess the efficiency of your vendor relationships and software utilization, ensuring you get the most value from your cloud investments. Tracking negotiation efficiency, software utilization, duplicate subscriptions, and vendor SLA compliance empowers you to optimize your cloud spending and hold vendors accountable for their commitments.

The following are important vendor management KPIs:

- *Contract Negotiation Efficiency*: Percentage of savings achieved through vendor negotiations. Skilled negotiation can secure better pricing terms and significant cost reductions.

- *Software Utilization*: Percentage of licensed software actively used within the organization. Identifying and eliminating underutilized software licenses prevents unnecessary spending on unused resources.

- *Duplicate Subscriptions*: Number of identified and eliminated duplicate or unused software subscriptions. Proactive management lowers unnecessary spending and gets rid of redundant subscriptions.

- *Vendor Service Level Agreement (SLA) Compliance*: The proportion of time that suppliers fulfill the terms of the service level agreements. Monitoring vendor SLA compliance guarantees to pay for the services you receive and reduces the likelihood of interruptions.

Automation KPIs

Automation is a cornerstone of efficient FinOps practices. Automation KPIs assess the effectiveness of your automation efforts in streamlining cloud cost management processes. Automation KPIs highlight the efficiency gains achieved through automating repetitive tasks in cloud cost management. They monitor cost reporting automation, resource provisioning, team self-service options, and the pace at which cost anomalies are resolved. Concentrating on automation can increase accuracy, expedite procedures, and encourage cost-conscious behavior in your teams.

Important automation KPIs include the following:

- *Automated Cost Reporting*: Percentage of cost reports generated and delivered automatically. Automating cost reporting saves time, improves accuracy, and ensures timely insights for cost optimization decisions.

- *Automated Resource Provisioning*: Number of resources that automation scripts provision and configure. Resource deployment delays are avoided, consistency is guaranteed, and human error is minimized.

- *Mean Time to Resolution (MTTR) for Cost Anomalies*: Average amount of time required to identify and resolve cost anomalies automatically. Automated anomaly detection and resolution reduce unexpected expense spikes and streamline cost management procedures.

Tracking and Evaluating FinOps KPIs

All the KPIs discussed in the previous sections are useful tools. However, their true potential can be realized only when you accurately know how to use the information that KPIs provide. Timely tracking and evaluation of FinOps KPIs ensures

- *Finding cost-saving opportunities*: KPIs let you know where too much money is being spent and where resources are being underutilized, which can help you devise cost-saving measures.

- *Boosting your cost-reduction efforts*: KPIs enable you to monitor the effectiveness of your cost-cutting initiatives and constantly improve your strategy.

- *Promoting shared accountability for cloud spending*: KPIs encourage a culture of shared accountability for cloud spending by linking costs to particular teams or projects.

- *Making informed decisions*: Cloud cost management decisions should be based on data, not intuition. KPIs provide the insights you need for informed choices.

Remember, FinOps KPIs are a continuous journey, not a one-time fix. Review your KPIs frequently, make any adjustments, and use them to improve your cloud financial management procedures continuously. You can achieve real cloud financial excellence and uncover considerable cost savings by adopting a data-driven approach and acting on your KPIs.

Beyond the Metrics: FinOps Team Success Indicators

Monitoring your FinOps team's success entails more than monitoring cloud usage. In this section, we examine KPIs from various FinOps perspectives to give an overall picture of the team's efficacy.

We suggest concentrating on KPIs in the following six crucial areas to gauge the efficacy of your FinOps practice. By monitoring these KPIs across various FinOps domains, you can get deep insights into your FinOps team's performance and pinpoint areas for development, allowing you to refine your FinOps strategy and achieve optimal cloud resource management within your organization.

Cloud Visibility KPI: Chargeback/Showback Percentage of Total Costs

This metric measures the percentage of your total cloud costs that are charged back or shown back to individual application owners. A successful FinOps team ensures service and shared service costs are allocated to the responsible teams, fostering cost awareness and accountability.

Why it matters: This KPI prevents the FinOps team from solely handling cost management and encourages individual teams to optimize their cloud spending.

Cloud Insights KPI: Unit Economics Metrics

During periods of growth, like global expansion, cloud costs can understandably increase. Unit economics metrics provide a clearer picture of cost efficiency by relating costs directly to business outputs (e.g., cost per customer acquisition). An upward trend in unit economics indicates potential areas for improvement in cloud resource optimization.

Why it matters: Unit economics metrics move beyond simple cost tracking and focus on cost efficiency in relation to business value.

Cloud Governance KPI: Cultural Shift: Engagement and Surveys

Regular engagement and surveys with engineering teams regarding their cloud usage and spending provide valuable insight into the FinOps team's effectiveness. An increasing level of engagement signifies a positive shift toward cost awareness and collaboration.

Why it matters: This KPI measures the FinOps team's success in fostering a cloud-conscious culture within the organization.

Cloud Cost Optimization KPI: Sustainability/Carbon Footprint

For environmentally conscious organizations, carbon footprint is an emerging metric. Cloud providers offer tools and data to assess your footprint. Tracking your progress in reducing environmental impact demonstrates the FinOps team's commitment to sustainability.

Why it matters: This KPI showcases the FinOps team's dedication to not just cost optimization, but also environmental responsibility.

Vendor Management KPI: Liaison/Collaboration

A successful FinOps team fosters collaboration between procurement, engineering, and finance teams during the procurement of new cloud products and services. This ensures financial and technical vetting, efficient resource utilization, and accountability for cloud spending across departments.

Why it matters: Strong collaboration across teams prevents unnecessary cloud expenses and ensures cost-effective solutions align with business needs.

Automation KPI: Time to Resolve a Cost Spike

Chapter 7 will discuss automated incident management for cost spikes. The time it takes engineering teams to react to and resolve a cost spike using the framework established by the FinOps team can be a powerful indicator of the team's success. A shorter resolution time showcases the effectiveness of automated solutions and the FinOps team's proactive approach.

Why it matters: This KPI emphasizes the FinOps team's ability to identify potential cost issues and implement solutions like automation to minimize financial impact.

Remember, KPIs are a continuous journey. Regularly review your KPIs, make adjustments, and use them to refine your cloud financial management practices. This data-driven approach, empowered by FinOps KPIs, unlocks real cloud financial excellence and significant cost savings.

Chapter Summary

This introductory chapter to Cloud FinOps provided the context for implementing Cloud FinOps in your organization. We covered the following key points:

- *What is Cloud FinOps*: Cloud FinOps is a methodology that gives teams the framework to establish accountability, visibility, and control over cloud costs.

- *The importance of FinOps*: FinOps enables businesses to realize the greatest possible return on their cloud investments and conduct cloud operations cost-effectively.

- *Vision, mission, and charter for FinOps teams*: The FinOps team aims to optimize costs as much as possible while maintaining and improving services and application performance.

- *The 6-Factor FinOps Formula*: This formula serves as a blueprint and road map to creating a strong FinOps practice in your organization.

Now that we've introduced the basic concepts of Cloud FinOps and provided a high-level structure for creating a FinOps practice, let's dive into the process. Building a FinOps practice from scratch can be daunting if you don't know where to start, but as you can see from my 6-Factor FinOps Formula, it starts with getting strong visibility into your existing cloud costs.

Cloud cost visibility is foundational to every other cost management and governance aspect. In the next chapter, we'll cover the importance of cost visibility and how to establish the foundations for cloud cost visibility.

References for Further Reading

https://www.finops.org/wg/finops-kpis/

https://blog.economize.cloud/finops-kpis-guide/

https://www.finops.org/framework/

https://www.finops.org/framework/maturity-model/

CHAPTER 2

Cloud Cost Visibility

Chapter 1 established the importance of a "construction project manager" (FinOps), using the analogy of building your dream house by acquiring materials from a cloud supply store. Imagine managing your house construction without blueprints or a clear understanding of the materials used. That's what operating in the cloud without cloud cost visibility is like. This chapter delves into the foundational element of successful FinOps practices.

Cloud computing has become a vital tool in today's fast-advancing technological world, making it an attractive option for businesses that want to improve operational efficiency, expand their capacity, and reduce operational spend. However, a lack of clear visibility into cloud costs can easily undermine these advantages.

Understanding your cloud costs is the most crucial step in controlling your spending. With adequate visibility into your cloud spending, you can identify issues such as cost spikes, cloud waste from unused/orphaned resources, and unauthorized purchases of cloud resources.

This chapter explores the importance of cloud cost visibility in scaling FinOps practices. We'll discuss the repercussions of not having cost visibility, including the absence of cost monitoring, disconnecting engineers from billing responsibilities, lack of shared cost allocation, punitive financial repercussions, and misalignment between finance and engineering. By understanding these issues, you can establish effective methods and best practices around cost visibility. This chapter also provides a comprehensive understanding of tag health, which, if not robust, can pose a prominent roadblock in a company's attempt to gain visibility in cloud spend.

We'll also provide a comprehensive strategy for properly tagging cloud resources, including ways to automate and enforce cloud tagging.

By building a solid foundation in cloud cost visibility, you'll be well equipped to navigate the construction of your cloud dream house efficiently and responsibly, just like a true FinOps champion!

© Sasi Kanumuri, Matthew Zeier 2024
S. Kanumuri and M. Zeier, *Scaling Cloud FinOps*, https://doi.org/10.1007/979-8-8688-0388-8_2

The Importance of Cloud Cost Visibility

Imagine a world without cloud cost visibility for a second, where your engineers operate in the traditional "billing is not my concern" mind frame. They do not know the cost of their cloud services nor how those costs are trending month over month. They can't answer the question "Are we over budget or under budget?" until the finance team sets off alarm bells for exceeding their cloud budgets. There is no way to install guardrails against out-of-control cloud spending without adequate visibility into cloud costs.

In today's cloud-driven world, understanding and tracking expenses related to cloud services and resources is crucial to promoting a culture of cost awareness (a topic we'll dive into in Chapter 5). Cloud cost visibility aims to change the traditional engineering mindset from "billing is not my concern" to "the economic impact of my work is my responsibility." Engineers can dynamically provision and decommission cloud resources, and with cloud services employing a consumption-based billing model, being aware of cloud costs is imperative to fostering a healthy FinOps practice for cloud cost management.

If it seems like we're focusing only on engineers here, it's because engineers have the most significant impact cloud cost spending. However, cloud cost visibility is also essential at the executive level, where strategic decisions are made about product portfolios (which services are profitable), staffing (which projects to assign engineers to), and budgets. Executives need strong visibility into cloud costs to make data-driven decisions that impact company direction.

The goal is to enable your organization to manage your cloud costs, prioritize cost visibility, and ensure every dollar is spent efficiently toward your cloud financial success. Proper cloud cost visibility unlocks the following strategic cloud cost management (CCM) and optimization activities that drive cost efficiency for your organization.

Resource Allocation

Cost visibility provides insights into resource allocation and distribution. Organizations can make educated judgments on resource allocation if they understand the correlation between the number of resources used, resource type, and the associated expenses. Resource allocation ensures accountability and often plays a pivotal role in eliminating waste and idle resources. Chapter 6 discusses identifying and eliminating waste in detail.

Cost Attribution and Distribution

Traditionally, a centralized engineering operations team, such as a DevOps, platform, or infrastructure team, holds primary responsibility for cloud costs within organizations. They support the finance team, which relies on them for cloud spending reports, and provide engineering leadership, which looks to enable application teams to run applications in the cloud. While this centralized approach simplifies accountability, true cost visibility is achieved by allocating and distributing costs to the departments consuming the resources. This fosters a shared understanding and encourages responsible resource usage across the organization.

Chargeback assigns expenses to individual departments or users based on the number of resources such departments or users consume, enabling cost responsibility and control. Finance can "charge" these teams for their cloud resource usage against their department budgets. On the other hand, *showback* provides expense reports to departments or users without charging them, the goal being to foster openness and cost transparency and encourage responsible resource utilization.

Chargeback and showback enable organizations to allocate and distribute cloud costs to different departments or business units. The model shown in Table 2-1 demonstrates how cloud costs are measured, calculated, and assigned based on usage or predefined cost allocation rules. This model promotes cost transparency and accountability among different stakeholders.

Whether your organization chooses to chargeback or showback cloud costs is a strategic financial accounting decision. It depends significantly on how budgets are set and whether finance decides to centralize cloud budgets to the DevOps (or similar) team or decentralize them to individual departments. Table 2-1 compares the chargeback and showback models.

Table 2-1. *Chargeback Model vs. Showback Model*

Criteria	Showback Model	Chargeback Model
Purpose	Provide expense reports to departments or users to increase cost transparency and awareness.	Assign expenses to departments or users based on usage for cost recovery and accountability.
Responsibility	A central DevOps team or a dedicated cost management team is responsible for reporting cloud resource usage to departments or users.	Departments or users are directly responsible for cloud resource usage costs.
Cost visibility	Provides visibility of cloud spending patterns and resource usage without direct charges.	Provides visibility of actual costs incurred by departments or users for cloud resources.
Cost control	Does not directly enforce financial responsibility but promotes cost awareness and potential behavioral change through cost transparency.	Encourages cost efficiency through direct financial responsibility and potential adjustments in resource consumption.
Billing	Does not involve direct billing to departments or users.	Involves charging departments or users for actual resource usage based on predefined rates or allocation methods.
Financial impact	Has an indirect financial impact by influencing user behavior and potentially leading to more efficient resource consumption and cost savings over time.	Has a direct and immediate financial impact on departments or users, potentially affecting budgets and resource allocation decisions.
FinOps Maturity Model phase	Crawl/Walk	Run

Budgeting, Forecasting, and Fiscal Planning

When not properly controlled, cloud computing costs can suddenly balloon. The best-laid financial plans can get blown apart when someone accidentally leaves a test system running or if the cost of supporting customers in SaaS applications doesn't align with expectations.

Business owners can plan and allocate budgets precisely when they have compelling expense insight. Companies can ensure that their cloud spending aligns with their financial goals and that they devote sufficient resources to satisfy their needs if they analyze historical cost data to make projections about future expenses. Budgeting enables more accurate financial planning and eliminates unanticipated cost increases. We'll cover advanced techniques in budgeting and forecasting in Chapter 3.

Cost Governance and Data-Driven Decisions

Organizations can make educated decisions about cloud strategies with visibility into costs. It enables them to evaluate the return on investment (ROI) for various cloud services, estimate the financial implications of shifting workloads to the cloud, and compare pricing alternatives from multiple cloud service providers (CSPs). Cost visibility is also beneficial to governance and compliance activities since it offers insights into cost allocation and makes it possible to verify that expenditures follows the rules of the business and any applicable regulations.

Organizations can use the many tools and services offered by CSPs and the cost management solutions provided by third-party vendors to achieve efficient cost visibility in cloud computing. These solutions allow businesses to thoroughly understand their cloud costs by offering capabilities such as cost tracking, budgeting, forecasting, and extensive cost breakdowns. These capabilities are offered in various degrees of granularity.

Cost Optimization

Before your teams can tackle the challenge of reducing cloud costs, they need to know what resources and services drive them and to whom they belong. Cloud services can incur variable expenses associated with numerous options and settings, and teams may not realize they are creating unnecessary cloud spending on unnecessary purchases they don't need.

Businesses can identify the factors contributing to costs, monitor their spending patterns, and optimize their resource allocation to reach the highest possible level of cost efficiency when they have access to cost visibility. Cloud cost visibility helps determine whether resources are unused or underutilized, enabling cloud instance rightsizing and purchasing strategies to take advantage of cloud service provider (CSP) discounts, such as employing reserved instances or spot instances in a planned manner.

Continuous Performance Evaluation

Cost visibility aids in identifying top spending resources, which further leads to investigating bottlenecks, monitoring application performance, and ensuring that resources are rightsized to meet the demands of the workload. This preventative method of resource management improves operational efficiency while cutting down on overprovisioning of resources that aren't necessary.

Tagging: Laying the Foundation for Cloud Cost Visibility

Before you can delve into the details of cost visibility, you have to do the groundwork that enables cost visibility and effective management of all your cloud resources. You do this by creating a tagging taxonomy and implementing an effective tagging strategy to ensure accurate tracking of expenses and that costs are allocated to the correct categories or entities. Collectively known as cost allocation, taxonomy, and tagging, they play vital roles in the financial and technical management of cloud resources.

Taxonomy and tagging allow for increased visibility into an organization's cost structure, which benefits the organization. Together, they offer a defined framework that makes it possible to disclose costs in a manner that is both consistent and visible throughout the entire organization. This insight enables the identification of cost causes, analysis of cost patterns, and making educated decisions about resource allocation.

With a well-defined taxonomy and tagging system, it's possible to appropriately assign costs to the various cost centers, projects, or activities. This includes cost allocation for shared services, where many departments may use cloud resources such as a Kubernetes cluster to reap the benefits of performance, efficiency, and scalability such services offer. Granular cost allocation enables businesses to evaluate the profitability or cost-effectiveness of the many business divisions, products, or initiatives they pursue. In addition, it helps locate areas of inefficiency and prospective chances to save costs.

Let's explore tagging and taxonomy and how they relate to one another for cloud cost allocation.

Tagging

Tags are key/value pairs attached to cloud resources such as virtual machines, storage buckets, databases, and load balancers. You can also use tags to search for specific information. Tags can reflect numerous qualities such as environment (e.g., production, development, etc.), project, department, application, or cost center. Within a taxonomy system, each individual cloud resource can be given its unique label or tagged through the tagging process.

Tags provide the foundation required for your FinOps teams to offer precise information about expenses, such as the specific activity, project, or department linked to each expenditure. For instance, a cost tag could show that certain charges are tied to a research and development project or marketing effort. Tagging enables granular cost management across engineering teams, making precise cost attribution and analysis easier.

As organizations rely more on cloud computing, understanding the hierarchy of cloud resources becomes crucial. Figure 2-1 provides an onion diagram that depicts cloud resource hierarchy. At the outermost layer are the cloud accounts (e.g., AWS accounts, Google Cloud Platform projects, Microsoft Azure subscriptions) through which CSPs enable cloud usage. The middle layer represents various cloud services categorized into Compute, Storage, Network, Database, etc., making it easy to group similar resources. Finally, the inner layer represents the cloud resources you provision to support your organization. Assigning tags to all taggable cloud resources enables granular breakdown and drill-down costs in any combination of factors to identify organizational cost factors. It's worth noting that not all cloud resources are taggable.

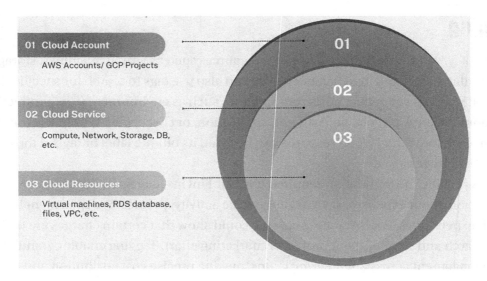

Figure 2-1. *Cost resource hierarchy*

Pro Tip   Leverage automation in developing taxonomies and applying tags. Manual tagging can be tedious and inconsistent, especially at scale. Look for solutions to ingest data and automatically categorize costs using the taxonomy hierarchies discussed in the "Taxonomy" section. Such solutions save significant human effort while improving accuracy and keeping taxonomies dynamic. Just be sure to have humans audit and validate auto-tagging results periodically. The right balance of human oversight and AI lays the foundation for scalability and cost visibility.

Taxonomy

A *taxonomy* defines the system you want to use to classify costs into various categories based on established criteria relevant to your business. Creating a systematic framework or hierarchy that organizes cloud expenses according to their nature, function, or purpose starts the cost allocation process.

For instance, a taxonomy might have entries for the cost center, operating environment, or application. Organizations implementing a consistent taxonomy can guarantee uniformity and comparability in cost reporting across various departments or entities.

Table 2-2 provides a short example of tag taxonomy, using the bare minimum required resource tags that any business operating in the cloud needs to manage their business.

Table 2-2. *Example Tag Taxonomy*

Tag Taxonomy	Description	Tag Key and Values
Cost Center	Identifies the department or team responsible for a resource.	cost_center • Dept A • Dept B • Dept C
Environment	Indicates whether the resource is for development, staging, or production.	env • Development • Staging • Production
Project	Associates the resource with a specific project or initiative.	project • Project A • Project B
Service	Associates the resource with a particular application or service.	service_name • App A • App B • App C
Owner	Identifies the individual or team responsible for the resource.	service_owner • Username 1 • Team Name 2 • Team Name 3
Lifecycle	Tracks the resource's lifecycle stage (e.g., active, archived, etc.)	lifecycle_stage • active • archived

While this would be a bare minimum taxonomy for cloud resources, as you will see in the next few sections, many possibilities can be considered part of your unique organizational taxonomy. An important point to remember is that your taxonomy will be a living master reference for your teams, and you will need to revisit your taxonomy periodically as your business grows and evolves to ensure your tag keys and values remain relevant to your business.

Tag Health

Tag health refers to the overall quality and effectiveness of your tagging practices. It encompasses aspects such as the following:

- *Completeness*: Are all resources tagged with the necessary information?

- *Accuracy*: Are the tags applied correctly and do they reflect the true nature of the resource?

- *Consistency*: Are tags applied consistently across different teams and resources?

- *Standardization*: Do you have a defined taxonomy that dictates how tags are used?

Why Is Tag Health Important?

Poor tag health can lead to several issues:

- *Erroneous cost allocation*: When inconsistent tags, it can be challenging to correctly allocate expenses to particular divisions, tasks, or individuals.

- *Wasted resources*: Inconsistent or imprecise tagging makes it challenging to discover underutilized or wasted resources.

- *Ineffective reporting*: Precise and insightful cost reporting is only possible with consistent tagging.

- *Compliance challenges*: Poor adherence to tagging standards may result in challenges with corporate governance or regulatory requirements.

Strategies for Maintaining Tag Health

Here are some key strategies to ensure your tagging practices are healthy and are consistent with your defined taxonomy structure:

- *Define a simple and clear tagging taxonomy*: Emphasize simplicity and clarity when creating a well-defined taxonomy that lists the required tags and their definitions. Avoid excessively complicated tag names and ensure everyone can understand them.

- *Be aware of case sensitivity*: Tags are case-sensitive. Keep case sensitivity in mind when creating and using tags. Erroneous data aggregation may result from inconsistent capitalization. For instance, the treatment of tags named "environment" and "Environment" will differ, which could distort cost reports.

- *Automate tagging*: Automate tagging during resource provisioning using cloud-native services like AWS CloudFormation or infrastructure as code (IaC) technologies like Terraform by HashiCorp. This reduces manual errors by ensuring consistent tag application and minimizing human error. Automating tagging via IaC is discussed in depth later in this chapter.

- *Remember to tag*: Ensure every cloud resource applies the proper tags. Untagged resources introduce blind spots into your cost data, which prevents you from effectively allocating expenses and obstructs your ability to recognize probable areas for savings.

- *Enforce tagging*: Implement tagging policies that mandate specific tags and enforce compliance. This ensures consistency and allows resources to be provisioned with proper tagging. Tagging enforcement

- *Cost governance*: Educates about best tagging practices and fixes any discrepancies or errors in your tagging. There's an elaborate discussion on tagging enforcement later in the chapter.

- *Tag governance*: Establish a clear ownership and governance structure for managing your tagging taxonomy and enforcing best practices.

- *Review and update*: Review and update your tagging taxonomy
  regularly and as your business needs and cloud environment evolve.

By implementing these strategies and maintaining good tag health, you can ensure your cloud cost data is accurate and reliable, enabling you to make informed decisions about resource optimization and cost control.

Recommended Tags and Taxonomy

The taxonomy you build for your FinOps practice will be specific to your organization's needs. This will enable you to correlate costs to teams and enable granular reporting on costs across various categories or entities.

As you start your tagging journey, consider how you want your costs organized for reporting and analysis. As shown in Figure 2-2, structure your cloud cost hierarchy by organizational business unit (BU), with applications assigned to teams (shared services are in blue), and teams reporting to business units.

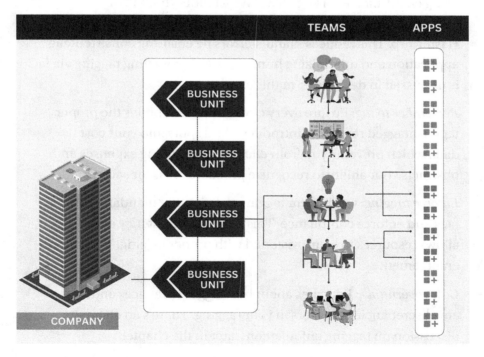

Figure 2-2. *Cloud cost hierarchy by BU*

This organizational-centric cloud cost hierarchy example drives most business financial reporting for cloud costs. You could also decide that you want a cloud cost hierarchy that reflects the infrastructure implementation, such as all resources that belong to development vs. all resources that belong to production, broken down by resource type.

In addition to the prevalent BU hierarchy, organizations can utilize an *executive leadership hierarchy* for cloud cost categorization. This approach aligns with existing leadership structures by assigning costs through tags like "VP," "Director," "Manager," and "Team Lead." This structure offers several advantages:

- Simplified cost allocation by leveraging the existing leadership chain

- Improved top-down visibility, as VPs can monitor departmental spending

- Increased accountability, as teams and individuals become responsible for their incurred costs

This hierarchy is well suited for organizations without a defined BU structure. Furthermore, it maintains flexibility, allowing customization based on specific organizational needs.

Whichever hierarchy you choose will help define the tags required in your taxonomy. The tagging suggestions presented in this section cover not only the tag name but also whether it's required for your taxonomy and the purpose of the tag. We'll break down the suggestions by:

- *Business-level tags*: Organizational-level tags that define account/ project information

- *Infrastructure resource tags*: The essential technical metadata for each cloud resource you leverage in your environment

- *Kubernetes cluster labels*: Additional technical metadata that is specific to Kubernetes (a.k.a. K8s) infrastructure

- *Management and security*: Metadata that assists with asset management and compliance

---

Note   Tagging nomenclature varies among CSPs. In AWS and Azure, key/value pairs for storing resource metadata are referred to as "tags," while in GCP and Kubernetes, these key/value pairs are called "labels" and tags have a different meaning/usage. We're keeping this discussion simple and using "tags" as a default.

Business-Level Tags

Business-level tags can help with cost attribution at an account level (AWS, Azure, etc.) or project level (e.g., GCP) and are the foundational information for budgeting, forecasting, and building chargeback/showback models. Recommended business-level tags are shown in Table 2-3.

Table 2-3. *Business-Level Tags*

Tag Name	Required?	Purpose
account_name **project_name**	Yes	Identify the name of the cloud account or project using the naming conventions of the organization.
account_owner	Yes	Specify the name of the engineering team that owns the account. A team alias works best in this scenario.
point_of_contact	Yes	Specify the username or email of the primary point of contact (POC) for the account.
executive_sponsor	Yes	Represent spend from an executive perspective. This helps to promote top-down budget alignment for cloud spend.
cost_center	Yes	Identify the cost center that the resource belongs to.
cob (cost_of_ business) **cogs (cost_of_goods)**	Yes	Indicate whether the tagged cloud resource direct production costs vs. R&D (non-production) with a true or false value. Use the term that matches your finance reporting standard.

Infrastructure-Level Tags

One or more teams will work on services and applications with a cloud account or project. Infrastructure-level tags enable additional granularity for cost attribution among multiple teams. Table 2-4 presents all recommended infrastructure-level tags.

Table 2-4. *Infrastructure-Level Tags*

Tag Name	Required?	Purpose
service_name	Yes	Identify the name of the service the resource belongs to. Example: service_name = front-end
service_owner	Yes	Specify the name of the engineering team that owns the service. A team alias works best in this scenario. If the resource is a shared service, add multiple owners separated by a comma.
shared_service	Conditional	Indicate whether or not the resource is shared across multiple users/teams. Takes Boolean values (yes or no as a value). If the value is yes, you have to add the name of all the service owners under the service_owner tag, separated by a comma. (We'll discuss shared services cost allocation later in the chapter.)
managed_by	Conditional	Identify the team alias/IC email of the team managing the service.
point_of_contact	Yes	Specify the username or email of the primary point of contact (POC) for the service.
requestor	Conditional	Specify the name of the team that requests the service might be required in creating an account.
env	Yes	Specify Dev, QA, Stage, Prod, Sandbox, etc. If the infrastructure falls under one of these categories, you must add this tag.
name	Conditional	Use any unique name with which the team can identify a resource meaningfully. This is for service owners to decide how to name their services to make them easier to identify. Example: us-west-2a-front-end-01.
iac_managed	Conditional	Indicates if cloud resource is managed via Terraform (tf), CloudFormation (cf), or other Infrastructure as Code (IaC) tool. (set to true if tf / cf managed, otherwise false)

> **Note**   From a cloud resource deployment perspective, the recommendation is to use the tag (Dev, QA, Staging, Prod, etc.) to identify resources from specific environments.

Kubernetes/Container-Specific Labels

Deploying microservice architecture on shared containers, especially Kubernetes, has become more popular over the past few years due to the agility of scaling clusters on demand. All Kubernetes resources (pods, nodes, etc.) must contain both the infrastructure-level tags listed in Table 2-4 and K8s-specific labels. Table 2-5 presents all recommended K8s-specific labels/tags.

Table 2-5. *Kubernetes/Container-Specific Labels/Tags*

Tag Name	Required?	Purpose
cluster_name	Yes	To specify the name for the cluster. Example: production-cluster-1
iac_managed	Conditional	Used to indicate if the cluster is managed by Terraform (true) or not (false). In an ideal world, it's recommended and a best practice to launch all cloud infrastructure via IaC.)

Resource Cleanup–Related Tags

You can add tags to help with resource housekeeping, especially if you leverage automation to look for and act upon these tags. Tags such as these can help with your cost optimization efforts and compliance. Table 2-6 presents all recommended tags that could be used for cleaning up unused resources.

Table 2-6. *Resource Cleanup–Related Tags*

Tag Name	Required?	Purpose
remove_after_date	Conditional	Required for resources created outside of the IaC (regular) process and other temp environments. If any additional infrastructure is created in response to an incident or for testing purposes, this tag helps remove cloud resources after the specified period when no longer needed. Example: remove_after_date = "12/21/2021"
shutdown	Conditional	Use for non-production workloads where resources can be turned off during non-business hours and weekends.

Pro Tip   The shutdown tag helps identify resources that can be stopped on a scheduled basis. For instance, if this is true, a lambda function or some automation script can turn off a resource with this tag at 5 p.m. and then bring it back online at 8 a.m. (You can set a schedule that works best for you.)

Security-Related Tags

This category is a curated list of tags that could be useful for security teams dealing with incidents and so forth. While these tags do not directly contribute toward cost allocation, they can help security teams implement guardrails and automate processes. Table 2-7 presents all recommended security-level tags.

Table 2-7. *Security-Related Tags*

Tag Name	Required?	Purpose
criticality	Conditional	This tag may help security teams inform security teams of the criticality of environments and resources. This could help set up incident response automation based on vulnerability criticality. • low • medium • high • business unit-critical • mission-critical
dr (disaster recovery)	Conditional	This tag may help cloud infrastructure teams identify failover environments during DR, which could help them determine the costs of running DR. • mission-critical • critical • essential
pii	Yes	This tag helps identify if the environment contains personally identifiable information (PII). This can help identify costs for securing environments and enable policies to be applied to Identity and Access Management (IAM). • False • True

Cloud Tagging Tools

Several methods exist for applying tags to cloud resources, ranging from almost fully automated to manually intensive. How you proceed with tagging will depend on your CSP and the DevOps tooling you have in place.

Ideally, your team should already use an infrastructure as code (IaC) tool from either a third party or the CSP to automate and manage your infrastructure deployments. IaC tools can automate tagging into resource provisioning, helping your teams maintain healthy tag hygiene.

Other options for tagging that are more manually intensive include leveraging the tagging feature of the CSP cloud console or applying tags via the command line interface (CLI) or application programming interface (API). Regardless of the method you choose to apply tags, remember that there are (rather generous) limits to how many tags can be applied to a cloud resource. For AWS and Azure, that limit is 50 tags (exclusive of system tags); for GCP, the limit is 64.

Infrastructure as Code Tools

IaC tools allow you to define and manage cloud resources using declarative configuration files. Tag definitions can be automated and included in the config file at any time, whether at initial configuration or updated post-deployment. Terraform is one of the most popular IaC tools on the market, but each of the CSPs have their own IaC offerings, including AWS CloudFormation, Azure Resource Manager (ARM), and Google Cloud Deployment Manager (CDM).

Tag management via IaC is the most preferred method for deploying your tag strategy, as it allows you to automate, standardize, and enforce tagging. IaC tools generally bring governance, repeatability, scalability, and automation to infrastructure provisioning and deprovisioning.

Listing 2-1 depicts how tags are defined in Terraform configuration files for standard infrastructure, and Listing 2-2 depicts how tags are defined in Terraform configuration files for Kubernetes clusters. In each example, you can see how account tags are defined and applied via the Terraform configuration files, with the Kubernetes example going one step further to define a worker group for the EKS cluster. For the book, we're limiting the examples to AWS.

Listing 2-1. Terraform Configuration for Standard Infrastructure

```
module "account_tags" {
  source      = "github.com/terraform-utils/modules/tags/account-
                 tags?ref=v0.1"
  account     = "devtest"
  owner       = "Ops"
  requestor   = "ops@Organization.net"
}
```

```
provider "aws" {
  region  = "us-west-2"
  profile = "Organization-devtest"
  default_tags {
    tags  = module.account_tags.tags #brings all the tags from the
            above module
  }
}
```

Listing 2-2. Terraform Configuration for Kubernetes Cluster

```
module "eks" {
source             = "terraform-aws-modules/eks/aws"
cluster_name       = local.cluster_name
cluster_version = "1.20"
subnets            = module.vpc.private_subnets
tags = {
environment        = "env"
service_owner     = "team1"
}
vpc_id             = module.vpc.vpc_id
workers_group_defaults = {
root_volume_type        = "gp3"
}
worker_groups    = [
{
name                    = "worker-group-1"
instance_type           = "t2.small"
additional_userdata     = "echo foo bar"
asg_desired_capacity = 2
}
]
}
```

Kubernetes Manifest File

In addition to using IaC tools, Kubernetes clusters can also be managed via third-party deployment tools such as Helm, specific to Kubernetes, whether deployed on-premises or in the cloud. The K8s manifest file uses YAML to define all relevant information about the cluster configuration, which is then read and executed by the deployment tool of choice.

As shown in Listing 2-3, the manifest file includes labels for the cluster, which can be used in automated templates for cluster management and manually edited as needed.

Listing 2-3. Applying Tags in the Kubernetes Manifest File

```
apiVersion: v1
kind: Pod
metadata:
  name: some-app
  labels:
    env: dev
    app: nginx
    service_owner: team-xyz
    service_name: nginx
```

CSP Management Consoles

Each CSP includes the ability to tag cloud resources via their cloud management console. The following example includes steps to add labels (as previously mentioned, tags in GCP are called labels) to a GCP project:

1. Navigate to the Labels page in the GCP cloud console.

2. Select your project from the project drop-down.

3. To add a new label, click the + Add Label button and enter a label key and value. Repeat for each label you want to add.

4. Save once you're finished adding labels.

Pro Tip   Tag Editor simplifies AWS resource tagging by offering an intuitive interface for searching and filtering. Users can target specific resource types (e.g., EC2 instances) or filter based on existing tags, encompassing all regions or selecting specific ones. Bulk operations empower efficient tag management: introducing new tags for the organization, editing existing values directly in search results, and swiftly removing unwanted ones (limited to 500 resources at once). While appropriate permissions are crucial, security best practices advise against storing sensitive information in tags. Benefits include enhanced organization for cost allocation and access control, improved visibility into resource usage and ownership, and streamlined workflows through efficient bulk management, leading to a comprehensive and streamlined tagging experience for technical professionals.

Manage Tags via CLI

Most CSPs offer command-line interfaces that allow you to interact with their services from the command line. Depending on the cloud provider, the CLI provides commands or options to set tags on cloud resources. Listings 2-4 and 2-5 show examples of tagging resources via the CLI for standard infrastructure and Kubernetes clusters, respectively.

Listing 2-4. Applying Tags via CLI for Standard Infrastructure

```
aws ec2 create-tags   --resources  ami-xxxxxx  --tags
Key=service_owner, Value=ops
```

Listing 2-5. Applying Tags via CLI for Kubernetes Clusters

```
Tag the cluster
aws eks tag-resource resource_ARN --tags
service_owner=devs
# Remove service_owner tag on cluster
aws eks untag-resource --resource-arn resource_ARN --tag-keys
service_owner
```

Tagging Enforcement

While tagging enforcement is crucial for data consistency, planning and communicating tagging enforcement effectively before implementing it across your organization is essential. This ensures everyone is on the same page and minimizes potential disruptions.

Not all tags hold equal importance. Focus on selecting a concise set of critical tags that are necessary for cost allocation, reporting, and compliance, considering your business context. Refer to the "Recommended Tags and Taxonomy" section for suggestions.

If you use Terraform for IaC, leverage tools like `tflinter` to enforce the presence of mandatory tags on your resources. This helps ensure consistent tagging practices and avoids potential data quality issues.

You could take this idea to your SRE/cloud team and ask them to implement something like `tflinter` with a mandatory (service_name = "xyz") tag on all your resources. `tflinter` can help with validation and enforcing tagging as well. Listing 2-6 presents a sample code snippet demonstrating how to use `tflinter` for tagging compliance.

Listing 2-6. Using `tflinter` to Enforce Tagging Compliance

```
#  Add your tflinter rule in a location like- docs/rules/aws_resource_
   missing_tags.md
# aws_resource_missing_tags

Require specific tags for all AWS resource types that support them.

## Configuration

```hcl
rule "aws_resource_missing_tags" {
  enabled = true
  tags        = ["service_name", "service_owner", "cost_center"]  #note that
              these are case sensitive
  exclude = ["aws_autoscaling_group"] # (Optional) Exclude some resource
            types from tag checks, here, aws_autoscaling_group resource
            type will be ignored.
}
```
```

```
#Assume you have a instance.tf file as follows:
resource "aws_instance" "instance" {
  instance_type     = "m5.large"
  tags  = {
    service_name  = "xyz"
    cost_center       = "abc@org.net"
  }
}
```

Once you have tflinter installed, you will now be able to execute tflint command in the terraform repository to check for any violations.

```
$ tflint
1 issue(s) found:
Notice: aws_instance.instance is missing the following tags:
"service_owner" (aws_resource_missing_tags)
```

Pro Tip   Leverage tags for cost optimization and automated resource management. Standardize tags (key and value naming), and utilize them for cost allocation (project/department), environment (dev/test/prod), and automation (opt-in/out for scaling). Use Tag APIs and IaC services from CSPs and other third-party software providers to programmatically tag your cloud resources. Prioritize informative tags and enforce tagging standards using organization service control policies (SCPs). This fosters cost visibility, streamlines resource management, and empowers informed financial decisions in your cloud environment.

Tagging Strategy for FinOps at Scale

Businesses that want to create and scale their FinOps practices need a solid tagging strategy. Effectively managing your business spend requires a tagging strategy that enables proper categorization and allocation of all cloud resources you deploy. However, even the most brilliant taxonomy will fail if you don't manage and enforce tagging among your teams consistently over time.

A tagging strategy can significantly improve financial visibility and optimize resource allocation and cost analysis. Defining, communicating, reviewing, automating, and enforcing the plan is crucial to creating a successful tagging strategy. Each component plays a significant role in ensuring the strategy is effective and efficient. Figure 2-3 represents the five-step tagging strategy for FinOps, described in the following list.

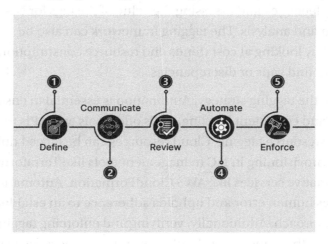

Figure 2-3. *Tagging strategy*

1. Define a tagging strategy. An explicit and comprehensive tagging taxonomy is essential for an efficient tagging strategy. This involves creating a set of standardized tags that capture information about cloud resources relevant to your organization's business. This step is necessary to ensure success. The specific tags may change based on the business needs; nonetheless, we'll discuss some examples of what tags to use in the next section.

2. Communicate the tagging strategy. Effective communication ensures the organization's adoption and comprehension of the tagging framework after it is created. The strategy should be well documented, along with instructions on consistently applying tags and what data each tag denotes. All parties involved in resource provisioning, including developers, IT administrators, and financial teams, should have easy access to this data. Regular workshops or training sessions can clarify the significance of tagging and resolving queries or worries.

3. Review the tagging strategy. Regular evaluation and auditing are essential to keep the tagging approach accurate and current. Evaluate the effectiveness of existing tags regularly and identify areas for improvement. Working with stakeholders from many departments, including finance, IT, and operations, entails gathering feedback and assessing the value of the tags for cost allocation and analysis. The tagging framework can also be improved by looking at cost trends and resource consumption patterns to find gaps or discrepancies.

4. Automate the tagging strategy. Automation is essential to ensure accurate and consistent labeling. CSPs offer tools and APIs to automate resource tagging. Cloud resources can be tagged during resource provisioning in IaC management tools like Terraform or cloud-native services like AWS CloudFormation. Automation minimizes human error and upholds adherence to an established tagging approach. Additionally, verifying and enforcing tagging compliance throughout the cloud environment is possible using third-party scripts and tools.

5. Enforce the tagging strategy. Establish governance and monitoring systems to enforce tagging. Third-party software/CSP-provided tools and automation ensure resource provision without proper tags is refused or highlighted. To ensure tagging when resources are mistagged, implement real-time notifications to notify users.

Tagging can be very tedious, especially without supporting automation, and it requires coordination with cross-functional partners to ensure accuracy, which may be why your teams haven't tackled this yet. However, the gains to your business in terms of cost visibility, which will drive hard dollar *cost savings* for your business, justify the effort involved in creating your tagging strategy The tagging strategy you create has to be well defined and communicated for tagging to be fruitful.

Slack's Case Study: Cloud Resource Tagging with the Tagging Strategy Adoption

Challenge

When I was the founding member of the Cloud Economics team at Slack, a Salesforce company and a leading communication/collaboration platform, only 40% of our cloud resources had mandated tags applied, which made it challenging to monitor expenses precisely and maximize resource use among various teams and apps. This lack of visibility impeded our ability to make well-informed judgments about cloud spending and resource management.

Solution

The Cloud Economics team implemented a comprehensive tagging strategy to improve cloud cost visibility. This strategy included the following key steps:

1. Define a tagging standard:

   a. *Collaboration*: We collaborated with Cloud Engineering and TPM teams to define a transparent and standardized tagging approach.

   b. *Mandatory tags*: Two mandatory tags were established that uniquely represent applications.

2. Communication and buy-in:

   a. *Documentation*: We developed comprehensive documentation explaining

      i. The importance of tagging for cloud cost visibility.

      ii. The specific tags to be used and how teams could tag their resources

      iii. The tagging process and best practices.

   b. Stakeholder engagement:

      i. *Executive buy-in*: We secured executive buy-in by highlighting the benefits of tagging for improved cost visibility and control.

    ii. *Broader communication*: We shared the documentation across various teams, including application developers, engineering managers, and the wider audience, for feedback and awareness.

    iii. *Transparency and collaboration*: We announced the mandatory implementation of these tags through public channels and encouraged collaboration with the Cloud Economics team for any assistance needed.

3. Review:

    a. *Regular audits*: We implemented periodic reviews and audits to assess the effectiveness of the tagging strategy. This involved

        i. Identifying any inconsistencies or gaps in tag usage.

        ii. Gathering feedback from stakeholders (finance, IT, operations) on the value of tags for cost allocation and analysis.

        iii. Analyzing cost trends and resource consumption patterns to pinpoint discrepancies.

    b. *Continuous improvement*: Based on the review findings, we refined the tagging strategy:

        i. Adjusted the taxonomy or tag requirements as needed.

        ii. Updated documentation and training materials to reflect any changes.

4. Automate:

    a. *Infrastructure as code*: We leveraged IaC tools like Terraform and cloud-native services (AWS CloudFormation) to automate tagging during resource provisioning. This ensured

        i. Consistent tag application across all resources.

        ii. Minimized human error.

        iii. Adherence to the defined tagging strategy.

    b. *Third-party tools*: We utilized additional scripts and tools to verify and enforce tagging compliance throughout the cloud environment.

5. Enforce:

   a. *Governance and monitoring*: We established clear governance structures to manage the tagging taxonomy and enforce tagging practices. This included

      i. Defining roles and responsibilities for tag ownership and enforcement.

      ii. Implementing processes for addressing noncompliance issues.

   b. *Tagging policies*: We enforced the use of specific tags through

      i. CSP-provided tools and APIs to prevent resource provisioning without proper tags.

      ii. Real-time notifications to inform users about missing or incorrect tags.

   c. *tflinter integration*: Using Terraform, we implemented tools like `tflinter` to enforce the presence of mandatory tags on resources. This ensured data consistency and adherence to tagging requirements.

Results

The tagging adoption rate surged from < 50% to over 90% within a quarter. This significant improvement has yielded several benefits:

- *Enhanced cost visibility*: Consistent tagging allowed us to track costs associated with specific applications and teams, enabling granular cost allocation and optimization strategies.

- *Accurate cost reporting*: Standardized tagging makes creating thorough and precise cost reports easier, which offers insightful information for efficient cloud cost management.

- *Data-driven decision-making*: By knowing where cloud expenditures are incurred, we can make data-driven decisions about resource allocation, budgeting, and other cost optimization initiatives.

This case study illustrates the success of a clear, coordinated, and cooperative tagging approach. We gained important insights for well-informed decision-making on cloud resource management. We considerably improved cloud resource tagging by enforcing necessary tags, involving stakeholders, and offering clear documentation.

Finding Untagged Resources

Untagged resources are a significant obstacle to efficient resource management, cost optimization, and infrastructure security. It's critical to find and remediate untagged resources at the outset of your FinOps journey and establish controls to maintain tag health over time. With ongoing monitoring, you ensure the accuracy of your cloud cost reporting remains strong.

Here are strategies for finding and remediating untagged cloud resources, from the most manual (and least effective) to the fully automated (and most effective):

- *Work with the CSP management console*: All CSPs include a management console with a GUI. Go to the console and the relevant service section to access your resources. To search or categorize materials based on tags, look for options or filters. To find untagged resources, exclude filters tied to specific tags.

- *Use CLI or SDKs*: Cloud service providers frequently offer CLIs or software development kits (SDKs) for programmatic access to their services. Using these tools, you can create scripts or commands to query the CSP's APIs and get a list of resources. Look for API methods or commands that let you use tags to filter resources, and specifically look for resources without labels applied.

- *Use tagging APIs*: Some cloud service providers have APIs that can be used to manage and look up tags on resources. Examine the tagging APIs currently offered and their documentation to learn how to search for untagged resources programmatically.

- *Consider third-party tools*: Third-party tools and services also manage, optimize, and secure cloud resources. Compared to native CSP tools, these technologies offer features to identify untagged resources and offer more sophisticated search and management capabilities.

- *Leverage automation and routine audits*: Create a procedure for conducting routine resource audits and tagging techniques. Use IaC technologies like AWS CloudFormation or Terraform, which may enforce tagging criteria during resource provisioning and prevent untagged resources when automating your processes. (Refer to Chapter 5 for more information.)

Pro Tip   Leverage cloud resource inventories and configuration management databases (CMDBs) to automatically track untagged resources. Solutions like AWS Config can record point-in-time configurations of your resources. You can identify missing tags by comparing these inventories against your expected tags. Schedule regular scans and automate alerts when newly untagged resources are detected. This removes the need for tedious manual audits and ensures you have ongoing visibility into untagged resources that may pose financial, security, or compliance risks if left unmanaged.

The best approach for remediating untagged resources is to update tags with IaC automation.

Now that we've provided the foundation for cloud cost visibility by creating a strong taxonomy and tagging strategy for your teams to follow, the next step for the FinOps teams is to communicate costs to the various stakeholders in the organization via reporting and executive dashboards.

Monitoring Costs Through Dashboards and Reports

Whether a single engineering team is working on one or two applications or many teams across divisions are working on a suite of products, the challenge leadership teams face remains the same: How does the leadership team see and understand their team's cloud usage and costs? The FinOps team is responsible for providing that information through executive dashboards and regular reports.

A significant portion of this chapter is dedicated to tagging because, without it, cost reporting becomes a labor-intensive exercise that often produces faulty or inadequate information about cloud costs. After an initial pass at implementing your tagging strategy, you can use the tag information to properly categorize and organize your cloud resource spend in whichever way best matches your organization's needs.

Cloud cost visibility results in a comprehensive set of dashboards that your teams can rely on to provide a high-level view of cloud spend and the ability to drill down into the data to provide deeper cost insights (which we'll cover in the next chapter).

Breaking Down Cloud Costs

Now that you've established a strong tagging strategy to determine how you will allocate shared costs and (hopefully) determine what tool you plan to use for CCM (detailed in the next section), it's time to define the reporting levels you need to establish to understand your cloud cost breakdown adequately. This starts with understanding how to segment your costs at the CSP account/project level and flow down to the individual resources.

Cloud Provider Billing Account/Subscription/Project

Organizations of any size generally have multiple billing accounts per cloud provider that roll into one master root group for billing and management purposes. However, each CSP uses different terminology for this entity (see Table 2-8). Separating departments, applications, or environments into different accounts, rather than having a single account, is a best practice for security and access management to cloud resources.

Having multiple accounts also provides cost segmentation for those departments or applications. Each account has a unique bill, making allocating and reporting on nonshared costs easy. Each CSP provides a hierarchical system for managing many accounts, and businesses can use this structure to better understand expenses at varying account levels. Table 2-8 presents billing entity name and master account name mapping for the three major CSPs.

Table 2-8. *CSP Billing Grouping Table*

CSP	Billing Entity Name	Master Account Name
AWS	Account	Root
Azure	Subscription	Root Management Group
GCP	Project	Organization

CSP Service Types

All cloud providers include system-level tags on resources as they are provisioned, identifying key attributes such as resource type (EC2 instances, Azure VM, GCP cloud storage, GKE, S3 buckets, RDS databases, and other services), regions/zones, and more. Reporting on cloud costs by resource type provides the information that finance or procurement departments need to negotiate commitment contracts with the cloud providers. It also provides the basis for additional cost insights—for example, drilling down into resource usage by application or workload—allowing companies to report, monitor, and promote efficient cloud resource usage.

Cost Centers

Utilizing cost centers allows businesses to get more detailed cost visibility. Departments, teams, projects, and business units are examples of the level at which cost centers may be defined for budgeting and planning purposes. By implementing the cost_center tag as part of your taxonomy, your organization can acquire granular visibility into how much each cost center spends on cloud resources. Reporting on cloud costs at the cost center level allows you to control costs better, create budgets, and optimize resource utilization within each cost center.

Applications/Services/Environments

SaaS applications and services built in the cloud generate revenue while driving cloud costs as part of doing business. By tagging cloud resources by the application or service they support, businesses provide visibility into their cost of business (cob) or cost of goods sold (cogs) for each application they deploy into the cloud.

Drilling Down into K8s/Microservices Spend

Kubernetes and microservices cost reporting is specialized because of their dynamic, shared nature among applications and teams. To provide granular reporting for these shared services, your tagging strategy needs to consider these factors:

- *Costs per label*: In K8s environments, labels are key/value pairs that can be assigned to resources. Organizations can associate costs with specific attributes such as microservices, applications, teams, or environments by leveraging tags or labels. This allows for granular cost reporting based on labels, providing insights into the cost breakdown of individual microservices or applications within a K8s cluster.

- *Costs per namespace*: K8s namespaces provide logical boundaries for isolating resources within a cluster. Organizations can associate costs with specific namespaces, enabling cost visibility at the namespace level. This helps them to understand cost distribution across cluster parts, teams, or projects.

- *Costs per service*: K8s employs the concept of services to enable communication and load balancing between microservices. Organizations can gain insights into each service's cost by associating costs with individual services. This allows for analyzing the cost efficiency and resource utilization of specific microservices or applications within the K8s ecosystem.

Cost Categories View: Grouping Applications with Teams and Leaders

Organizations can build cost category views aligned with applications, teams, or business units to provide a holistic perspective. This involves grouping relevant microservices or applications and associating them with the respective teams or leaders responsible for them. By aggregating costs at this level, organizations can understand cost allocation across different teams or business units, enabling better accountability and decision-making.

Cost Trends over Time

Analyzing cost trends over different periods is crucial for understanding cost fluctuations and identifying patterns. Organizations can compare costs on an hour-over-hour (HoH), day-over-day (DoD), week-over-week (WoW), or month-over-month (MoM) basis for identifying cost spikes, unusual spending patterns, or potential areas for optimization. Historical cost data enables trend analysis and proactive cost management.

As the previous subsections demonstrate, by building reports and dashboards covering multiple levels of cost breakdowns, organizations can gain deeper insights into their cloud costs. This enables better decision-making, cost optimization, and resource allocation within their cloud environment.

Dashboards covey a story. They provide an easy way to monitor actual spending against the budget so that unplanned spending can be proactively controlled. Many CCM tools incorporate forecasting features into their dashboards, using previous spending data and patterns to project future costs. This enables executives to plan for and distribute resources more effectively.

Dashboards and Reports

A cloud cost dashboard (illustrated in Figure 2-4) provides an overview of the organization's cloud spend. It typically includes graphs and charts showing cost trends, cost breakdowns by services or departments, and alerts for cost anomalies. The dashboard is a central hub for tracking and managing cloud costs effectively. This section navigates through how you can build reports and dashboards using tags for various personas, from executives to team members.

Figure 2-4. *Cloud cost executive dashboard example*

It's important to note that you won't have just one dashboard for your cloud costs; you will have multiple dashboards depending on which persona the dashboard caters to.

Executive-Level Dashboards

Executive-level dashboards provide a high-level view of the entire organization's cloud spending, including reports and graphs covering the overall amount spent in the cloud, cost trends over time, and cost allocation by department, service, or account. These dashboards focus on crucial cost metrics impacting the business's health.

Pro Tip   Use dashboard filters at account, date, cost_center, service_name, region, usage_type, pricing option, CSP, and other tag levels to gain cost visibility across various dimensions.

Here's how you can use tags to monitor your costs with reports and dashboards.

Pie Charts/Donut Charts

The following list describes the numbered pie charts and donut charts shown in Figure 2-4:

1. Use the account_name/project_name tag to access the costs at the account level. If you can sort your accounts in descending order, you will have a report/widget depicting your top-spending accounts.

2. The following diagram shows the top cloud services in this example, such as EC2, GKS, or S3. To build a report on these services, use the CSP's services and sort them in descending order to get to the top-spending services.

Pro Tip   Use cost categories to group services into spend categories like compute, storage, network, or other services. For instance, a "database" category can be used to group services like RDS, Dynamo DB, or Aurora.

The cost categories concept can be extended to group multiple applications into a category to determine the costs of running a POC by tagging the resources with specific or multiple tags grouped under one category to determine their costs.

3. Vendor split depicts the cost split between multiple CSPs. Use this widget when you have a multi-cloud environment.

4. Use the **cost_center** tag to report costs at a cost-center level. The widget reports the organization's five top-spending cost centers. With this tag, you not only know what the top-spending areas are but also where you should focus to optimize. We'll discuss more cost optimization techniques in Chapter 6.

5. With the **service_owner** tag, you can identify application owners for top-spending areas/applications within the organization.

Trend Graphs

For executive dashboards, keep the trends, represented at the center of the graph, at a year-over-year (YoY), quarter-over-quarter (QoQ), or month-over-month (MoM) level to provide a high-level summary of cost data to executives.

- Use the cost categories graph at the center-left to depict costs across top-spending categories, which can help identify where the bulk of costs come from and allows executives to focus in the top spending areas.

- Going one step deeper, the Service Name graph at the lower left identifies top-spending CSP services and their trend over time.

- The next graph depicts spend across applications with the service_name tag.

- The final graph represents cost-split across service_owners/leaders responsible for the applications in the organization.

Technical/Team Deep-Dive Dashboard

Depending on the size and structure of your organization, you may tailor the cost visibility dashboards to your team's cloud costs and thus create team-level dashboards, such as the example shown in Figure 2-5. These dashboards focus on actionable insights for cost optimization, such as workloads/applications with high expenses, deep-dive into cost categories where most spending comes from, and identifying the underlying cloud resources responsible for cost trends. Once the underlying cloud resources responsible for cost trends are identified, leverage monitoring tools such as CloudWatch to identify utilization and rightsize as necessary.

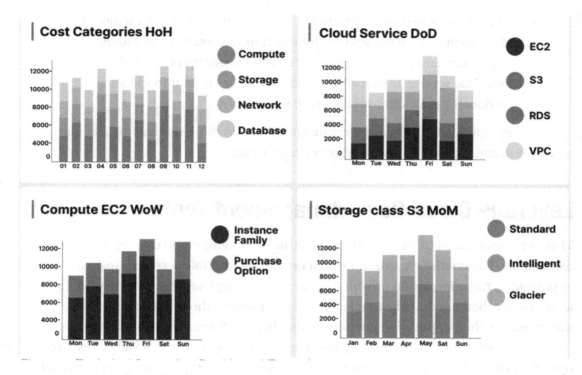

Figure 2-5. *Technical deep-dive dashboard example*

Build trend graphs more granularly at MoM, WoW, DoD, or HoH for technical deep-dive dashboards. Note that CSPs provide HoH cost reporting for the last 14 days, which you can utilize to get more granular insights into costs. You can identify changes and utilization patterns on an hourly basis. Technical/team deep-dive dashboards should include all the executive summary dashboards and more granular spending details like the following:

- Cost category view at the top left, is similar to the executive dashboard but more granular level reporting at HoH and WoW to identify top spending buckets.

- Similar to the executive dashboard, build cloud services granular dashboards that can depict trends with appropriate filters.

- Build trend graphs for compute costs, for instance, the bottom-left graph, including detailed costs like instance type, family, usage hours, and purchase option (on-demand, spot, reserved, savings plans), with a combination of tags and filter to your applications and cloud accounts.

- Granular storage costs for instance, the bottom-right graph, including all types of storage classes over time and storage services including object, file, and block storage can depict your storage cost trends over time. Use service_owner and service_name tags to go into specific workload/application-level storage costs.

You can expand on the idea and create graphs across more services for granular reporting according to your organization's cloud usage.

Leverage Cloud Cost Management Tools

There's no shortage of CCM tools for creating and managing cloud cost reports and dashboards. For smaller organizations that don't have multiple accounts/teams/ applications, the information provided by the CSP management console may be adequate for their needs. However, larger organizations or those that leverage Kubernetes in their application environments will benefit from investing in a third-party CCM tool to aid their reporting (not to mention providing cost insights, resource optimization, and savings opportunities). Cloud cost reporting via spreadsheet *should not* be considered a viable approach for scaling FinOps.

With your tag strategy in place, a CCM tool (whether from the CSP or a third party) will enable users to examine the cloud costs attributed to the various categories created by the tagging taxonomy. For instance, you can analyze the overall costs of an environment, project, or department and see a consolidated view of costs at the account or cloud provider level.

You can also drill down into different combinations of cost attribution to drive greater cost insights. For example, you could answer questions such as "What is the storage bandwidth usage by team A," or "What is the cost of an application by environment (prod/non-prod)?"

Whichever tool you choose, you can improve visibility into your cloud costs and dive deep into cloud cost analysis based on the data you surface. Cost management software frequently uses graphical representations like charts, graphs, and heat maps to visualize cost allocation across tags. These representations make recognizing patterns, anomalies, or trends in costs easier.

CCM tools generally include historical cost data, which enables users to compare costs over time. By analyzing previous trends and looking for patterns, you can detect cost spikes, seasonality, or usage patterns affecting your overall spending. This analysis enables you to optimize the allocation of resources, discover possibilities to save costs, and make educated decisions regarding the utilization of cloud computing.

In most CCM solutions, you can set up cost alerts and notifications based on tag-specific thresholds and spikes. Thanks to this functionality, you can proactively monitor spend associated with tags. For instance, you can schedule alerts/notifications that will inform you once the costs of a specific department or project reach a predetermined limit.

Beyond cost reporting and visibility, CCM tools generally have features that enable cost optimization, budgeting/forecasting, chargeback/showback, and compliance. We'll cover those aspects of scaling FinOps later in the book. The next section will discuss a framework for choosing a CCM tool for your business needs.

Selecting the Right CCM Tool

As previously mentioned, the information provided by the CSP management console might suffice for smaller organizations with limited accounts/teams/applications, but larger organizations and those utilizing Kubernetes within their application environments will significantly benefit from investing in a third-party CCM tool. These tools offer a wider range of capabilities beyond reporting, enabling you to optimize your cloud spending and gain valuable insights.

Features of Effective CCM Solutions

Effective CCM solutions offer the following features:

- *Consolidated visibility*: View costs across multi-cloud environments, including public, private, and hybrid cloud deployments.

- *Cost monitoring and analytics*: Gain insights into usage, spending, and forecasts, including amortized costs, custom reporting, and reservation tracking. Advanced analytics using AI/ML can identify potential waste and suboptimal resource utilization.

- *Optimization and automation*: Automate actions like shutting down idle resources, resizing instances, and scheduling instances for real-time optimization.

- *Unified platform*: Manage costs across multiple cloud environments and platforms through a single interface, fostering better governance.

- *Flexibility*: Adapt to your existing workflows and infrastructure with flexible deployment options, custom data ingestion, and extensibility through APIs.

- *Usability*: Intuitive dashboards tailored for different stakeholders with self-service access, alerts, and recommendations improve user adoption.

Choosing the Right CCM Tool Is Controlling Cloud Expenses

Due to the increasing use of cloud computing, organizations now value controlling cloud expenditures. Although the cloud's on-demand resource paradigm offers flexibility and potential cost savings, a lack of visibility and control can quickly lead to unforeseen expenses.

Respondents cited optimizing cloud expenses as the most prominent cloud challenge in the *RightScale 2024 State of the Cloud Report from Flexera*. Choosing the appropriate CCM tool can help you confront that challenge by tackling the following issues to optimize your cloud ROI:

- *Lack of visibility*: Public cloud services like AWS, Azure, and Google Cloud Platform charge only for consumed resources, offering flexibility and potentially obscuring the true cost picture. Costs can quickly escalate across numerous accounts, subscriptions, projects, and business units. Issues Addressed by CCM Tools.

- *Inefficiencies and waste*: Gaining visibility into cloud resource utilization and spending patterns is the foundation for cost optimization. CCM tools collate and analyze usage and billing data to provide insights across multi-cloud environments.

Boosting Cloud ROI with CCM Tools

CCM tools boost cloud ROI through the following:

- *Providing granular visibility*: Gain insights into utilization and spending across cloud environments, enabling informed decision-making.

- *Eliminating waste*: Identify and eliminate waste from idle or underutilized resources.

- *Optimizing resources*: Optimize cloud workload size, configuration, and resource allocation.

- *Enforcing governance*: Enforce budgets, policies, and governance based on business needs.

- *Promoting accountability*: Foster cost awareness through chargeback and showback reporting.

- *Forecasting and planning*: Accurately forecast future spending to optimize budgets.

- *Ongoing optimization*: Use automatic actions and suggestions to monitor and optimize costs continuously.

Build vs. Buy

Should you build your own CCM tool or buy one? The answer depends on your resources and priorities.

Building a CCM tool offers greater customization and control. A knowledgeable FinOps team can modify the tool to meet your unique requirements. However, this route necessitates a large initial investment of time and funds for development, as well as continuous maintenance costs.

Purchasing a prebuilt CCM tool offers faster implementation and lower upfront costs. However, you'll need to factor in licensing fees and potential subscriptions. These tools may not be as customizable, but some offer prebuilt features that suit your industry or needs. Consider how well the tool integrates with your existing systems. While building your own tool offers more control over integration, a prebuilt solution can streamline the process.

Visibility, Insights, and Actions Framework to Evaluate CCM Tools

When evaluating potential CCM tools, consider the Visibility, Insights, and Actions (VIA) framework, represented in Figure 2-6, to ensure that you choose the solution that best aligns with your organization's specific needs.

Figure 2-6. *VIA framework for CCM*

Visibility

Effective cloud financial management begins with gaining comprehensive visibility into your cloud environment. This involves understanding costs at various levels and identifying trends to inform strategic decisions.

- *Cloud service level*: Gain cost overviews for various services, such as compute, storage, networking, databases, and monitoring.

- *Tag level*: Understand cost attribution granularly to foster cost awareness across teams and executives.

- *Hierarchy needs*: Ensure the tool accommodates your organization's unique hierarchy structure for effective cost attribution, chargeback, and management.

- *Drill-down*: Drill down into costs at various levels, including accounts, projects, regions, cloud services, teams, and even resource IDs for deeper insights.

- *Trend analysis*: Analyze cost trends over time to identify potential issues and forecast future spending.

- *Container/microservice visibility*: Gain insights into costs associated with containers and microservices for accurate chargeback and cost awareness within these environments.

- *Multi-cloud single pane of glass*: View costs across all your cloud deployments from a single, unified platform, simplifying cost management for multi-cloud environments.

Insights

To optimize cloud usage and manage costs effectively, the value of actionable insights into your cloud environment cannot be overstated. These insights are the key to understanding resource utilization, setting budgets, and identifying areas for improvement, giving you the tools for success.

- *Unit economics*: Understand costs per unit, such as per user or customer, to identify trends and calculate net profits.

- *Resource utilization*: Identify underutilized compute resources and optimize their usage to eliminate waste.

- *Container optimization*: Gain insights into container memory and CPU utilization to optimize containerized workloads and infrastructure.

- *Budgeting*: Set budgets and receive alerts when exceeded, promoting cost awareness and enabling proactive management.

- *Forecasting*: Receive forecasts for financial planning, discount renegotiation, and cost allocation based on priorities.

- *Customizable dashboards*: Create customized dashboards for specific roles so that users can view expense data in a way that best suits their needs.

- *Cloud cost alerting*: Receive alerts for budget overruns, cost spikes, and other anomalies, allowing you to take immediate action and prevent unnecessary costs.

- *Waste identification*: Identify idle, orphaned, or underutilized resources that contribute to wasted spend and optimize their use or removal.

- *Recommendations*: Receive recommendations from the CCM tool to rightsize resources, optimize configurations, and utilize cost-saving features like reserved instances.

- *Anomaly detection*: Be alerted to unexpected cost behavior so you can investigate and mitigate potential issues before they escalate.

Actions

Taking informed actions based on visibility and insights is key to effective cloud financial management. Automation and integrations can streamline these actions and enhance accountability.

- *Automation*: Automate actions like auto-stopping idle resources for non-business hours, autoscaling resources based on usage, and auto-tagging cloud resources for simplified cost attribution.

- *Integrations*: To expedite the settlement of suggestions and enhance accountability, integrate with current ticketing systems (such as Jira and ServiceNow), and other third-party software providers.

- *Integration of collaboration tools*: Connect with Slack and Teams, among other communication platforms, to exchange suggestions and useful information with the appropriate parties.

- *Training and support*: Leverage the educational resources and support offered by the CCM provider to maximize the tool's effectiveness and efficiently onboard new users.

- *Advanced optimization features*: Explore advanced features like reservations automation, enhanced Kubernetes bin packing, and the launch of spot instances (if supported by the tool) for significant cost optimization opportunities.

By leveraging a robust CCM tool and following the VIA criteria, organizations can gain the necessary insights and control to optimize their cloud spending, maximize their cloud ROI, and ensure cost efficiency throughout their cloud journey.

Shared Services Cost Allocation

When you implement your tagging strategy, you fundamentally enable cost allocation for cloud resources dedicated to teams, applications, or environments, which is then visualized via reporting. However, cloud resources shared among teams or projects need additional consideration to distribute those resources' costs properly. This is known as *shared services cost allocation*, and it's a key component of any FinOps practice, enabling cost transparency, accountability, and equitable cost allocation.

Examples of shared services include infrastructure such as Kubernetes clusters and databases, SaaS or CSP Marketplace services, and committed use discounts. While not all shared services can be tagged, a successful strategy remains essential for shared cost allocation for infrastructure such as K8s and databases. As we defined in the previous section, your tagging taxonomy will include tags to identify whether a resource is a shared service and which teams are using the resource.

To successfully implement shared cost allocation, organizations must establish a precise cost allocation model that shows how expenses are allocated among various cost centers or organizational entities. The organization's structure, business goals, and reporting requirements should all be considered while designing the model.

It's best to think of shared cost allocation as an ongoing process that may be honed and enhanced. Organizations should seek stakeholder input and continually assess the efficiency of the cost allocation model, tagging method, and allocation process. Organizations may improve shared cost allocation precision, equity, and effectiveness by examining cost patterns. They may also identify optimization opportunities and consider lessons learned.

Steps to Build a Successful Shared Services Cost Allocation Model

Let's explore the steps needed to build a successful shared services cost allocation model:

1. Identify shared cloud costs. Review your cloud bill to identify the primary cost drivers for shared services. Taggable infrastructure such as Kubernetes and databases are easy examples; however, there are also untaggable costs, such as the support cost, SaaS services/tools purchased via the CSP marketplace, or even discounts/credits that must be distributed among the teams. When designing proper shared cost allocation procedures, it's essential to have a solid understanding of the elements that contribute to costs.

2. Determine the methodology for distributing costs. Several methodologies can be used to divide up shared cloud costs. The simplest is to evenly split costs across entities (departments, projects, etc.), regardless of other factors such as cloud usage or activities. Alternatively, you can proportionally allocate shared costs based on fixed factors, such as headcount, or variable factors, such as resource usage or activities. Proportional shared cost allocation relies heavily on a proper tagging strategy to ensure accurate team cost distribution.

3. Communicate effectively and transparently. Conveying the shared cost allocation process to all parties involved is crucial, primarily if your organization has implemented chargeback policies for cloud costs. Doing so maintains transparency, reducing disagreements or misconceptions regarding cost allocation. Establishing confidence and mutual comprehension among the departments is facilitated by clear documentation and consistent communication.

4. Continuously monitor and modify. Continuously perform systematic reviews and adjust the shared services cost allocation technique as the business progresses through its various development stages. Alterations in company priorities, changes in resource consumption patterns, or introduction of new services could necessitate revisions to ensure fair and accurate cost allocations.

Shared Services Cost Attribution for Specific Scenarios
Attributing Taxes, Support Fees, and Credits

The CSP typically applies these costs at the account level, meaning they are not inherently tied to specific resources or teams. Therefore, allocating these costs fairly requires alternative strategies:

- *Even split*: Regardless of each department's unique consumption, this approach equally splits the overall cost of shared services. While this strategy is simple to implement, it can be unfair if some departments utilize shared services significantly more than others.

- *Proportional split*: This approach distributes shared costs based on each team's overall cloud spending percentage. It assumes that teams utilizing more cloud resources proportionally contribute more to these shared expenses.

Here's the formula for the proportional split method:

Cost Allocation per Team = Shared Cost * (Team's Cloud Spend / Total Cloud Spend)

Example:

- Shared Support Fee: $1,000

- Team A's Cloud Spend: $5,000

- Team B's Cloud Spend: $3,000

Cost Allocation for Team A: $1,000 * (5,000 / 8,000) = $625
Cost Allocation for Team B: $1,000 * (3,000 / 8,000) = $375

Shared Services like RDS and K8s

Chargeback models for Relational Database Services (RDS), Kubernetes (K8s), and similar services can be intricate due to each team's varying workloads. These services often serve multiple teams, making it crucial to identify relevant metrics, such as CPU, memory, network utilization, storage per team, to attribute their costs accurately.

Identifying Relevant Metrics

Accurately attributing costs for shared services like Relational Database Services (RDS) and Kubernetes (K8s) requires a detailed understanding of the specific metrics that reflect each team's resource consumption. Identifying and monitoring these relevant metrics is crucial to ensure fair and precise cost allocation.

- *Data-intensive workloads*: Metrics like storage used and network IOPS (input/output operations per second) can be employed to measure data storage and transfer activities. This helps gauge the proportional resource consumption by different teams.

- *Compute-intensive workloads*: When working on tasks requiring a lot of processing power, measurements like CPU, memory or network utilization are quintessential factors that cannot be forgotten. These indicators clearly and accurately depict each team's usage of computational resources.

Combining Metrics

Since different workloads prioritize different resource types, more than a single metric might be required for fair cost allocation. Therefore, a weighted combination of relevant metrics is often employed to distribute resource costs proportionally. This involves assigning weights to each metric based on its relative importance in reflecting a team's resource usage.

Here's a simplified example formula for combining metrics:

Cost Allocation per Team = Shared Cost * ((Metric1_Weight * Metric1_Value) + (Metric2_Weight * Metric2_Value) + ...)

Example:

- Shared K8s Cost: $1,500

- Team A:
    - Average CPU utilization: 50%
    - Average Memory utilization: 30%

- Team B:
    - Average CPU utilization: 30%
    - Average Memory utilization: 70%

Assuming equal weights (0.5) for both CPU and memory utilization:

Cost Allocation for Team A: $1,500 * ((0.5 * 0.5) + (0.5 * 0.3)) = $675

Cost Allocation for Team B: $1,500 * ((0.5 * 0.3) + (0.5 * 0.7)) = $825

It's important to remember that these are oversimplified examples and that the metrics selected and their weights may vary depending on each person's workload and the company's demands. Consulting with cloud cost management tools and cloud service provider documentation can provide further guidance on cost allocation calculations specific to your platform and services.

Benefits of Effective Shared Services Cost Allocation

The following are several benefits of effective shared services cost allocation (SSCA):

- *Improved cost transparency*: A well-defined SSCA model helps decipher the often-opaque world of cloud billing, providing departments with a clear understanding of their cost drivers. By identifying their proportionate share of shared services costs, departments gain valuable insights into how their activities contribute to overall cloud expenses. This transparency fosters awareness and ownership among teams, enabling them to identify potential areas for cost optimization.

- *Enhanced accountability*: Effective SSCA fosters a sense of accountability within organizations. The model encourages responsible resource utilization by holding departments responsible for their share of shared service costs. Teams become more mindful of their cloud resource consumption, leading to improved resource optimization and potentially less waste. This shift in mindset can significantly impact overall cloud spending and optimize resource allocation across the organization.

- *Informed decision-making*: Strong SSCA models provide facts and insights to leaders, enabling them to make well-informed decisions about cost optimization and resource allocation. By knowing the costs associated with different cloud services and how different departments use them, leaders can choose services, allocate resources, and even implement cost-saving measures. Furthermore, by giving managers a comprehensive view of historical and current expenses, SSCA enables data-driven decision-making. This enables managers to predict future spending patterns and create well-informed budgets.

- *Increased collaboration and communication*: Stakeholders within an organization must frequently work together and communicate to build and sustain an effective SSCA model. Finance, IT, and individual teams must collaborate to establish acceptable cost allocation procedures, identify pertinent KPIs, and guarantee that all parties understand and approve the model. This fosters transparency, trust, and a shared understanding of cost ownership, ultimately leading to better cooperation and alignment between departments in managing cloud resources effectively.

- *Improved ROI and business value*: A higher ROI for cloud services can be achieved through effective SSCA, which enhances cost transparency, accountability, and decision-making. Enterprises may optimize the return on their cloud computing investments by efficient resource allocation and reducing unnecessary expenses. Furthermore, by using SSCA, firms can show stakeholders that they are cost-effective and efficient, which strengthens the overall value proposition of their cloud adoption plan.

Implementing an effective structure for shared cost allocation ensures that departments or business units fully understand the costs incurred through cloud usage. Understanding and taking responsibility for their proportionate share of expenses encourages accountability while discouraging wasteful resource usage. It also empowers leaders to make well-informed decisions based on accurate information, such as recognizing opportunities for enhancing processes or delegating tasks.

Chapter Summary

This chapter on cloud cost visibility explored various strategies and practices to gain insights into cloud costs. Here's a recap of the key points discussed:

- *Monitoring costs*: Cloud cost visibility is crucial to understanding and controlling cloud costs. By actively tracking and analyzing costs, organizations can identify trends, anomalies, and areas for optimization.

- *Tagging resources*: Tagging cloud resources enables organizations to associate costs with specific attributes or entities such as applications, projects, departments, or cost centers. This fosters a culture of resource ownership and accountability and facilitates accurate cost attribution.

- *Financial impact awareness*: Engineers and developers need to understand the financial impact of their work. Shifting from the traditional engineering mindset of "billing is not my concern" to a contemporary mindset of "the economic impact of my work is my concern" cultivates a culture of cost awareness and encourages responsible resource utilization.

- *Shared services cost attribution*: Shared services should not be taken for granted. By implementing shared resources cost attribution methodologies, organizations ensure that shared services costs are accurately allocated to the respective users or departments. This promotes fairness, accountability, and informed decision-making regarding collective resource utilization.

Chapter 3 will focus on cloud cost insights. Building upon the foundation of cost visibility, cloud cost insights provide organizations with more profound analysis, optimization opportunities, and strategic decision-making based on cost data. Organizations can unlock valuable insights to drive cost optimization and achieve better financial efficiency by leveraging advanced analytics, machine learning, and predictive modeling.

Chapter 3 will explore techniques and tools for cloud cost insights, including advanced cost analytics, anomaly detection, cost forecasting, and optimization recommendations. These insights will empower organizations to make data-driven decisions, optimize costs, and maximize cloud value.

References for Further Reading

https://www.apriori.com/blog/3-tips-for-creating-a-powerful-cost-transparency-culture/

https://fellow.app/blog/leadership/how-to-build-a-strong-engineering-culture/

https://www.indellient.com/blog/cloud-infrastructure-how-proper-tagging-saves-time-and-money/

https://blogs.centilytics.com/what-is-tagging-and-why-does-your-cloud-need-tagging-today/

https://bootcamp.uxdesign.cc/cloud-tagging-part-1-tagging-101-a38325a1f3e1

https://medium.com/aws-in-plain-english/finops-cloud-tagging-what-tags-key-value-to-use-abe6228e9abf

https://medium.com/aws-in-plain-english/finops-cloud-tagging-the-tagging-strategy-17440117191

https://www.capitalone.com/software/blog/cloud-cost-optimization/

https://www.c-facts.com/blogs/15-tips-for-a-more-cost-conscious-culture/

https://aws.plainenglish.io/shared-services-cost-attribution-allocation-cloud-costs-46bbbd8be583

https://resources.flexera.com/web/media/documents/
rightscale-2019-state-of-the-cloud-report-from-flexera.pdf

https://docs.aws.amazon.com/tag-editor/latest/userguide/
tagging.html

https://cloud.google.com/resource-manager/docs/creating-
managing-labels

CHAPTER 3

Cloud Cost Insights

You have gone to great lengths to build your dream house. It has a solid foundation, sturdy walls, and a proper roof that shields the house. Even though you've reached a noteworthy achievement, there is much more to accomplish. Now begins the crucial task of interior designing, decoration, and furnishing. This is where your vision truly comes to life, transforming a basic structure into a comfortable and personalized space.

Similarly, in cloud cost management, achieving cost visibility is akin to building the house's core structure. You understand where your resources are located and the overall cost. However, true optimization requires delving deeper—that's where cloud cost insights come in.

This chapter explores the art of transforming raw cost data into actionable intelligence. We'll delve into techniques for studying resource usage patterns, identifying cost anomalies, and leveraging this knowledge to optimize cloud spending. Think of it as furnishing your cloud environment—maximizing efficiency and value within the established framework.

After spending significant time and effort laying the groundwork for cloud cost visibility, the FinOps team hands the executive team a comprehensive report showing the company's cloud costs. It's a massive improvement over previous cost reporting, but what does the data mean? What conclusions can be drawn from the data, and what actions can be taken? The first step is gaining cloud cost visibility; the next step is diving deep into insights from that data.

As the name implies, cloud cost insights provide insights into cloud resource costs. Cloud cost insights are the product of acquiring in-depth knowledge of your cloud spend and comprehending those expenses in detail. Leveraging cloud cost insights becomes vital when creating and scaling FinOps practices from the ground up so businesses can maximize spending efficiency and make well-informed decisions.

© Sasi Kanumuri, Matthew Zeier 2024
S. Kanumuri and M. Zeier, *Scaling Cloud FinOps*, https://doi.org/10.1007/979-8-8688-0388-8_3

This chapter will discuss what generating cloud cost insights entails. This includes studying different facets of cloud resource usage, identifying cost patterns and anomaly trends, and using this information to promote cost-effectiveness for enterprises. We'll also cover the concept of unit economics, which delves deeper into measuring the efficiency of cloud spending.

Understanding Resource Utilization and Cloud Waste

When starting from scratch to establish and scale FinOps practices, acquiring insights into how efficiently cloud resources are used provides the baseline for cloud cost optimization and reducing cloud waste. Insights into effective resource utilization provide an understanding of which cloud resources are being well utilized and which are contributing to cloud waste and should be addressed to improve performance and save costs.

Efficient cloud resource usage entails ensuring that cloud resources are provided only as needed, rightsized to match the demands of the workload, and utilized in the most effective way possible. Several ways to measure resource utilization can offer beneficial insights into resource consumption. Depending on the types of resources being used, the metrics in question could include CPU utilization, memory usage, network bandwidth, storage consumption, request rates, and concurrent connection counts. These indicators help companies not only better understand how much they utilize their resources but also locate potential bottlenecks or inefficiencies.

Effective resource utilization is not a one-time activity; it requires ongoing monitoring and optimization. Businesses can spot shifts in patterns, adjust resource allocations, and optimize utilization under new circumstances if they routinely analyze utilization measurements. This iterative strategy lets companies adapt to shifting requirements while ensuring continued cost-effectiveness.

Effective cloud cost management hinges on understanding how efficiently you utilize your resources. This section dives into *cloud waste*—resources that are either unused, underutilized, or failing to deliver optimal value. Cloud waste can significantly impact your cloud bill, reduce overall resource efficiency, and limit your ability to scale effectively.

In this section, we will explore how to gain insights into resource utilization and identify potential areas of cloud waste. We will leverage the cost visibility techniques covered in Chapter 2 and build upon them to identify resource consumption patterns and potential inefficiencies. This section will equip you with the foundational knowledge to identify cloud waste. We will also briefly touch upon advanced techniques for more granular analysis.

Implementing these strategies can provide valuable insights into your cloud resource usage and identify opportunities for optimization. This will ultimately reduce cloud waste and create a more cost-effective cloud environment.

Resource Utilization Insights

Multiple tools are available for understanding cloud resource performance and utilization, all of which build upon the cost visibility strategies covered in Chapter 2. That's not surprising since the methods for allocating cloud costs go hand-in-hand with understanding the performance of the resources contributing to costs.

CSPs offer built-in monitoring tools that provide insights into resource consumption data. These tools typically include dashboards, logs, and monitoring metrics to determine resource usage. Utilization visibility can be effectively gained using these cloud-native tools, which might be a practical starting point.

Third-party tools can provide sophisticated monitoring and analytics capabilities, delivering more detailed insights and configurable dashboards. These technologies can interact with many CSPs, consolidate data, and provide a centralized view of resource use across various contexts.

Businesses can also gain visibility into resource configurations and maintain consistency by implementing techniques associated with infrastructure, such as code, and utilizing tools related to configuration management. This insight helps detect instances that are misconfigured or overprovisioned, enabling adjustments to maximize resource use.

Identifying and Quantifying Cloud Waste

The proportion of the cloud bill devoted to resources that either are not being used at all, are being used insufficiently, or are not giving enough value is an example of cloud waste. Cloud waste can be caused by overprovisioning, orphaned or idle resources, incorrectly configured deployments, or ineffective workload management, among other things. The extent of the problem can be better understood by organizations when they calculate the percentage of waste in the cloud bill, and this calculation also establishes a baseline for future progress.

According to the Flexera 2024 State of the Cloud Report, approximately 30% (~ one-third) of cloud resources are waste.[1] This means that a significant portion of the cloud bill is underutilized and must be spent on effectively administering resources or providing concrete value. Identifying and addressing this waste is crucial for cost optimization and implementing effective FinOps or cloud economics strategies.

Several factors contribute to cloud resource waste:

- Unused/orphaned cloud resources that were provisioned for a workload but never shut down once the workload was complete

- Idle resources for workloads that are required for extended periods but only run intermittently

- Overprovisioning, where resources are allocated over what is needed

- Incorrectly configured deployments and ineffective workload management

Calculating the percentage of waste in the cloud bill is a fundamental step for organizations to understand the extent of the problem. It provides a baseline for measuring future progress in reducing waste and optimizing costs. Companies can make informed decisions to eliminate waste, improve resource utilization, and optimize costs in their cloud environments. This is done by continuously monitoring and analyzing resource usage.

Negative Impacts of Idle Resources

In cloud computing, *idle resources* are cloud resources that have been provisioned but are not being actively used or utilized. These resources consume computing power, storage, and other cloud services without providing meaningful value or a workload.

---

[1] https://resources.flexera.com/web/pdf/Flexera-State-of-the-Cloud-Report-2024.pdf?elqTrackId=6c729f23c1084d56a076074c31462307&elqaid=7675&elqat=2&_gl=1*1mn4zqw*_gcl_au*MjAxMTEwMDc3My4xNzA4NTMzOTU0

Idle resources in a cloud computing environment can have several negative impacts, including

- *Increased costs*: Idle resources consume computing power, storage, and cloud services without providing meaningful value or a workload. This results in unnecessary expenses for organizations, as they continue to pay for resources that could be more actively utilized.

- *Resource waste*: Idle resources waste valuable computing power, storage capacity, and network bandwidth. These resources must be utilized more effectively to serve other workloads or applications.

- *Reduced efficiency*: Idle resources reduce overall efficiency in the cloud environment. The resources allocated to sluggish instances could have been used to scale or support other critical workloads, resulting in decreased resource utilization and slower application performance.

- *Environmental impact*: Idle resources also have an indirect environmental impact. Cloud data centers consume significant energy to power and cool the infrastructure. By leaving idle resources running, unnecessary energy is expended, resulting in a larger carbon footprint and increased environmental impact.

- *Limited scalability*: Idle resources tie up available capacity and limit the scalability of the cloud environment. When resources are idle and underutilized, allocating additional resources to meet increasing demands or scale applications effectively becomes challenging.

- *Reduced ROI*: Investing in idle cloud resources reduces the organization's return on investment (ROI). The resources do not generate value or support business objectives, resulting in wasted financial resources that could have been allocated more effectively.

- *Virtual machines running 24/7*: The situation in which a virtual machine (VM) continues to run even though it is only actively used for a few hours at a time is a typical example of resource inefficiency. This could happen for different reasons, including the following:

- *Environments for development or testing*: Software developers and quality assurance analysts frequently need VMs during a typical workday. However, if these VMs are allowed to run continually, this contributes to optional costs. It is possible to drastically cut waste by implementing automation and scheduling systems that turn off VMs when they are not being used and deallocate their resources. This will be addressed more in Chapter 6 of this book.

- *Incorrect configuration or omission*: Virtual machines are often deployed with default settings that keep them running continuously. This could be a mistake or an oversight, or it could be due to a need for more information regarding cost optimization practices. Correct configuration and ongoing monitoring are necessary to avoid these scenarios and ensure that resources are provided according to actual requirements.

Finding Idle Resources

Here are some things to consider when identifying idle resources:

- *Monitoring and metrics*: Businesses can track resource use metrics using CSP monitoring tools or third-party solutions. When evaluating metrics such as CPU utilization, network traffic, or disk activity, it is possible to identify idle resources based on extended periods of low or no training by comparing these indicators over time.

- *Activity logs and access patterns*: Analyzing activity logs and access patterns can provide valuable insights into resource utilization. Suppose a resource has no or very little activity for a prolonged period. This indicates that the cloud resource may be dormant and should be examined for optimization.

- *Scheduled usage and business requirements*: Understanding the anticipated usage patterns and the business requirements for the available resources is essential. It indicates the potential idle time that can be eradicated through optimization. This is particularly valuable if a resource is supplied to run continuously 24 hours a day but is actively used only for a few hours.

- *Tagging and metadata*: Utilizing tagging and metadata can help discover idle resources. Tags attached to a cloud resource can indicate a resource's purpose, owner, project, or environment. Examining tags and metadata can assist in locating resources connected to projects that are no longer being worked on or obsolete.

The following are CSP tools that can help you to identify idle resources:

- AWS Trust Advisor

  1. Open the AWS Management Console and navigate to Trusted Advisor.

  2. In the left navigation, select Cost Optimization.

  3. On the right are cost optimization options. On the Idle Load Balancers recommendation, click View Details.

  4. Here, inactive load balancers are displayed. From this list, you can choose whether load balancers can be deactivated or activated again.

  5. The recommendation "Low Utilization Amazon EC2 instances" allows you to check underutilized (10% or less utilization) EC2 resources.

- Google Cloud Recommender

  - For your project, enable Google Cloud Monitoring and Logging. These services will log and analyze resource measurements.

  - Set up metrics and logs to monitor activity and resource utilization. You can keep track of CPU use, network activity, disk I/O, and resource creation, deletion, and use.

  - Google Cloud Monitoring supports resource analytics dashboards. CPU usage, network activity, and other indicators can eventually disclose idle resources.

  - Examine resource creation, deletion, and user activity logs using Google Cloud Logging. Look for sparing resources. Unused logs may indicate inactive resources.

- Azure Advisor from Microsoft Azure

    - Provides insights into utilization and cloud cost optimization recommendations on underutilized resources.

    - You can get recommendations at a subscription and resource group level.

Benefits of Cloud Cost Insights

Leveraging cloud cost insights provides many benefits:

- *Enables simplified cost examination and optimization*: Businesses can detect cost drivers by analyzing CSP cost data. Examples of cost drivers include resource use, storage, networking, and data transfer. These insights allow for optimizing resource allocation, infrastructure rightsizing, implementing cost-saving measures, and identifying areas for automation and improvement. Understanding resource utilization helps pinpoint areas where these cost drivers are high, allowing for targeted optimization efforts to reduce cloud waste.

    Cloud cost insights help determine whether or not there is an opportunity to use reserved instances or savings plans. These plans offer price reductions in exchange for long-term commitments. Enterprises can optimize the purchase of reserved instances by evaluating previous usage patterns. This allows enterprises to save costs without overcommitting themselves.

- *Comprehensive cost anomaly detection and overspending alerting*: The ability to recognize unusual cost anomalies and expenditure patterns enables businesses to benefit from cloud cost insights. Stakeholders can be notified automatically via automated alerts when expenses surpass established criteria. This assists them in investigating and resolving potential issues such as runaway resources, inefficient procedures, or misconfigured installations. This benefit of cloud cost insights is discussed in depth in the next section.

- *Unveiling cost-effectiveness with business alignment*: When paired with business intelligence tools, cloud cost insights allow businesses to see where their money is going and how effectively they are using their cloud resources. This makes it possible to allocate resources based on data and makes it easier to spot any cloud waste problems that can be fixed to increase cost-effectiveness.

  CSPs' cost insights can be combined with various business intelligence tools to attribute expenses to specific customers, initiatives, or income streams. This link allows businesses to comprehend the cost-effectiveness of diverse business activities, make decisions based on the data they collect, and strategically deploy resources according to the impact those resources will have on their finances.

- *Enables informed cost governance*: Cloud cost insights are the basis of effective/actionable cost governance policy and cost control. When businesses are thoroughly aware of cost patterns and trends, they can achieve cost efficiency by establishing rules, implementing cost controls, and creating frameworks for resource tagging, provisioning, and access management.

Comprehensive Cost Anomaly Detection and Overspending Alerting

Cost anomaly detection is essential to creating and scaling FinOps or cloud economics strategies from the ground up. It helps discover and handle unexpected cost spikes, utilization patterns, and unit cost variations. Organizations can gain insights into abnormalities within their cloud cost data and proactively optimize expenses and increase overall efficiency by employing anomaly detection techniques. This enables organizations to boost overall productivity. Let's investigate how anomaly detection can be utilized in CCM.

Cloud cost spikes can be caused by various factors, including rapid increases in resource use, configuration errors, workloads that are not optimized, or unanticipated usage patterns. Techniques for detecting anomalies can help identify such cost spikes and provide early warnings of the possibility of cost overruns. Businesses can detect anomalies in their cost data by establishing thresholds or employing machine learning algorithms. These algorithms can trigger alerts or automated actions to explore and correct the underlying causes of anomalies.

Analyzing historical cost data, establishing baseline patterns, and evaluating current cost trends against established norms are necessary to find anomalies in cloud cost spikes. (An *anomaly* is a deviation that exceeds a predetermined threshold or is statistically significant.) This allows companies to analyze the underlying reasons for cost spikes. They can optimize resource allocation, alter provisioning, or implement automated cost controls to reduce the adverse effects of cost increases. The notification bell icon shown in Figure 3-1 represents a sample anomaly in cost trend.

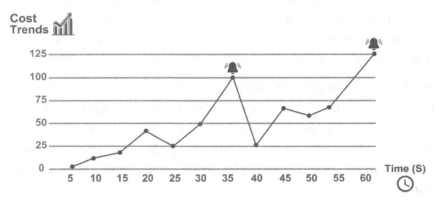

Figure 3-1. *Sample cost trend analysis graph illustrating cost spikes*

Monitoring resource utilization and detecting abnormalities in that utilization are both crucial steps in the process of locating ineffective or underutilized resources. These resources may contribute to wasteful costs. Businesses can spot resource utilization anomalies by evaluating CPU usage, memory usage, network traffic, or disk activity. These anomalies indicate less-than-optimal resource utilization.

To discover anomalous utilization patterns, anomaly detection requires either the setup of thresholds or the application of machine learning methods. The abnormality of consumption rates indicates inefficiency and possible cost reductions. For instance, if your CPU utilization is continuously low during peak hours, this could indicate overprovisioning. Still, abrupt increases in network traffic could mean unexpected workload increases. Businesses can take the right actions to optimize resource allocation, alter scaling policies, or adopt automation to improve usage efficiency if they first discover these abnormalities and then monitor their effects.

Analyzing historical cost data and looking for departures from expected patterns or benchmarks can detect cost anomalies. Businesses can detect cost anomalies by setting thresholds or using statistical approaches. These abnormalities may signal price changes, billing mistakes, misconfigured resources, or consumption that could be more optimal. For instance, if the cost of storing a data unit suddenly increases without a commensurate shift in the amount of labor to be done, this can hint that there are faults or inefficiencies in the system.

By exploiting anomaly detection in unit prices, businesses can reveal possibilities for cost optimization, identify areas for negotiation with CSPs, or build automated systems to ensure proper invoicing and cost allocation. These opportunities can be used to achieve any of these goals.

Thanks to implementing anomaly detection techniques in CCM, businesses can acquire timely insights, spot inconsistencies, and take proactive steps. This allows organizations to optimize expenses and enhance efficiency. Organizations can improve their decision-making processes, reduce their exposure to financial risks, and strengthen their overall CCM strategies when properly leveraging anomaly detection.

Cost Anomaly Detection with CSPs

Cost anomaly detection enables users to identify and analyze cost anomalies or unusual spending patterns across CSPs. It leverages machine learning algorithms and historical cost data to automatically detect deviations from normal spending behavior, allowing users to investigate and address potential cost-related issues promptly. CSPs have built-in anomaly detection tools that can help.

Figure 3-2 outlines an anomaly detection process, representing a high-level overview of how cost anomaly detection works and how anomalies can be detected.

Figure 3-2. *Cost anomaly detection process*

The following list explains the phases of the anomaly detection process:

- *Cost data collection*: The CSP anomaly detection tools collect and analyze cost and usage data from various cloud services, such as compute, storage, databases, etc. The tools gather detailed cost information on resource usage, data transfers, storage, and other service-specific metrics.

- *Data analysis*: The CSP anomaly detection tools build a baseline model using historical cost and usage data. This model represents the cloud accounts' expected spending patterns and normal behavior over time. It considers factors like day-of-week patterns, seasonality, and usage trends.

- *Anomaly detection*: The CSP anomaly detection tools use machine learning techniques to compare current cost data against the baseline model, which identifies deviations or anomalies that indicate unusual spending patterns that deviate significantly from expected behavior. Detected anomalies are ranked based on their severity or impact. The severity ranking helps prioritize investigating and resolving cost anomalies based on their potential impact on the overall cost structure.

- *Alerting and notification*: The CSP anomaly detection tools generally provide a user-friendly interface and visualizations to present anomalies and insights. Users can access detailed reports, charts, and graphs highlighting irregularities and delivering insights into potential cost drivers. Users can set custom thresholds based on their specific cost patterns and define alerts to trigger when spending exceeds or deviates from these thresholds.

- *Third-party cost management tools*: There are various third-party cost management tools available in the market that offer advanced anomaly detection capabilities. These tools can integrate with cloud provider APIs, collect cost data, and apply sophisticated algorithms to identify anomalies.

Once anomalies are detected, CSPs' native tools can be used for in-depth investigation and resolution. Users can drill down into specific cost anomalies to understand the root cause. Tools like AWS Cost Explorer, Azure Cost Management + Billing, and Google Cloud Cost Management provide detailed breakdowns of cost drivers, allowing users to identify misconfigurations, over-provisioned resources, or unexpected usage. Users can then take corrective actions, such as resizing instances, adjusting resource allocations, or implementing budget controls to prevent future anomalies. Utilizing these native tools ensures a streamlined and integrated approach to managing and resolving cost anomalies within the CSP environment.

Cost Alerting Framework

Businesses can monitor their cloud expenditure, keep spending within their budgets, uncover cost anomalies, and take early actions to optimize cost structures when setting up cost alerts. By integrating these alerts into communication channels such as Slack and email, relevant stakeholders are guaranteed to receive timely notifications and can respond efficiently. Let's get into the nitty-gritty of constructing an all-encompassing framework for expense warnings.

Notifications Determined by Budgets

Businesses can more carefully monitor their expenditure on cloud services and ensure they stick to predetermined budget boundaries when setting up alerts based on their budgets. This entails setting budget limitations for cost categories, projects, or departments. It also involves configuring alarms to activate when expenditure gets close to or passes these restrictions.

With a cost overrun alerting system, stakeholders have real-time visibility into cost overruns and can react quickly. For instance, if the total cost of a project's cloud computing services exceeds the budget allotted, an alert can be sent to the project manager, the finance team, or any relevant stakeholders. This allows them to analyze the reasons behind excessive spending, optimize the usage of resources, or change the budget allocation as necessary.

Notification in Response to Unusual Expenses

Anomalies in cost can help identify inconsistencies in cloud expenditure patterns, pointing to inefficiencies or unanticipated shifts if the anomalies are found and investigated. When there are significant deviations from predicted cost trends, such as rapid spikes in cost, unexpected patterns, or anomalous variations in unit costs, anomaly-based alerts are produced. Establishing baseline cost patterns and identifying anomalies exceeding predetermined criteria is the first step, for organizations. Notifications can be send out for any anomaly detected for further investigation from the FinOps and Engineering teams. For instance, if the cost per storage unit suddenly jumps substantially, an alarm might be generated to determine the cause. The reason for the sudden increase in cost per storage unit might include misconfigured resources, data leakage, or unexpected usage patterns.

Anomaly-based alerts can help a corporation proactively address cost inefficiencies, optimize resource use, and discover potential billing problems or unauthorized usage.

Integrated Support for Slack/Teams and Email

Integration with communication channels such as Slack, Teams, and email improves the efficacy of expense alerts by ensuring that timely and targeted messages are delivered to the appropriate stakeholders. Businesses can expedite communication and enable quick responses to cost-related concerns if they integrate cost-warning systems with various communication channels.

When an alert is triggered, it can be immediately broadcast to Slack channels or persons. This enables quick visibility and communication among the affected teams. In a similar vein, email integrations can send notifications directly to the inboxes of people who have been designated as recipients. This ensures stakeholders are updated quickly.

When cost alerts are integrated into Slack and email, they facilitate collaboration among several teams, speed up the decision-making process, and efficiently convey cost-related insights and actions.

Personalization and Fine-Grained Approach

A comprehensive framework for cost alerting should offer several levels of flexibility to cater to the individual requirements of various teams, projects, or cost categories. This includes setting different alarm levels, configuring alert frequencies, and defining alert recipients.

Granularity in cost alerts enables firms to focus on cost dimensions, such as individual resources, service categories, geographical regions, or cost centers. Granularity can also describe the degree of detail in a cost estimate. With this high level of personalization, you can rest assured that the expense alerts your firm receives are specifically adapted to meet its requirements and focus areas.

Pro Tip   Leverage alerts for overage analysis and underutilization. Cost alerts typically focus on overspending budget thresholds. However, you can also set alerts for potential savings by flagging underutilized resources. For example, schedule an alert if CPU usage drops below 20% for a sustained period, indicating instance size reduction. Or trigger an alert if a storage volume stays below 50% complete, suggesting it is overprovisioned. Broadening alerts beyond budget overages provides more holistic visibility into optimization opportunities and waste. The most cost-efficient cloud usage stays within budget while maximizing resource utilization. Comprehensive alerts help strike this balance.

Cost Spike Analysis Framework

Imagine a company that operates its infrastructure in the cloud and utilizes various cloud services like virtual machines, storage, databases, and more. This company wants to monitor and analyze cost spikes or sudden increases in cloud expenditure to identify the underlying causes. It intends to take appropriate actions to optimize costs. To achieve this, the company has decided to implement a cost spike analysis framework, represented in Figure 3-3.

Figure 3-3. *Cost spike analysis framework*

Cost spike analysis gives companies a more in-depth understanding of their cost structures, one of the most significant advantages of this framework. This research pushes organizations to investigate the underlying issues generating cost changes rather than accepting these fluctuations as an inherent part of the business. This preventative strategy gives decision-makers the ability to make educated decisions founded on accurate facts and take necessary actions to reduce changes in costs in the future.

Businesses building and scaling FinOps or cloud economics practices from the ground up must master the art of identifying and remedying these cost anomalies. Let's follow the journey from the identification to the remediation of a cost spike as our FinOps investigators unravel the mystery and restore cost efficiency.

Phase 1: Detection and Alert

The investigation begins with implementing advanced monitoring systems that serve as the first line of defense against cost spikes. These systems continuously scrutinize cloud billing data, employing sophisticated algorithms to detect unusual patterns or sudden surges in expenses. When anomalies are identified, alerts are promptly generated, indicating the potential occurrence of a cost anomaly.

It's critical to establish crystal-clear criteria for a significant cost surge based on historical data, industry benchmarks, or established targets and document these criteria. This enables the analysis to focus on the most considerable cost swings.

Phase 2: Evidence Collection and Analysis

Upon receiving an alert, the FinOps investigators spring into action, meticulously collecting and analyzing evidence related to the cost spike. They delve deep into billing details, resource usage logs, and configuration settings to uncover the underlying cause of the sudden surge. By leveraging historical cost trends, usage patterns and employing data analytics techniques, investigators (FinOps teams) gain valuable insights into cost anomalies, gradually unraveling the mystery behind the crime scene (cost spike).

Phase 3: Forensic Examination

Equipped with a comprehensive understanding of the evidence, FinOps investigators conduct a rigorous forensic examination. They meticulously examine resource allocation practices, identifying instances of overprovisioning, idle resources, and inadequate workload management. Additionally, investigators scrutinize deployment configurations and assess compliance with industry best practices to identify misconfigurations or ineffective resource utilization. This detailed examination reveals clues and exposes the culprits responsible for wasteful spending.

Phase 4: Remediation and Optimization

With a clear understanding of the origin of the cost spike, the FinOps investigators implement remedial measures. They develop a targeted action plan encompassing rightsizing overprovisioned resources, optimizing workload management strategies, and deactivating idle resources. Automation tools and intelligent cost management techniques ensure sustained cost efficiency. Regular monitoring is instituted, enabling ongoing optimization efforts to mitigate future cost anomalies and maintain financial harmony.

In the automation chapter (Chapter 7), we'll discuss how you can incorporate cost spikes into your incident management strategy and treat cost spikes as incidents with severity.

Case Study: Unsurfaced Cost Spike in KMS Service

This case study explores a scenario where a company utilizing cloud services encountered an unexpected cost increase in its AWS Key Management Service (KMS). We will analyze the limitations of anomaly detection for gradual increases and the importance of comprehensive cost monitoring across all services.

Background

The company regularly monitored its cloud spending, focusing on top AWS services like EC2 and S3. However, cost monitoring for less frequently used services like KMS was less rigorous.

Problem

Despite utilizing anomaly detection tools, a significant cost spike in the KMS service went unnoticed. The anomaly detection system was designed to identify sudden spikes, not gradual increases. Additionally, the lack of regular cost monitoring for KMS services made detecting the anomaly early on complex.

Investigation

After discovering the cost increase, the company initiated a manual investigation. They reviewed historical data and identified a steady rise in KMS usage over time, which the anomaly detection system did not flag.

Root Cause Identification

The investigation revealed that a new application with increased KMS usage was deployed without proper cost considerations. The lack of comprehensive cost monitoring across all services made identifying the rising KMS costs difficult.

Resolution

The company took the following actions to resolve to problem:

- *Implemented cost monitoring for all services*: Regular cost monitoring was established for all services, including KMS. This included alerts for unusual cost patterns across services, regardless of their typical usage volume.

- *Optimized KMS usage*: The company reviewed KMS usage patterns and identified opportunities for optimization, which included using different pricing tiers and implementing alternative key management solutions.

- *Improved communication*: Enhanced communication channels were established between development teams and FinOps to ensure cost considerations are integrated into application deployments.

Lessons Learned

The company followed up resolution of the problem by identifying the following lessons learned:

- *Limitations of anomaly detection*: Anomaly detection excels at identifying sudden spikes but might miss gradual increases. Businesses require a multipronged approach, including regular cost monitoring across all services.

- *Importance of comprehensive cost monitoring*: Monitoring all services, regardless of usage volume, is crucial for early detection of cost anomalies.

- *Collaboration between teams*: Effective communication between development and FinOps teams ensures cost-conscious application deployments.

This case study highlights the limitations of anomaly detection in identifying gradual cost increases. It emphasizes the importance of comprehensive cost monitoring and collaboration between development and FinOps teams for effective cloud cost management. Early detection and proactive steps can significantly reduce the impact of unexpected cost spikes.

Unit Economics

Within cloud computing, resources are frequently provided under a payment model based on consumption. This implies that the quantity of resources or services you use will determine how much you are charged. Although this flexibility has many benefits, it also presents a problem in efficiently controlling and optimizing expenses.

Unit economics is relevant in this situation. Unit economics is a paradigm that aids companies in comprehending the cost ramifications of using specific cloud services. By examining these expenses, businesses can arrive at well-informed decisions regarding the distribution of resources, pinpoint opportunities for cost reduction, and eventually attain fiscal stability within their cloud infrastructure.

Here's a breakdown of the key elements of Unit Economics:

- *Consumption-based billing*: Typically, cloud providers bill according to the number of resources used, including data exchanged, storage used, and virtual machine hours.

- *Unit Economics Metrics*: These metrics analyze the costs and value associated with each unit of a chosen resource (e.g., cost per VM hour, cost per GB of storage).

- *Cost optimization*: A proper grasp of unit economics can help businesses find ways to save cloud costs by investigating different pricing options, properly scaling resources, or streamlining service setups.

- *Informed decision-making*: Unit economics empowers businesses to make data-driven choices regarding resource selection, workload management, and overall cloud strategy.

In simpler terms, unit economics helps you see the bigger financial picture associated with your cloud usage. It allows you to move beyond simply paying the bill to understand the cost drivers and make strategic decisions to optimize your cloud investment.

Understanding Unit Economics: The Cornerstone of Cloud Cost Management

Unit economics serves as the foundation for analyzing the financial health of your cloud environment. It focuses on dissecting the costs and value associated with individual units of resources relevant to your business operations. These units can be anything from virtual machines and storage volumes to network bandwidth and API requests.

Here's a breakdown of its core aspects:

- *Analyzing costs and value*: Unit economics is more than just keeping track of your entire cloud service spending. It looks more closely at the price per unit of each resource used. This offers insightful information on the cost effects of using particular resources. You can find out how much a VM hour costs, how much storage costs in gigabytes (GB), or how much an API call costs per million.

- *Cloud cost insights*: You can get a detailed insight into the real cost of executing your workloads and apps in the cloud by knowing the cost per unit. This gives you the ability to

  - *Identify cost drivers*: Unit economics assists in identifying the resources that have a major impact on your cloud bill. This enables you to concentrate optimization efforts on the areas where the financial benefit is greatest.

  - *Compare pricing models*: If you understand unit costs well, you can quickly evaluate cloud providers' pricing alternatives. This allows you to select the most affordable option for your particular requirements.

- *Purpose*: Unit economics serves two critical purposes in cloud cost management:

  - *Assessing financial viability*: You can evaluate the financial feasibility of utilizing particular cloud resources by comparing the cost per unit with the value obtained from the resource. This helps you determine whether the expenses associated with a certain resource outweigh its advantages.

  - *Maximizing cost-effectiveness*: Unit economics can help pinpoint areas for cost optimization. Knowing how much each unit costs, you can look for ways to save costs. Depending on your workload requirements, this may entail rightsizing resources (allocating the proper number of resources), investigating alternate pricing options (such as committed use discounts), or optimizing service settings.

Unit economics gives you the expertise to do more than just pay for your cloud computing services. It offers a data-driven method for comprehending your cloud expenses, empowering you to decide wisely and optimize the return on your cloud investment.

Cloud Unit Metrics: Building Blocks for Cost Optimization

Cloud unit metrics are the fundamental measurements used to quantify cloud resource utilization. These granular metrics provide a vital starting point for analyzing cloud spend and identifying opportunities for cost optimization.

Here's an overview of some common cloud unit metrics aligned with the FinOps perspective:

- *Cost per VM hour*: This metric reflects the financial cost of running a virtual machine for one hour. By analyzing this metric, businesses can

  - *Examine the relative costs of several VM types*: By knowing the cost per hour for different VM configurations (e.g., CPU, memory), businesses can select the most economical VM configuration that satisfies their performance needs.

  - *Identify underutilized VMs*: Focusing on VMs with low usage compared to their cost can help pinpoint opportunities to optimize resource allocation. This might involve rightsizing the VMs or shutting down inactive ones.

- *Expense per storage gigabyte (GB)*: This metric shows the cost of storing 1GB of data in the cloud. Businesses can leverage this metric to

  - *Optimize storage choices*: Businesses can determine which storage tier is the most economical based on performance requirements and data access frequency by comparing the costs per gigabyte of various storage tiers (e.g., standard vs. high-performance storage).

  - *Investigate substitute storage options*: Companies with a lot of rarely accessed data could consider affordable archive storage solutions.

- *The price per gigabyte (GB) of sent data*: This metric shows how much money is spent on moving 1GB of data into or out of the cloud. Analyzing this metric helps

  - *Evaluate data transfer charges*: Businesses can assess the impact of data transfer costs on their overall cloud bill, especially for applications involving frequent data movement.

  - *Explore bandwidth optimization strategies*: Implementing data compression techniques or leveraging geographically closer storage solutions can reduce data transfer costs.

- *Cost per million API requests*: This metric represents the cost of processing one million API requests within a cloud service. Understanding this metric allows businesses to

  - *Identify cost-intensive APIs*: Analyzing the cost per million API requests can reveal services contributing significantly to the cloud bill. This information can guide efforts to optimize API usage or explore alternative pricing models.

  - *Assess serverless functions*: To ascertain the most economical course of action, businesses might contrast the cost per API call of serverless functions with that of standard application deployments.

- *Cost per computing unit (e.g., vCPU)*: This measure shows how much it costs to use a single virtual CPU (vCPU) for a predetermined time. Analyzing this metric helps

  - *Rightsize compute resources*: Businesses can assess the cost-effectiveness of allocating vCPUs to workloads. Scaling down overprovisioned instances can lower expenses and optimize resource usage.

  - *Compare price models*: Businesses can evaluate pricing structures provided by various cloud providers and select the most affordable solution for their unique compute requirements by clearly understanding the cost per virtual CPU.

Businesses can obtain critical insights into how their cloud resources are being used and the related cost ramifications by tracking and evaluating these cloud unit metrics. They can use this information to make well-informed judgments about:

- *Resource selection*: Choosing the most cost-effective resources based on specific workload requirements.

- *Service configuration*: Optimizing service configurations to minimize unnecessary resource usage.

- *Pricing models*: Exploring alternative pricing options offered by cloud providers.

Essentially, data-driven cost management in the cloud is built upon cloud unit metrics. They give companies the knowledge they need to pinpoint improvement areas and ensure their cloud investment yields the most return.

Leveraging Unit Costs for Cloud Optimization: Making Informed Choices

Understanding unit economics empowers businesses to go beyond simply monitoring cloud spending. By analyzing unit costs, businesses can unlock a range of optimization strategies.

Cost Comparison: Choosing the Right Fit

Unit costs allow businesses to compare pricing across different resources:

- *VM types*: Companies can evaluate the price per VM hour for different CSP-offered VM configurations (such as CPU and RAM). This allows them to choose the solution that best suits their needs for workload while staying within their budget. For example, a web server with modest resource requirements might not need a high-performance VM type, which could result in financial savings by selecting a less expensive choice.

- *CSPs' offerings*: Unit prices are another useful tool for comparing CSPs' pricing structures. Companies can determine which CSP offers the most affordable solution for their requirements by examining each provider's cost per unit resource (such as storage per GB). This could entail shifting workloads to a new supplier who charges less per unit for particular resources.

Rightsizing Resources: Avoiding Overprovisioning

Analyzing unit costs of resources (CPU, memory, storage) empowers businesses to identify the optimal size for their workloads. This combats overprovisioning, where businesses pay for excess resources they don't fully utilize, ultimately saving on cloud expenses.

Here's how unit costs facilitate rightsizing:

- *Identifying underutilized resources*: High unit costs relative to utilization can indicate overprovisioning. Businesses can identify underutilized resources with low utilization hours and potentially rightsize them by scaling down instances or choosing a lower-tier resource configuration.

- *Optimizing resources for workload needs*: Unit cost insights empower businesses to allocate resources precisely. This minimizes the costs related to overprovisioning while guaranteeing workloads have the resources needed for maximum performance.

Service Optimization: Identifying Possibilities for Cost Savings

Unit costs act as a guidepost for optimizing cloud services. By analyzing cost structures, businesses can pinpoint areas for potential savings:

- *Data storage optimization*: Exorbitant data storage unit costs may indicate that other storage choices must be investigated. Companies can consider using archive storage solutions for long-term data retention or moving rarely accessed material to a more affordable storage tier.

117

- *Optimizing service configurations*: Service configurations may be improved by examining the unit costs connected to particular services. For instance, companies may lower resource consumption and related expenses by modifying autoscaling settings or utilizing managed services.

Cost Allocation: Promoting Accountability and Transparency

Unit costs enable businesses to allocate cloud costs accurately based on specific units (e.g., project, department, customer). This allocation promotes accountability within teams and fosters transparency around resource usage in several ways:

- *Project-level cost tracking*: Businesses can track cloud expenses associated with specific projects by allocating costs based on unit usage. This enables them to monitor project budgets and identify potential cost overruns early.

- *Departmental cost visibility*: Assigning unit costs to departments provides insights into cloud resource utilization across different business units. This promotes departmental accountability and encourages responsible resource usage within teams.

- *Customer chargebacks*: Unit costs can be used to implement a chargeback model for cloud services used by customers. This provides customers a clear understanding of their cloud resource usage and associated costs, potentially promoting responsible cloud consumption.

Unit economics empowers businesses to leverage unit cost insights for strategic optimization across various aspects of their cloud environment. By making informed choices through cost comparison, rightsizing resources, optimizing services, and allocating costs accurately, businesses can achieve significant cost savings and maximize the value they extract from their cloud investment.

Benefits of Using Cloud Unit Economics

Businesses can gain many advantages by adopting cloud unit economics, including the capacity to make well-informed decisions and attain long-term financial sustainability in their cloud environment. Here are a few more details on the main benefits:

- *Improved decision-making*: Unit economics equips businesses with the data necessary to make strategic choices regarding various aspects of their cloud operations:

  - *Cost forecasting*: Businesses can obtain insight into future cloud expenses by examining past unit cost trends and resource utilization patterns. This allows them to plan budgets and resource allocations efficiently and proactively.

  - *Resource selection*: By grasping the unit prices linked to various resources (such as virtual machine types and storage alternatives), organizations can select the most economical options corresponding to their workload demands. This could entail investigating different storage tiers depending on data usage patterns or choosing the appropriate instance type for a VM.

  - *Deployment configurations*: Unit economics enables companies to optimize deployment configurations by finding ways to reduce resource use. This could entail using serverless services for transient activities, scaling instances up or down in response to demand, or rightsizing resources (allocating the proper amount of resources for the workload).

  - *Workload management*: Businesses can decide where to place and manage their workloads more effectively by knowing the financial effects of various workloads. This could entail moving workloads to more economical areas of a cloud provider's infrastructure or looking at other cloud providers with lower unit pricing for particular services.

- *Enhanced financial visibility*: Unit economics sheds light on cloud resource usage and the associated financial impact. This transparency enables businesses to

  - *Gain granular insights*: Unit costs give an accurate idea of the price of each cloud resource unit, such as a virtual machine hour or gigabyte of storage. This allows businesses to pinpoint the regions where their costs are the highest.

- *Track cost drivers*: Businesses can identify resources or services that substantially contribute to their overall cloud bill by tracking unit expenses over time. This information allows them to focus their optimization efforts on the areas with the largest financial impact.

- *Make informed budget allocations*: A better understanding of cloud expenses can help businesses manage their budgets more effectively and ensure they maximize their investment in the cloud.

- *Scalability and growth*: Unit economics ensures businesses can effectively increase their cloud resources while controlling costs:

  - *Predictable costs*: Using unit economics, businesses may estimate the costs of growing their cloud environment. This information is essential for financial planning purposes and to ensure that there is enough budgetary allocation to sustain future growth.

  - *Cost-conscious scaling*: Businesses can allocate resources wisely based on workload needs if they know the unit cost implications of scaling up or down. As a result, they can prevent overspending and resource overprovisioning.

- *Continuous optimization*: Unit economics fosters a culture of continuous improvement in cloud cost management:

  - *Identify optimization opportunities*: Businesses can always find areas for improvement by routinely examining unit costs and resource consumption trends. This could entail investigating other price structures, haggling with cloud service providers, or implementing automated cost-cutting techniques.

  - *Data-driven decision-making*: Unit economics offers a data-driven framework for deliberating on cloud resource optimization tactics and consumption. This guarantees that companies continuously work to get the most out of their cloud investment.

Calculating and Analyzing Unit Economics

Calculating and analyzing unit economics is crucial in understanding the cost and value of individual cloud resources. By assessing the financial performance of these units, businesses can make informed decisions, optimize resource allocation, and maximize the value derived from their cloud investments. Let's explore the critical steps in calculating and analyzing unit economics:

- *Define the unit*: Start by defining the analysis unit. It could be a virtual machine, storage volume, network bandwidth, or any other cloud resource that aligns with your business operations. The unit should be specific enough to enable accurate cost allocation and analysis.

- *Gather cost data*: Collect all relevant cost data associated with the unit, including direct costs (e.g., resource usage fees, storage costs) and indirect costs (e.g., support, maintenance). Ensure that you have access to detailed billing data or cost management tools that provide a breakdown of the expenses at the unit level.

- *Identify revenue or value drivers*: Determine the revenue or value drivers associated with the unit. For example, if the unit is a virtual machine, consider the revenue generated by applications or services running on that VM. This step is essential for analyzing the ROI and understanding the value derived from each unit.

- *Calculate unit costs*: Calculate the total cost associated with each unit by summing up all direct and indirect costs. This will give you the cost per unit and the financial foundation for unit economics analysis. Divide the total cost by the number of units to obtain the average cost per unit.

- *Analyze revenue or value generation*: Assess the revenue or value generated by each unit. This can be done by evaluating the revenue or value drivers identified earlier. Compare the revenue or value generated by the department against its cost to determine the unit's profitability and overall contribution to the business.

- *Evaluate unit efficiency*: Analyze each unit's efficiency by assessing resource utilization, performance metrics, and operational effectiveness. For example, consider CPU utilization, storage utilization, or network bandwidth usage. Identify any underutilized or inefficient units that may drive costs without proportional value.

- *Optimize iteratively*: Continuously monitor and analyze unit economics to identify improvement opportunities. Consider factors such as pricing changes, alternative resource configurations, workload optimization, or technology upgrades that could positively impact unit economics. Iterate and refine your analysis to drive ongoing cost optimization and value maximization.

- *Consider scalability*: Assess the scalability of your units and associated economics. Understand the incremental costs and revenue or value potential when scaling up or down. This analysis helps determine the most cost-effective growth strategies and ensures scalability aligns with business objectives.

- *Incorporate future projections*: Forecast future costs, revenue, and value drivers to understand the potential impact on unit economics. Consider business growth, usage pattern changes, or pricing model shifts. This enables proactive decision-making and long-term planning.

Case Study: Optimizing Security Services with Unit Economics

Problem

A Security as a Service company needed a clearer understanding of the profitability of individual customer relationships. They knew their overall revenue but needed to know the cost of servicing each customer. This made it challenging to identify areas for optimization and ensure long-term financial sustainability.

Solution

The company implemented a unit economics framework, focusing on the amount of data ingested (GB) per customer as the unit of analysis. This metric provided valuable insights into customer size and resource consumption.

Resolution

By analyzing unit economics, the company discovered a critical issue: the top ten customers, while ingesting significant data volumes, needed to generate more revenue to cover the associated cloud storage and processing costs.

Results

Analyzing cloud services' financial performance and customer segmentation provides critical insights that drive strategic decisions and operational improvements. By examining unit economics and customer behaviors, organizations can uncover hidden cost drains, identify distinct customer segments, and derive actionable insights that inform sales strategies, product development, and customer retention efforts.

- *Profitability analysis*: Unit economics revealed a hidden cost drain. Large data volumes from specific customers needed to translate into sufficient revenue.

- *Customer segmentation*: The company identified two distinct customer segments:

  - High-value customers with significant data ingestion but lower profitability

  - Low-value customers with minimal data ingestion and potential profitability

- *Actionable insights*: This analysis triggered several actions:

  - *Customer relationship management*: The sales team prioritized renegotiating pricing with high-volume, low-profit customers.

  - *Product development*: The product team explored tiered pricing models based on data ingestion volumes.

- *Customer churn reduction*: The company could identify and potentially retain low-value customers through targeted promotions or service adjustments.

Overall Impact

Implementing unit economics provided a data-driven approach to customer profitability analysis. The company gained valuable insights into:

- *Cost structure*: Understanding the costs associated with serving different customer segments

- *Pricing strategy*: Identifying opportunities to improve pricing models to align with resource consumption

- *Customer focus*: Enabling the sales and product teams to prioritize high-value customers and develop strategies for retaining smaller, potentially profitable clients

Lessons Learned

The company learned the following valuable lessons:

- Unit economics can be a handy tool when identifying hidden cost drivers and improving pricing strategies.

- Finding the right analytical unit is essential to deriving insightful conclusions.

- Opportunities for focused marketing and product development initiatives can be found by segmenting customers according to how they use resources.

This case study illustrates how unit economics can alter a company's perception of client profitability. This particular firm used this methodology to obtain insightful knowledge that enabled them to optimize their business model for long-term performance and make data-driven decisions.

Unit economics is an excellent framework for seeing the real value of cloud services, enabling organizations to understand business profitability, growth, expansion benefits, etc. Unit economics also helps to realize cost spikes associated with expansion, which are suitable for business while keeping unit economics at the same rate.

Chapter Summary

FinOps investigators successfully restore cost efficiency within the cloud environment through meticulous investigation and proactive remediation. Businesses can promptly detect and address cost spikes by implementing the following practices:

- Advanced monitoring systems to rapidly detect anomalies

- A thorough analysis of cost evidence and data

- Proactive remediation strategies to resolve issues

- Mature processes for ongoing optimization

Establishing these capabilities enables sustained financial harmony in the cloud. Just as crime scenes are unraveled through diligent investigation, CCM demands:

- Perseverance to understand cost drivers

- Attention to detail when analyzing costs

- Continuous vigilance and optimization

As we conclude this chapter on cloud cost insights, we recognize the critical role of effective cloud cost governance. The insights gained from FinOps investigations shed light on the importance of a robust cost management framework.

Fundamental principles of cost governance include:

- Implementing clear policies

- Defining cost allocation methodologies

- Enabling granular monitoring

- Promoting cross-functional collaboration

In the next chapter, we will delve deeper into the concept of Cloud Cost Governance by exploring the fundamental principles and strategies that empower businesses to maintain control over their spend. We will discuss the significance of establishing clear policies, defining cost allocation methodologies, and implementing granular monitoring mechanisms. Furthermore, we will explore the role of cross-functional collaboration between finance, operations, and IT teams in optimizing cloud costs and achieving financial harmony.

Cloud Cost Governance transcends cost optimization; it serves as the foundation for sound financial management in the cloud. By embracing the principles of transparency, accountability, and continuous improvement, businesses can navigate the complexities of CCM and drive sustainable growth.

References for Further Reading

https://www.youtube.com/watch?v=7zIBL2DrYRw&pp=ygULY2xvd WQgY29zdCA%3D

https://www.vmware.com/topics/glossary/content/ cloud-cost-management.html#:~:text=Cloud%20cost%20 management%20(also%20known,maximize%20cloud%20usage%20 and%20efficiency

https://www.techtarget.com/whatis/Breaking-Down-the-Cost-of-Cloud-Computing

https://www.hpe.com/us/en/what-is/cloud-cost-management.html

https://granulate.io/blog/cloud-cost-management-complete-guide/

https://www.cloudwards.net/understanding-cloud-storage-pricing/

https://www.forbes.com/sites/forbestechcouncil/2023/01/ 19/the-hidden-costs-of-cloud-and-where-to-find-overspending/

https://techmonitor.ai/technology/cloud/cloud-spending-wasted-oracle-computing-aws-azure

https://resources.flexera.com/web/pdf/Flexera-State-of-the-Cloud-Report-2024.pdf?elqTrackId=6c729f23c1084d5 6a076074c31462307&elqaid=7675&elqat=2&_gl=1*1mn4zqw*_ gcl_au*MjAxMTEwMDc3My4xNzA4NTMzOTU0

CHAPTER 4

Cloud Cost Governance

Your dream house wouldn't be complete without a smart home system to manage its various aspects efficiently. This chapter of your FinOps journey is about establishing cloud cost governance, the smart home system for your cloud environment. Traditionally, managing the expenses of a house includes manually switching lights on and off—leaving the lights on all the time increases the electricity bill and wastes resources. With a smart home system, you can automate that task by setting up smart lights that automatically adjust based on time or occupancy.

Similarly, uncontrolled cloud spending can lead to unnecessary costs. Cloud cost governance helps you avoid this waste. Setting up routines and teaching everyone to turn off lights when not in use is part of good home management. Cloud cost governance involves establishing similar processes for cloud resource usage and assigning clear roles for cost management within your organization.

This system helps you proactively control and optimize your cloud spending. It goes beyond simply monitoring costs (turning on the lights) and provides automated features (smart lights with timers) to ensure you're not wasting resources (leaving all the lights on). By implementing cloud cost governance, you build a smart system for your cloud environment, ensuring efficient resource usage and optimized costs.

Depending on the context, governance can mean different things, but when applied to managing how your teams use cloud resources, it means taking control of and creating proactive processes to manage your cloud spend. Implementing effective cloud cost governance policies is critical to controlling and optimizing cloud expenditures for businesses and organizations.

As organizations rely more on cloud services to satisfy their computing needs, monitoring and efficiently managing cloud computing costs is becoming increasingly essential. Governance of cloud costs entails implementing policies, processes, and tools to measure, control, and optimize spending in alignment with business objectives. This is a proactive approach to managing cloud costs rather than reacting to unexpected cost spikes.

127

© Sasi Kanumuri, Matthew Zeier 2024
S. Kanumuri and M. Zeier, *Scaling Cloud FinOps*, https://doi.org/10.1007/979-8-8688-0388-8_4

This chapter will investigate the fundamental ideas, obstacles, and solutions for creating effective cloud cost governance processes. We'll focus on the people and processes of cloud cost governance in this chapter and Chapter 5 and take a deep dive into automating cloud cost governance in Chapter 7.

Benefits of Cloud Cost Governance

It is impossible to overestimate the significance of cloud cost governance as part of efficiently managing cloud resources and optimizing expenses. As more companies move their operations into the cloud, it is imperative that they put in place efficient cost governance policies to avoid unnecessary expenditures. This will enable them to maximize resource utilization and ensure cloud expenses align with their business goals. Let's go deeper into the myriad facets of its general significance, shall we?

Cost Management and Financial Resources

When implementing cost governance in the cloud, organizations can regain control over costs and avoid running over budget. Businesses can limit spending by introducing budget thresholds, approval processes, and cost-tracking mechanisms and ensuring costs remain within acceptable bounds. These mechanisms enable organizations to ensure costs remain within acceptable thresholds. This level of control allows enterprises to allocate their cloud budgets properly and make well-informed decisions regarding cloud provisioning and utilization.

Optimize Resources Utilization

Cloud cost governance is vital to maximizing available resources and reducing unnecessary expenditures. Organizations can identify underutilized or idle resources and take corrective steps when monitoring and analyzing cloud costs. These corrective actions include resizing instances, terminating excessive resources, and adopting autoscaling capabilities. Optimizing resource allocation can help organizations maximize the value they obtain from cloud investments while eliminating optional expenses.

Cost Transparency and Accountability

Cloud cost governance makes spending in the cloud more transparent and accountable. It lets companies accurately manage and assign costs to the various departments, projects, and teams that make up the firm. Businesses can see which teams or projects are responsible for specific expenditures if they use cost allocation systems and tag their resources. This transparency cultivates accountability, encourages cost-conscious behavior, and enables efficient cost optimization at the granular level.

Structure for Implementing Cost Optimization Efforts

Cloud cost governance offers a structure that may be utilized to implement cost-reduction measures. Constant monitoring and analysis of cloud costs are required to find potential cost reduction and improvement areas. Organizations can gain considerable cost savings by leveraging technologies and strategies such as rightsizing instances, leveraging reserved instances or savings plans, and automating resource provisioning. These cost savings can be accomplished without compromising the system's scalability or performance. Cloud cost governance guarantees that cost optimization evolves continuously and systematically.

Financial Planning and Forecasting

Cloud cost governance is necessary for accurate financial planning and forecasting. Companies can acquire insights into patterns, trends, and factors influencing costs by conducting historical cost analyses. Businesses can more properly allocate budgets and prepare for future growth or scaling requirements if they have access to this information, which enables improved forecasting of future cloud expenses. Businesses are better positioned to make educated decisions and avoid unpleasant financial surprises if their financial planning and cloud cost governance are aligned.

Scalability and Agility

Governance of cloud costs is crucial in determining whether cloud environments are scalable and agile. When expenses are optimized, businesses can allocate resources more effectively and grow their infrastructure in response to changing demands. Because of its scalability, organizations can quickly adapt to shifting market conditions and customer requirements without spending additional resources. Cloud computing is dynamically supported by cloud cost governance, which allows enterprises to scale up or down without interruption while preserving cost-effectiveness.

Administration of Compliance Risks

With effective cloud cost governance, businesses can assist in effectively managing compliance and risk mitigation related to cloud expenditure. Businesses can verify that cloud resources are provisioned and utilized under regulatory standards and industry best practices if they develop policies, guidelines, and approval processes. It helps prevent the use of cloud resources in a way that is not allowed or monitored. This decreases the chance of security breaches, data loss, or noncompliance concerns, which could result in losses to a company's finances and reputation.

Cloud cost governance is essential for companies who want to manage cloud resources effectively and reduce operating expenses. It enables enterprises to maximize resource consumption, adopt cost optimization techniques, and align cloud expenditures with business objectives by providing control, transparency, and cost accountability. By establishing comprehensive cost governance policies, businesses can generate cost savings, improve financial planning, and foster scalability and agility in their cloud environments.

Pro Tip   Automate policy enforcement through infrastructure-as-code. Manual governance processes can catch up to the pace of cloud usage. Leverage infrastructure as code (IaC) tools like Terraform or CloudFormation to embed governance controls directly into provisioning workflows. For example, tagging standards are required, budget alert thresholds are set, and instance types are limited through code. This bakes governance into cloud deployments from the start. Make policy guardrails version controlled, auditable, and scalable. Automated enforcement turns administration from a reactive process into a proactive safeguard.

Cloud Cost Governance Goals and Objectives

It is vital to have a strong understanding of cloud costs and the reasons behind them before entering into the process of cloud cost governance. This is because managing cloud costs presents several challenges in today's dynamic business environment due to the following:

- *The dynamic nature of cloud systems*: Tracking the actual cost of services and applications is difficult due to the provisioning and decommissioning of resources on demand.

- *Lack of visibility into cost drivers*: Identifying areas of overspending within the cloud infrastructure is challenging due to limited insight into specific cost drivers.

- *Fragmented cloud adoption*: Lack of centralized control and accountability for cloud expenditures results in decentralized and fragmented cloud adoption within enterprises.

Cloud cost governance aims to address these challenges. Its primary goals are to control costs, maximize resource utilization and ROI, and align cloud costs with business priorities. The following subsections describe how to implement cloud cost governance to achieve those goals.

Control Costs

Establish budget controls and spending limits for cloud resources. This ensures that you stay within your financial limitations and helps prioritize resource allocation (consider it like setting a budget for your house's electricity usage).

Implement cost allocation methods to identify cost drivers and hold teams accountable. Chargeback models can be implemented to attribute cloud costs to specific departments or projects, fostering a sense of ownership and encouraging resource optimization (similar to how smart meters can track individual appliance energy consumption within a house).

Utilize automation for tasks like rightsizing resources and shutting down idle instances. Automating these processes ensures efficient resource utilization and reduces waste (like setting timers on smart lights to automatically turn off when not in use).

Maximize Resource Utilization and ROI

Employ resource optimization and monitoring techniques to find underutilized resources. By giving you insights into resource utilization patterns, cloud monitoring solutions help you identify underutilized or idle resources that can be retired or optimized (imagine utilizing sensors in your smart home to recognize regularly unused rooms and modify the heating or cooling system accordingly).

Encourage cloud users to be cost-conscious by providing incentives and training. Users are better equipped to choose cloud resources wisely by learning about cloud pricing structures and best practices. To encourage even more responsible resource use, provide teams with incentives when they reach or surpass cost-saving goals.

Utilize tools like autoscaling to optimize resource allocation based on demand. With autoscaling, you may adjust your cloud resources automatically in response to changes in your real-time usage patterns. This way, you can be sure that you have the resources to manage high demand while preventing wasteful spending during low consumption (somewhat like a smart thermostat that optimizes energy use by automatically adjusting heating and cooling according to occupancy).

Align Cloud Costs with Business Priorities

Tag resources with relevant business units or projects for cost allocation and chargeback models. By adding tags to cloud resources, you can keep track of the expenses related to particular departments or projects, which helps you allocate resources wisely (like allocating portions of your house's overall utility bill to different rooms or roommates).

Prioritize cloud investments that directly support business objectives. Evaluate cloud spending to ensure it aligns with your strategic goals. Focus on cloud resources that directly contribute to achieving business objectives and eliminate unnecessary expenses (Imagine prioritizing energy-efficient upgrades for the areas of your house that are used the most).

Conduct regular reviews of cloud spending to ensure alignment with strategic goals. Regularly assess your cloud spending patterns and identify areas for improvement. Examine cost allocation data to make sure resources are going to projects that will benefit the company the most (akin to going through your monthly electricity bills to find places where you may cut back on energy use).

Strong cost governance policies provide a robust foundation for achieving cost predictability, transparency, and accountability. This requires establishing transparent cost allocation methods, defining budget thresholds, and facilitating cost tracking on several levels, including individual resources, departments, and projects. The objective is to reduce costs as much as possible while maintaining high operational efficiency and innovativeness.

Strategies for Cloud Cost Governance

Organizations can use many different approaches to achieve effective cloud cost governance, and the most successful companies leverage a combination of techniques to accomplish their goals.

Education and awareness of cloud costs across the engineering and leadership teams are among the most important first steps in cost governance. Raising awareness among stakeholders regarding the impact of cloud costs on the company, including chargeback/showback enforcement as described in Chapter 2, begins establishing a culture of cost consciousness among teams.

Cultivating a culture of cost awareness also includes establishing comprehensive expense monitoring and alerting methods using CSPs native tools or third-party tools so that cost reports can be reviewed regularly. Create regular cost review meetings, schedule alerts when cost thresholds are met, watch for discrepancies, and take steps to reduce unnecessary expenditures.

This section will highlight important governance policies and procedures you should implement, including resource provisioning criteria, budget thresholds, and approval processes. The establishment of guidelines can assist in the enforcement of cost control measures and ensure compliance throughout the entire organization. It's important to note that governance of cloud computing costs is an ongoing task. Review your cost optimization tactics regularly and make any necessary adjustments in light of shifting business demands, new technological developments, and updated offerings from cloud service providers.

For advanced cloud cost governance, you should also look into third-party tools that provide cost optimization and governance capabilities. These solutions offer functional capabilities, including cost tracking, budget alerts, resource efficiency advice, and cost analyses. Automated solutions have the potential to expedite cost governance processes and provide real-time insights into costs, enabling enterprises to take preventative measures. We'll explore these capabilities further in the automation and vendor management chapters (Chapters 7 and 8, respectively).

Let's dive deeper into the cloud cost governance strategies your teams can leverage to scale your FinOps practices.

Driving Buy-in for Cloud Cost Optimization and Governance

If you are just starting to investigate implementing FinOps in your organization, your first challenge may be to drive buy-in for investing in cloud cost optimization and governance programs. Without buy-in from key stakeholders and engineering leaders, your FinOps initiatives will be much more difficult to implement. To effectively garner support and enthusiasm for such initiatives, it is essential to highlight the benefits and value of efficient cloud cost management.

Efficient cloud cost management directly contributes to an organization's financial stability and profitability. Optimizing cloud costs can enhance businesses' bottom lines and improve economic performance. Emphasizing this aspect helps stakeholders understand that cloud cost optimization is not just a cost-cutting exercise but a strategic approach to long-term financial success.

Cloud cost optimization programs free up financial resources for innovation and growth initiatives. Organizations can allocate funds toward research and development, new product development, market expansion, or strategic partnerships by reducing unnecessary cloud costs. Demonstrating how cost optimization supports innovation and growth can inspire stakeholders to focus on long-term success and expansion.

Organizations that prioritize sustainable financial practices can expect a highly engaged and devoted workforce aligned with the company's mission. Optimizing operational cloud costs helps maintain financial stability, positively impacting employee engagement and job security and reducing the risk of layoffs or downsizing. Highlighting the connection between cost optimization and job security can garner support from the workforce and foster a sense of collective responsibility.

Organizations need to be agile and adaptable in today's dynamic business environment. Efficient cloud cost management enables companies to respond quickly to market changes, economic fluctuations, and industry disruptions. Organizations can weather uncertainties and maintain their competitive edge by reducing costs and enhancing operational flexibility. Highlighting the role of cost optimization in fostering agility can garner support from stakeholders who value resilience and adaptability.

Cost optimization programs often align with sustainability goals and responsible business practices. By minimizing waste, optimizing energy consumption, and adopting environmentally friendly practices, organizations can reduce their ecological footprint and contribute to a greener future. Presenting cost optimization as a means to promote sustainability and responsible business practices can appeal to stakeholders who prioritize environmental consciousness and social responsibility.

Tailoring the messaging to different stakeholders' specific interests and priorities is crucial to driving buy-in for cost optimization programs. By highlighting the diverse benefits and value of efficient cloud cost management, you can build a compelling case for these programs and secure the necessary support to drive meaningful change and improvement.

Collaborate and Align on Cost Governance Goals

Collaborating with finance, FinOps, and cloud infrastructure teams allows for a holistic approach to cost management. Each team brings a unique perspective and expertise to the table. Finance provides financial insights and overall budgetary guidance. FinOps specializes in optimizing cloud costs and usage. The cloud infrastructure team possesses technical knowledge to assess infrastructure requirements and make cost-effective decisions. By leveraging the strengths of these teams collectively, organizations can develop comprehensive cost optimization strategies that consider both financial constraints and technical requirements.

Governance cadence meetings offer an opportunity to align cost optimization goals and strategies across teams. Finance may have specific financial targets, such as reducing expenses or optimizing cost categories. FinOps may focus on cloud cost optimization through rightsizing instances, utilizing reserved instances, or leveraging cost management tools. The cloud infrastructure team may prioritize resource allocation, infrastructure automation, or architecture optimizations. By bringing these teams together, organizations can ensure that their cost optimization efforts are synchronized, minimizing conflicts and maximizing overall effectiveness.

Collaboration in governance cadence meetings facilitates sharing insights, challenges, and best practices. Finance can provide financial analytics, cost trends, and benchmarks that help teams understand the financial impact of their decisions. FinOps can share cloud cost optimization techniques, such as tagging strategies, resource usage analysis, or recommendations for leveraging CSP discounts. The cloud infrastructure team can contribute technical insights, such as optimizing resource provisioning, utilizing serverless architectures, or implementing efficient containerization strategies. These knowledge exchanges foster innovation, cross-pollination of ideas, and continuous improvement in cost optimization strategies.

Governance cadence meetings enable collaboration in budget management and forecasting. Finance can provide budgetary guidelines, cost forecasts, and insights into spending patterns. FinOps can contribute by analyzing historical cost data, forecasting future cloud expenses, and giving cost-saving recommendations. The cloud infrastructure team can provide input on infrastructure requirements, capacity planning, and cost implications of architectural decisions. By working together, these teams can develop accurate budget forecasts, identify potential cost overruns, and proactively take measures to optimize costs and align spending with financial goals.

Collaboration in governance cadence meetings ensures continuous monitoring and optimization of cost optimization initiatives. Regular meetings allow teams to review cost metrics, track progress toward goals, and identify areas that require further attention or adjustment. By analyzing cost data, sharing insights, and discussing challenges, teams can iteratively refine their strategies, implement corrective measures, and drive ongoing improvements. This iterative process helps organizations stay on track, adapt to changing business needs, and continuously optimize costs.

To ensure effective collaboration in governance cadence meetings, follow these essential practices:

- *Clearly define meeting objectives*: Establish the purpose and scope of the meetings and ensure that cost optimization goals, financial targets, and critical metrics are communicated to all teams involved.

- *Regular meeting cadence*: Schedule regular meetings for governance to maintain a consistent forum for collaboration. Monthly or quarterly meetings are ordinary, depending on the organization's size, complexity, and cost optimization priorities.

- *Cross-functional representation*: Invite critical stakeholders from the finance, FinOps, and cloud infrastructure teams to attend the meeting, ensuring diverse perspectives and promoting a collaborative environment.

- *Agenda and preparation*: Develop a well-structured agenda covering relevant topics such as cost trends, cost optimization initiatives, budget forecasts, and each team's challenges. Share the agenda and supporting materials in advance to allow participants to come prepared and contribute effectively.

- *Data-driven discussions*: Encourage data-driven discussions by sharing relevant cost metrics, financial analyses, and performance reports. Use visualizations and dashboards to communicate complex information effectively and facilitate team understanding.

- *Action-oriented outcomes*: Document the meeting's action items, decisions, and responsibilities. Ensure clear ownership and deadlines for follow-up actions and track progress at subsequent meetings.

- *Knowledge sharing and training*: Facilitate knowledge-sharing sessions or training workshops where teams can educate each other in their respective domains, building a shared understanding of financial concepts, cost optimization techniques, and technical considerations.

- *Continuous improvement*: Regularly evaluate the effectiveness of governance cadence meetings by seeking participant feedback. Identify areas for improvement and adjust the meeting structure, agenda, or format as necessary.

Monthly Cost Reviews with Engineering Managers and Leadership

Everyone in your organization is wearing multiple hats and juggling competing priorities for their time. When critical production deadlines approach, reviewing cloud cost reports can often get deprioritized. Monthly cost reviews with engineering managers (EMs) and leadership provide dedicated time for all leaders to review cost metrics and progress to cost savings goals. These are crucial for any organization that aims to manage its financial resources and optimize its operations effectively.

Monthly cost reviews enable organizations to monitor and analyze key metrics such as operational expenses, capital expenditures, cost per unit, and cost trends over time. These metrics help identify areas of excessive spending, cost overruns, or opportunities for improvement. By regularly reviewing these metrics, organizations can take proactive measures to control costs, optimize resource allocation, and enhance overall financial performance.

Monthly cost reviews also facilitate collaboration and accountability among different stakeholders. These reviews promote cross-functional communication, transparency, and a shared understanding of financial objectives by bringing together engineering managers and leadership. When EMs present their cost metrics and initiatives, they are held accountable for their department's performance, fostering a sense of ownership and responsibility for cost management.

Cost reviews provide engineering managers and leaders a platform to share and discuss cost-saving initiatives. These initiatives may involve process improvements, technology optimizations, vendor negotiations, or resource reallocation strategies. By leveraging the EMs responsible for day-to-day operations and resource management, organizations can tap into their expertise and ideas to uncover potential cost-saving opportunities that need to be apparent at a higher level.

Cost reviews provide a structured framework for evaluating the effectiveness of cost-saving initiatives and determining their impact on the organization's financial health. By reviewing the progress made toward cost reduction targets and assessing the ROI of implemented initiatives, organizations can gauge the success of their strategies. This evaluation process helps identify successful approaches that can be replicated in other areas while highlighting areas requiring further attention or adjustment.

Overall, regular cost reviews contribute to a culture of continuous improvement within the organization. By consistently evaluating costs and seeking opportunities for optimization, organizations can foster a mindset that encourages innovation and efficiency. Use the insights gained from these reviews to refine cost-saving initiatives, adapt strategies to changing business needs, and drive ongoing improvements across different departments and functions.

Figure 4-1. *Cost reviews framework*

To conduct effective monthly cost reviews, it is vital to establish a well-defined structure, represented in Figure 4-1, and follow certain best practices:

- *Set clear objectives and agenda*: Define the purpose of the review, outline the specific metrics to discuss, and establish an agenda that covers critical topics and initiatives.

- *Prepare comprehensive reports*: Before the meeting, EMs should provide detailed reports on cost metrics, trends, and initiatives, allowing leadership to review the information beforehand and come prepared with questions or suggestions.

- *Foster open and constructive discussions*: Encourage active participation and open dialogue during the review sessions. Create an environment where EMs feel comfortable sharing challenges, proposing ideas, and seeking guidance.

- *Document action items and follow-up*: Document action items, decisions, and next steps resulting from the cost reviews, ensuring accountability and providing a reference for tracking progress between meetings.

- *Share learnings and best practices*: Encourage the sharing of successful cost-saving initiatives and best practices across different departments. This cross-pollination of ideas can inspire innovation and generate new approaches to cost management.

- *Adapt and iterate*: Regularly assess the effectiveness of the cost review process itself. Seek participant feedback to identify improvement areas and make adjustments as necessary to ensure the reviews remain valuable and impactful.

Incorporating Cost into Cloud Architecture Reviews

How your SaaS products are architected can significantly impact your cloud costs, especially as your customer base grows. On a small scale, having your application make two database calls instead of three isn't significant cost-wise. But when your application performs that function 1,000 times or 10,000 times per hour, that 50% increase in database access fees becomes very relevant to your cloud costs.

Incorporating cost elements into architecture review processes is crucial for understanding the cost implications of new services or features. By considering cloud costs early in the architectural design phase, organizations can make informed decisions on architecture, optimize resource allocation, and avoid expensive surprises.

Cost-driven architecture focuses on designing systems and solutions that balance functionality, performance, and cost-effectiveness. For example, investing in high-performance infrastructure might have higher upfront costs but result in lower maintenance costs or an improved user experience. The architecture review is where decisions are made regarding cloud costs and other attributes, such as performance, scalability, security, and maintainability.

Architecture reviews should include a deliberate assessment of the cost implications of each design decision. This involves analyzing the financial impact of various architectural choices, such as infrastructure components, technology stack, scalability options, data storage, and integration points. Organizations can select the most cost-effective options by considering costs at the design stage without compromising functionality or quality.

Incorporating cost elements into the architecture review process is a collaborative effort between architects and financial stakeholders. Effective communication of cost implications and trade-offs helps stakeholders understand the economic impact of architectural decisions and align their expectations accordingly.

Cost-driven architectural reviews should be ongoing throughout the system's lifecycle. Regular cost monitoring and control allows organizations to track actual costs against estimated ones, identify cost overruns, and take corrective actions promptly. Lessons from previous projects can inform the refinement of cost estimation methods and improve future cost assessment accuracy. Over time, this helps maintain cost discipline and optimize resource allocation in alignment with architectural decisions.

Integrating Cost Considerations into Architecture Reviews: A Case Study

Many organizations implement an architecture review board to review applications and Slack has one too. Previously, cost was a minor consideration during their architectural review processes. However, the company recognized the importance of integrating costs into the design phase.

To address this, the company made the crucial change of *incorporating a dedicated cost section* within its architectural review process specifically focused on cost implications. This section involves cloud architects, cost analysts, and potentially other stakeholders collaboratively assessing the cost impact of proposed design decisions.

This seemingly simple change has yielded significant benefits, primarily *better business alignment*. The cloud economics team guarantees better alignment with business objectives by specifically taking cost into account during architecture assessments. Financial stakeholders make better decisions since they are more aware of the financial effects of different architectural options.

This case study exemplifies the power of integrating cost considerations into architecture reviews. By following a similar approach, your organization can achieve better cost control and ensure alignment between technical decisions and financial objectives.

The following are a few additional tips for integrating cost considerations into the architecture review process:

- *Leverage cloud cost management tools*: Use the cloud cost management resources offered by your cloud provider or outside vendors. These technologies can help estimate costs during architecture reviews by providing insightful information about resource usage and cost patterns.

- *Develop cost estimation models*: Establish cost estimation models based on historical data and cloud provider pricing structures. These models can help predict potential costs associated with different architectural choices.

By incorporating these suggestions and learning from the case study, you can empower your organization to make cost-conscious architectural decisions that optimize cloud resource utilization and deliver long-term financial benefits.

The Role and Importance of Technical Program Management in Cloud FinOps

In the context of cloud computing, cost optimization and effective utilization of resources are critical considerations. Technical program management (TPM) becomes a strategic driver in this situation. TPM encompasses the principles and processes for organizing, directing, and managing the lifetime of technical initiatives. Within the framework of cloud economics, TPM concentrates on encouraging stakeholder engagement, utilizing data-driven insights for ongoing cost optimization, and seamlessly integrating cost considerations throughout the whole cloud project lifecycle. Organizations may ensure that their cloud expenditures provide optimal value by firmly establishing a basis for cost governance by successfully implementing TPM procedures. Let's examine how TPM helps create a well-oiled cloud cost governance system.

Technical program management is critical in optimizing cloud economics and ensuring cost-effective cloud resource utilization. Here's how TPM contributes to a well-oiled cloud cost governance machine:

- *Streamlined cost considerations into project lifecycles*: Effective TPM integrates cost considerations seamlessly into the entire project lifecycle. Intake forms, a core TPM tool, capture crucial information upfront, including the following:

  - *Anticipated usage patterns*: Identifying potential high-demand features allows for proactive cost optimization strategies like data compression or cost-effective storage solutions.

  - *Scalability requirements*: Understanding scalability needs helps to estimate future costs and to choose solutions that scale efficiently without incurring unexpected expenses.

  - *Third-party service dependencies*: Determining third-party service costs ensures a holistic view of project expenses.

  - *Cost limitations*: Defining budget constraints early guides resource allocation and prevents exceeding financial limitations.

  Through the early collection of this cost-related data, TPM promotes a cost-conscious culture throughout the project.

- *Enhanced visibility and collaboration for informed decisions*: TPM tools like Jira provide a centralized platform for cost discussions and data sharing. Stakeholders from various departments (IT, finance, operations) can collaborate on cost analysis within Jira tickets, ensuring all perspectives are considered.

  - *Issue-tracking features*: Jira allows documenting and discussing cost implications for specific features, promoting transparency and informed decision-making.

  - *Task tracking and status monitoring*: Teams can track progress on cost-related tasks (analysis, optimization techniques, implementation) within Jira, ensuring timely cost considerations throughout the project.

  - *Customizable workflows*: Customizable workflows can mandate cost-related tasks at specific stages of the software development process, further solidifying cost considerations

- *Data-driven insights for continuous improvement*: TPM empowers data-driven decision-making through:

  - *Analytics and reporting*: Jira creates reports on cost-related activities that allow stakeholders to monitor developments, spot spending trends, and assess the effectiveness of cost-optimization initiatives.

  - *Combining cost analysis tools*: When Jira and cloud cost management (CCM) solutions are integrated, Jira tickets can automatically populate with cost information. This offers real-time insights on expenditures, estimates, and suggestions for cost minimization for improved decision-making.

- *Increased transparency and accountability*: TPM enables discussions, project management through:

  - *Comments and discussions*: Collaboration features like comments and discussions within Jira tickets promote transparency and shared responsibility for cost management.

  - *Assigning cost analysis tasks*: Assigning specific cost analysis and optimization tasks fosters accountability among team members.

Organizations can effectively leverage TPM practices to ensure their cloud spending is aligned with business objectives and delivers optimal value. This strong foundation sets the stage for the more granular cost governance practices discussed in the following sections.

Technical Program Management Strategies

Effectively managing your engineering team's work priorities is a major task that requires strong program management to keep your teams focused on the right goals. Program management tools like Jira, Asana, Monday.com, etc., are essential to keeping your engineers on task. The most effective cloud cost governance programs integrate into existing technical program management procedures to provide transparency and control to cost optimization and governance tasks.

Alongside effective program management tools is the need to create a structured and organized method to collect pertinent information regarding planned changes to cloud infrastructure. Without a consistent structure for capturing critical data such as a project's scope, goals, timeframe, technical needs, and estimated budget, changes to cloud infrastructure can have unplanned impacts to cost, performance, and stability. Intake forms are generally used for this purpose, and the goal is to collect as much information as possible about a planned project so that an accurate evaluation of its viability and an estimate of its future expenses may be performed.

Program Management Tools

As a tool for managing projects, Jira and other similar tools provide a consolidated platform for recording and organizing information relating to new applications or features. Jira's issue-tracking features allow teams to document and debate cost-related considerations. With thorough documentation on cost considerations, you can rest assured that all pertinent information will be saved in a single spot, making it simple for team members to access it while conducting cost analysis and optimization.

Jira task-tracking tools allow teams to create and monitor cost-related activities throughout a project's lifecycle. When specific tasks relating to cost analysis, cost optimization techniques, and implementation are defined, teams can track progress and ensure cost considerations are addressed promptly. Additionally, because Jira's workflows and status monitoring tools are fully customizable, businesses can designate phases of the software to complete cost-related tasks, making monitoring and reporting on cost optimization endeavors easier.

Jira includes reporting options that users can employ to produce cost-related insights and analytics for their projects. Organizations can use Jira reporting features to monitor cost-related tasks, assess progress, and spot patterns over time. These reports have the potential to play a vital role in the decision-making process by enabling stakeholders to evaluate the efficiency of cost optimization methods, locate areas in need of improvement, and make decisions regarding resource allocation and budgeting based on accurate information.

Jira can be coupled with many cost analysis tools and platforms, allowing data flow without interruptions and improving cost visibility. By integrating Jira with CCM tools or services, teams can automatically populate cost-related information within Jira tickets. Examples of this type of information include current spending, predicted costs, and recommendations for cost minimization. This integration increases openness and supports data-driven decision-making during development and deployment.

Stakeholders from multiple fields can communicate their viewpoints and areas of expertise with one another through comments and discussions contained within tickets. This approach to collaboration helps cultivate a sense of shared responsibility for efficiently managing costs. In addition, the built-in assignment features of this type of tool allow teams to delegate cost analysis and optimization duties. This makes it possible to ensure that the appropriate employees are held accountable for driving cost-related projects.

Utilizing technologies such as Jira and intake forms to record concerns related to costs and enhance transparency delivers some benefits to companies. It makes it possible to gather information, provide early awareness of costs, collaborate, be accountable, monitor tasks, generate reports, integrate with cost analysis tools, and document processes. As a result of using these tactics, companies can better integrate cost concerns into development and deployment processes, leading to more cost-conscious decision-making and efficient resource allocation.

Structured Intake Forms

Intake forms provide an organized framework for collecting vital information on programs that will introduce new applications or features. Completing an intake form is essential in ensuring cost considerations are included in the evaluation for switching to new infrastructure or adjusting existing infrastructure.

Organizations can encourage stakeholders to contribute pertinent information at the beginning of the process by establishing a separate section inside the intake form to address cost-related factors, including anticipated usage patterns, the anticipated requirements for scalability, the dependency on third-party services, and the anticipated cost limitations. The standardized format of intake forms makes it easier to collect data invariably and makes it more likely that cost considerations will not be neglected.

By incorporating cost-related questions into intake forms, teams can acquire early visibility into potential cost implications. This enables stakeholders to explore cost optimization methods right from the beginning of the project, which is a significant advantage. For instance, if a feature needs considerable data storage, the team can proactively examine possibilities such as adopting data compression techniques or using more cost-effective storage solutions. Early awareness of costs allows teams to make informed decisions and lowers the risk of unanticipated expense increases.

A strong, comprehensive intake form should include the following elements:

- *Project goal and scope*: The intake form must record a project's objectives and scope. This helps stakeholders understand the aim of infrastructure modifications and their expected effects. It enables them to properly connect cost concerns with project goals and prioritize resources for those objectives.

- *Technical requirements and specifications*: Compiling comprehensive technical requirements and specifications lists is necessary before producing an accurate cost estimate. The intake form should have parts describing the existing infrastructure, the planned changes, and the essential resources. This could comprise hardware, software, network infrastructure, security measures, and other pertinent components. Identifying potential cost drivers and assessing alternative solutions is aided by precise specifications.

- *The budget and the distribution of costs*: The intake form must have a distinct section to record the estimated cost of infrastructure adjustments. Estimating costs for procurement, installation, maintenance, and continuous operational expenditures could be part of this process. The decision-makers in an organization can guarantee that cost concerns are matched with available resources and organizational priorities if they define budget and cost allocation in as much detail as possible.

- *Risk evaluation and prevention measures*: Alterations to existing infrastructure can involve additional risks. The intake form should have a section dedicated to risk assessment to determine potential dangers and associated costs. This helps evaluate the possible spending linked to risks and devise methods for mitigating such costs. When businesses consider risk management, they can better prepare for unanticipated expenses and reduce the impact of these costs on the entire budget.

- *Stakeholder involvement*: The intake form should include a stakeholder analysis to determine the prominent individuals or departments involved in the decision-making process and cost considerations. Involving essential stakeholders from other departments, such as IT, finance, and operations, helps ensure a holistic perspective on the costs and advantages of the changes to the infrastructure. It also assists in developing teamwork and securing buy-in from all relevant parties.

- *Evaluation criteria*: The intake form should offer clear criteria to facilitate an efficient evaluation of the suggested alterations to the infrastructure and the expenditures connected with them. This could involve considerations like scalability, performance, security, compliance, and the capacity to maintain costs over the long term. Decision-makers can objectively analyze the various possibilities and choose the course of action that results in the lowest overall cost.

- *The procedure for documentation and approval*: The paperwork and approval process for any infrastructure changes should be outlined in the intake form. This ensures that all parties know the timing for decision-making and the actions required to evaluate and approve cost considerations. An open and easy-to-understand method encourages accountability and allows accurate expenditure tracking throughout a project's lifecycle.

When it comes to putting in place intake forms for various infrastructure projects, they shouldn't be a one-off deal. It is essential to conduct regular reviews and keep the intake form template up to date depending on the knowledge gained and the shifting requirements of the firm. Continuous improvement allows businesses to enhance their cost analysis process and better react to shifting technological landscapes, evolving market conditions, and limiting financial parameters.

The Importance of Budgeting and Forecasting for Effective Cost Management

Budgeting and forecasting are essential tools for effective cost management in any organization. They are crucial for planning, decision-making, and maintaining financial stability. This section describes the importance of budgeting and forecasting in detail.

Planning and Goal Setting

Budgeting and forecasting allow organizations to set financial goals and objectives. Businesses can estimate their revenue, expenses, and profitability for a specific period by analyzing historical data and market trends. This information helps in setting realistic targets and identifying areas for improvement. Proper planning makes allocating resources efficiently and achieving desired financial outcomes easier.

Resource Allocation

Budgeting helps allocate resources effectively. It allows organizations to determine how much money should be allocated to different departments, projects, or activities. Organizations can prioritize their investments by setting spending limits and ensuring funds are distributed optimally. This prevents overspending and wasteful expenses and promotes cost control.

Expense Control and Cost Reduction

Budgeting and forecasting provide a framework for monitoring and optimizing spend. Organizations can identify overspending and take corrective actions by comparing actual expenditures with budgeted amounts. It facilitates early detection of cost overruns, allowing managers to make necessary adjustments to stay within budget. Forecasting also helps predict future expenses, enabling proactive cost-reduction strategies.

Decision-Making and Risk Management

Budgeting and forecasting assist in informed decision-making. When evaluating potential investments or business decisions, organizations can rely on budget and forecast data to assess the financial impact. Budgeting enables management to prioritize projects based on expected returns and aligns them with the organization's strategic objectives. It also helps identify potential risks and uncertainties, allowing organizations to implement risk mitigation strategies and develop contingency plans.

Performance Evaluation and Accountability

Budgeting and forecasting serve as benchmarks for performance evaluation. Organizations can measure their financial performance by comparing actual results with budgeted or forecasted figures. Variances between planned and actual outcomes highlight areas of success or concern, enabling management to take appropriate actions. Moreover, budgeting promotes accountability as departments and individuals are responsible for adhering to allocated budgets and achieving financial targets.

Communication and Stakeholder Management

Budgeting and forecasting help communicate financial information effectively to stakeholders. Whether they are shareholders, lenders, or internal teams, having a well-defined budget and forecast enhances transparency and credibility. It helps stakeholders understand the organization's financial position, growth prospects, and resource utilization. Additionally, budgeting and forecasting facilitate effective communication between different departments, aligning their goals and fostering collaboration.

Long-Term Financial Planning

Budgeting and forecasting are not limited to short-term planning; they are crucial for long-term financial sustainability. Organizations can develop multiyear budgets and forecasts by considering long-term trends and strategic objectives. This enables them to project future financial needs, plan for investments, and ensure long-term viability.

Techniques to Visualize Cost Data in Cost Governance Context

Not every organization is ready to invest in advanced third-party tools to provide cost visibility and insights into your cloud data, especially if your cloud costs are relatively small and simple (one use case or department, for example).

Leveraging simple tools such as Excel sheets and coloring techniques, represented in Figure 4-2, to visualize cost data can significantly enhance the effectiveness of cost discussions within an organization.

| Enhanced data comprehension | Improved decision-making | Effective communication | Highlighting key insights and metrics | Tracking progress and performance |

Figure 4-2. *Techniques to visualize cost data*

With its versatile features and capabilities, Excel allows the creation of visualizations that make complex cost data more accessible and understandable. The following list describes the benefits of using Excel and coloring techniques for cost data visualization and how they can facilitate discussions:

- *Enhanced data comprehension*: Coloring techniques in Excel, such as conditional formatting or color-coded charts, can significantly improve data comprehension. By assigning different colors to specific cost categories, trends, or performance indicators (typically green and red), stakeholders can quickly grasp the information at a glance. This visual representation helps highlight patterns, outliers, and areas that require attention by making it easier to understand complex cost data and facilitating more meaningful discussions.

- *Improved decision-making*: Visualizing cost data using Excel enables stakeholders to make informed decisions based on clear and concise information. By using colors to represent different aspects of costs, such as expenses, savings, or cost variations, decision-makers can quickly identify opportunities for cost optimization or areas where corrective actions are needed. Visualizations can also help compare cost metrics across different periods, departments, or projects, enabling more effective decision-making and resource allocation.

- *Effective communication*: Colorful visualizations created in Excel are powerful communication tools during cost discussions. They provide a common visual language that different stakeholders can easily understand, regardless of their finance or data analysis expertise. Visual representations enable more transparent communication, facilitate discussions, and encourage collaboration among team members. Stakeholders can share insights, identify trends, and discuss cost-related challenges more productively and with greater focus.

- *Highlighting key insights and metrics*: Excel's color-based visualizations highlight key insights and metrics in cost data. For example, different colors can be assigned to indicate high- and low-cost items, cost variances from budget, or cost outliers. By drawing attention to these critical metrics, discussions can be centered on specific areas that require attention or further investigation. This focus on critical insights helps prioritize conversations and drive actionable outcomes.

- *Tracking progress and performance*: Coloring techniques in Excel can be utilized to track progress and performance against cost targets or benchmarks. By assigning colors to represent goal attainment or performance thresholds, stakeholders can quickly identify whether objectives are being met or corrective actions are necessary. This visual tracking of progress fosters accountability and encourages discussions about performance, enabling timely adjustments to cost optimization strategies.

When leveraging tools such as Excel and coloring techniques for cost data visualization, consider the following best practices:

- *Choose appropriate visualization types*: Select the most suitable visualization types, such as column charts, bar charts, or heat maps, based on the nature of the cost data and the specific insights you want to convey. Experiment with different chart options to find the most effective representation for your audience.

- *Utilize conditional formatting*: Excel's conditional formatting feature applies colors based on specific criteria or thresholds. For example, use color scales to show variations in cost data or apply color rules to highlight specific cost ranges.

- *Keep it simple and intuitive*: Avoid cluttered or complex visualizations that may need to be clarified or modified for stakeholders. Strive for simplicity and clarity, ensuring the visual representation is intuitive and easy to interpret.

- *Provide clear legends and labels*: Clearly label the colors used in the visualization to indicate their meaning. Include a legend or a key that explains the color-coding system, ensuring that all stakeholders understand the significance of each color.

- *Update visuals regularly*: As cost data evolves, update the visuals to reflect the most recent information. This ensures that discussions are based on up-to-date and accurate data.

- *Use complementary visuals*: Combine different visualizations to view cost data comprehensively. For example, charts can be used to show overall trends, and tables can provide detailed breakdowns.

- *Customize visuals to fit the audience*: Tailor the visuals to the audience's preferences and needs. Consider factors such as their level of financial expertise, familiarity with Excel, and specific requirements when designing visualizations.

Chapter Summary

This chapter introduced cloud cost governance, focusing on goals and processes for creating cloud cost governance strategies in your organization. Key topics included

- *What is cloud cost governance?* Cloud cost governance is a collective set of policies and procedures for proactively controlling and optimizing cloud expenditures for businesses and organizations.

- *The importance of cloud cost governance*: Effective cloud cost governance enables organizations to maximize cloud resource utilization and ensure cloud expenses align with business goals.

- *Strategies for cloud cost governance*: Cost governance provides a set of guidelines for creating the processes needed for effective awareness, education, and control cloud costs.

Cloud cost governance provides the foundation for managing and optimizing spend at scale. By implementing robust governance practices, organizations can take control of cloud costs and drive financial success.

The strategies discussed in this chapter for governing cloud costs set the stage for creating a culture of cloud cost awareness in your organization. In Chapter 5, we'll dive deep into why it's essential to shift left on cloud cost awareness. Chapter 5 also introduces an innovative new strategy for cost awareness called the #Piggy-Bank Framework.

Cultivating Cost Awareness Culture

Continuing the journey of building your smart cloud home, this chapter focuses on cultivating a culture of cloud cost awareness. Imagine this chapter as the guide to transforming your smart home into a truly efficient and cost-effective environment.

Like everyone in a household benefits from understanding how their actions impact energy usage, everyone in an organization that utilizes cloud resources can contribute to cost optimization. This chapter explores how to empower everyone, from CEOs to developers, to be mindful of cloud costs and actively participate in achieving savings.

Cultivating a culture of cloud cost awareness is like unlocking a treasure chest of savings and optimization. It's all about empowering every organization member, from top-level executives to developers, to understand the impact of their cloud-related decisions on costs and actively contribute to optimization efforts.

Cultivating a culture of cloud cost awareness involves education, cost visibility and accountability, collaborative cost optimization, cost-conscious design principles, continuous monitoring, optimization, recognition, and incentives, and integrating cost-related metrics and goals. It seeks to "shift left" cloud cost efficiency into the engineering teams, directly impacting cloud costs.

Shift Left in Engineering and FinOps

Let's examine the idea of "shift left" in the context of engineering and FinOps before delving into the tactics for fostering a culture of cloud cost awareness. In traditional software development, many activities, such as performance optimization and security testing, were frequently postponed phases of the development lifecycle. Many software development responsibilities, such as performance optimization and security testing,

© Sasi Kanumuri, Matthew Zeier 2024
S. Kanumuri and M. Zeier, *Scaling Cloud FinOps*, https://doi.org/10.1007/979-8-8688-0388-8_5

were traditionally handled later. This strategy, sometimes called "shift right," often resulted in delays and costly solutions if issues were found later in the project.

The shift left paradigm strongly emphasizes resolving these issues as early as feasible. This entails proactively incorporating best practices and factors into the first phases of the development process. "Shift left" in the context of FinOps and cloud cost management refers to incorporating cost optimization techniques early on in the lifespan of a cloud project rather than later.

Here's how this shift left approach applies to FinOps:

- *Early cost considerations*: Possible cost problems can be found and resolved before substantial resources are used by implementing cost estimation and optimization techniques throughout the planning and design stages.

- *Cost-conscious design guidelines*: A shift to the left promotes the use of economical design patterns and architectures that place an early emphasis on resource efficiency. This could entail autoscaling, choosing appropriately sized resources, and implementing effective data storage techniques.

- *Developer accountability and visibility*: Giving developers access to tools that clearly show their costs gives them the power to decide how best to use their resources. As a result, development teams benefit from having a greater sense of accountability and ownership for cloud charges.

Organizations can proactively control cloud expenses throughout the development lifecycle and achieve considerable cost savings and better resource efficiency by adopting a shift left approach in FinOps. This lays the groundwork for the tactics covered in the subsequent sections of this chapter, which focus on encouraging an awareness of cloud costs throughout the company.

Essential Elements for Culture Creation

Creating a cultural shift isn't a one-time activity that magically creates a new mindset in your teams. It requires a strategic approach and a long-term commitment by leadership to build a culture of cost awareness that enables businesses to manage cloud expenses effectively, drive efficiency, and maximize the value of cloud services. Leaders should emphasize cost optimization, clearly communicate goals, and align those goals with broader business objectives.

Executive buy-in for creating a culture of cost awareness is essential to every other aspect of culture. Leaders can promote shared responsibility among teams, convey the relevance of cost minimization, and provide resources for training and growth. When senior leaders actively advocate and participate in a cultural shift, it sends a strong message about the significance of the shift to the rest of the organization.

- **Visibility and Accountability via the #Piggy-Bank Framework**

What if every team member could see the direct impact of their actions on cloud costs? Transparency and visibility into cloud costs provide employees with access to cost dashboards, reports, and user-friendly tools, enabling them to uncover the financial impact of their decisions. With this knowledge, they can make informed choices about resource utilization and create cost-driven architectural decisions. Regularly sharing cost-related updates and information further fuels the culture of cost awareness, ensuring everyone is on board.

One key to success in the quest for cost awareness lies in establishing effective cost allocation measures and ensuring teams take responsibility for cloud expenses. Organizations create a sense of responsibility by assigning costs to specific departments, projects, or teams. Teams take ownership of actively managing and optimizing cloud usage within allocated budgets. Responsible resource utilization and cost-conscious decision-making become ingrained in their actions.

The #Piggy-Bank Framework provides the methodology for ensuring your teams have the visibility they need to understand their cloud costs and be held accountable. It establishes a forum and dedicated channels for exchanging cost optimization ideas, strategies, and tips, fostering a collaborative environment where employees learn from each other and collectively drive cost optimization efforts.

- **Effective Collaboration**

Focus on making cost optimization a team effort rather than an individual burden. Engineers are more likely to embrace cost consciousness if they feel supported and that it is a shared responsibility across the organization. Encourage cross-functional collaboration between engineering, finance, and operations to analyze costs, brainstorm ideas, and implement optimizations. Make it about working together to maximize efficiency and resources for the company's good, not singling people out over expenses.

Framing it as a team effort also results in better ideas and avoids the tendency to cut corners or sacrifice quality to save costs. The most sustainable path is when engineers feel empowered and incentivized to optimize costs while delivering robust systems and innovation.

Conduct periodic cost reviews at various levels, analyzing cloud costs to identify overspending or inefficiencies. Involve relevant stakeholders to foster shared responsibility and ownership. Organizations can continuously refine cost optimization strategies by analyzing cost trends, patterns, and anomalies, ensuring that the culture of cost awareness always retains momentum.

- **Ongoing Education to Cultivate a Culture of Cost Awareness**

Educating employees about cloud costs and optimization techniques is critical to fostering cost awareness. It's like equipping them with a map to navigate the cloud expense landscape. Engaging training programs and immersive workshops unveil the mysteries of cost implications tied to different cloud resources and services. Employees become cost-conscious developers with best practices like rightsizing instances, uncovering cost-effective storage options, and navigating data transfer optimizations.

- **Reward Successes and Celebrate Wins**

Encourage employees to share their cost optimization experiences, challenges, and triumphs. Recognizing and rewarding cost-conscious behavior will motivate and inspire your teams. Establishing programs acknowledging individuals or teams contributing significantly to cost optimization creates a positive and competitive environment. Employees become eager to do more, constantly seeking innovative ways to uncover cost-saving opportunities and claim their share of success.

Fostering a culture of cloud cost awareness requires strong leadership, effective communication, education, and transparent visibility into cloud costs. Organizations embark on a cost optimization journey by empowering employees with knowledge, promoting accountability, and nurturing continuous improvement and knowledge sharing. This culture leads to significant cost savings and aligns costs with strategic objectives, unveiling the hidden financial potential in the cloud.

Visibility and Accountability: Introducing the #Piggy-Bank Framework

Effective communication is the cornerstone of visibility and accountability in cultivating an organization's culture of cloud cost awareness. Imagine a scenario where the FinOps team has worked to create a comprehensive reporting structure for cloud costs but then struggles to disseminate that information effectively to all the key stakeholders. What the FinOps team needs is a robust communication framework, one that is built upon existing tools already in use by their teams.

Transparency and visibility into cloud expenditures empower employees with access to cost dashboards, reports, and user-friendly tools, enabling them to discern the impact of their decisions on the organization's finances. Regular sharing of cost-related updates and information further fuels this culture of cost awareness, ensuring alignment across teams and reinforcing the collective responsibility and accountability for managing cloud expenses.

What Is the #Piggy-Bank Framework?

Cloud computing has emerged as an indispensable tool for modern enterprises because of its scalability, flexibility, and cost-effectiveness advantages. Nevertheless, with adequate cost management and awareness, cloud charges can quickly get out of hand and become unmanageable. To address this issue, the #Piggy-Bank Framework encourages openness, accountability, and education on cloud charges within a business.

The #Piggy-Bank Framework empowers organizations to make informed decisions about cloud spending by integrating cost considerations into the technology development process. This framework rests on four key pillars:

- *Visibility*: Granular cloud usage and cost data is the foundation. Engineers gain insights into how their choices, like instance types and resource sizing, impact the bottom line by seeing detailed monthly expenditure breakdowns.

- *Literacy*: Understanding cloud billing, pricing models, and cost-effective configurations is crucial. Training equips engineers with the knowledge to interpret usage reports and optimize configurations for cost savings. They learn how provisioning and resource allocation decisions translate into real dollars.

- *Shared accountability*: The #Piggy-Bank Framework promotes a collaborative approach to cost optimization, shifting the focus from blame to shared responsibility. This fosters a sense of ownership among teams, encouraging them to work together to identify and eliminate waste.

- *Thrift*: Regular cost reviews and resource optimization become ingrained practices. Teams dedicate time to analyzing usage trends, identifying areas for savings, eliminating unused resources, and rightsizing instances. By institutionalizing thrift, organizations can achieve significant cost reductions.

FinOps Champions: Dedicated FinOps teams play a pivotal role in driving the adoption of the #Piggy-Bank Framework. They equip teams with the necessary tools, training, and frameworks to foster financial accountability. By leading this cultural shift, FinOps teams ensure that cloud costs are no longer an afterthought but a central consideration in technology decision-making.

This framework is a proven road map for organizations to cultivate cost consciousness at scale. By promoting visibility, education, accountability, and a culture of thrift, FinOps teams can empower a grassroots movement that maximizes cloud ROI.

The #Piggy-Bank Framework enables teams to actively participate in managing and optimizing cloud expenditures by exploiting the collaborative nature of the widespread communication and collaboration platform Slack/ Teams. At its core, implementing #Piggy-Bank Framework involves setting up a dedicated Slack/ Teams channel for employees to exchange information, insights, and best practices for managing cloud costs.

This channel is common for conversations, questions, and updates regarding cloud storage and computing costs. It encourages collaboration and expertise sharing among team members from various areas, such as engineering, finance, operations, and management. When implemented as a Slack/Teams channel, the #Piggy-Bank Framework is a creative approach to establishing a culture of cloud cost awareness across enterprises.

The #Piggy-Bank Framework in Action

The #Piggy-Bank Framework is an example of a collaborative strategy in which different teams work together to find possibilities to save money, optimize spending, and increase overall financial efficiency. Creating the Slack/Teams channel is easy; the challenge is ensuring teams participate and engage in the framework over time. The following are ways to meet that challenge:

- *Define precise goals and objectives*: Establish crystal-clear goals and objectives for the #Piggy-Bank Framework to encourage team involvement and participation. Communicating the overall financial goals for cloud costs and each team's role in reaching those goals is crucial. This alignment guarantees that all teams comprehend the reason for establishing the communication channel and the significance of their contributions to those goals, which encourages active participation.

- *Emphasize shared responsibility*: Emphasize that engineering, financial, and procurement departments all have equal responsibility for cost optimization. This cultivates a culture where everyone feels accountable for discovering unnecessary cloud expenditures, maximizing resource use, and promoting financial efficiency. Participants are encouraged to take an active role within the #Piggy-Bank Framework to encourage everyone to work together to achieve cost goals and foster a sense of cost ownership.

- *Facilitate data access and transparency*: Ensure that all participating teams have easy access to the pertinent FinOps data. Open and honest data exchange enables teams to better comprehend the economic repercussions of their choices and locate weak spots in which they may make improvements. Make it possible to see expenditure patterns, the factors that affect costs, and other critical performance metrics connected to financial efficiency. Data-driven discussions encourage well-informed decisions and stakeholders' active participation in cost-reduction efforts.

- *Foster collaboration between teams*: A great way to encourage cross-functional collaboration is to facilitate frequent meetings, workshops, or forums where engineering, finance, and procurement representatives can discuss cost optimization ideas. Establish a secure and welcoming setting for all participants that promotes open dialogue and exchange of ideas. This collaboration helps break down silos, fosters understanding across different perspectives, and enhances the effectiveness of initiatives to optimize costs.

- *Provide ongoing educational programs*: Make educational resources and training sessions available to acquaint engineering, finance, and procurement teams with cost control fundamentals and practices. Thanks to this newfound knowledge, they can now see opportunities to save costs and make decisions based on accurate information. Putting money into training can give companies the ability to equip their workers with the skills necessary to actively contribute to the #Piggy-Bank Framework and develop a shared comprehension of their monetary objectives and plans.

- *Motivate and praise*: Establishing recognition and incentive initiatives is paramount to acknowledging and rewarding individuals and groups who successfully reduce expenses. It is imperative to show appreciation for profitable collaborations, ingenious concepts, and effective cost-cutting strategies. Not only does this acknowledgment enhance morale, but it also emphasizes the significance of involvement and participation within the #Piggy-Bank Framework.

- *Evaluate performance regularly*: Including goals and indicators for cost optimization in the routine performance assessments conducted by the engineering, finance, and procurement teams is essential. This integration guarantees that individuals are assessed based on their contributions to cost management and encourages continued involvement in the #Piggy-Bank Framework. Additionally, this integration ensures that individuals are evaluated based on their contributions to cost management. Feedback on performance opens the door to coaching and growth, thus strengthening both engagement and accountability.

- *Continually seek to improve the framework*: Soliciting feedback from engineering, finance, and procurement teams is crucial to fostering continuous development. Make it a habit to ask for their feedback regularly regarding the efficiency of the #Piggy-Bank Framework, methods, and instruments. Pay attention to what they have to say, answer any problems they may have, and make changes based on their suggestions and comments. This iterative strategy helps cultivate a culture of lifelong learning and demonstrates to participants that their contributions are valued.

Benefits of the #Piggy-Bank Framework

The key goal and benefit of the #Piggy-Bank Framework is to foster open communication among the FinOps team, key stakeholders, and engineering. Sharing information, establishing common goals, and providing a forum for cross-department collaboration foster a culture of cost awareness.

Employees are encouraged to offer ideas, tips, and cost-saving solutions they have discovered or executed. For instance, individuals might collaborate to share their views regarding optimizing infrastructure configurations, identifying and eliminating idle resources, utilizing reserved or spot instances, or using cost-effective cloud services. Collective intelligence makes knowledge dissemination and empowerment of individuals possible to contribute to cost optimization.

In addition, the architecture of the #Piggy-Bank Framework enables the formulation of cost-related measurements and key performance indicators (KPIs), which are made visible to all team members through the Slack/Teams channel. These metrics can include monthly cost trends, the cost of providing an application or service, cost savings obtained from optimization initiatives, or any other pertinent financial data. When such information is easily accessible, teams can monitor progress, keep track of changes, and identify areas that need further attention.

The #Piggy-Bank Framework concept fosters awareness, teamwork, education, and ongoing learning. Organizations can invite finance professionals, cloud cost experts, or representatives from cloud service providers to share their knowledge and assist with cost management techniques. They can also ask them to participate. These special guests can participate in live question-and-answer sessions or hold webinars within the Slack/Teams channel, providing employees with unique education possibilities.

Integration of cost monitoring and analysis tools is another feature that may be included in the framework. These tools may consist of cloud service providers' cost dashboards, third-party cost optimization solutions, or scripts written specifically for the business. These systems can automatically gather cost data, generate reports, and provide insights to boost cost awareness. By integrating with Slack/Teams, reports are shared, discoveries are discussed, and ideas for potential solutions are generated.

In addition, the #Piggy-Bank Framework can incentivize and reward personnel for their contributions to cost-optimization efforts. For instance, firms can recognize individuals or teams that have generated cost savings or implemented novel cost management strategies through recognition programs or gamification aspects. When introduced at scale within the organization, these acknowledgments help cultivate a healthy culture centered on cost consciousness and encourage active engagement.

Enterprises must establish explicit norms and expectations about the #Piggy-Bank Framework to maximize its efficacy. This includes defining communication manners, facilitating respectful dialogue, and encouraging inclusive participation from all team members. The Slack/Teams channel should be monitored and moderated regularly to ensure quality and relevance. It should also address any potential problems or complaints that may arise.

The #Piggy-Bank Framework structure, whether implemented as a Slack/Teams channel or framework, is a valuable method for organizations to cultivate a culture of cost awareness about cloud services. This framework enables employees to manage cloud expenses through collaboration, transparency, education, and incentives. Consequently, spending can be minimized, productivity can be raised, and the culture can become more cost-conscious.

Effective Collaboration

Encouraging collaborative efforts across teams is crucial for fostering a culture of cloud cost awareness. By emphasizing collective responsibility, engineers are more likely to engage with cost optimization initiatives and feel supported and empowered within the organization.

Facilitating cross-functional collaboration between engineering, finance, and operations allows for comprehensive analysis and implementation of cost-saving measures, ensuring efficiency without compromising quality. Conducting periodic cost reviews involving relevant stakeholders ensures ongoing refinement of optimization strategies, sustaining a culture where cost awareness remains integral to organizational success.

Create an Atmosphere That Encourages Collaboration

Establishing a cooperative atmosphere where team members can quickly express their thoughts and viewpoints is essential to starting meaningful conversations. Leaders should encourage open and transparent communication and ensure everyone's thoughts and feelings are considered. This setting fosters collaboration, cultivating a culture of shared responsibility for cost reduction.

Individuals on cross-functional engineering teams have various skills and expertise in their respective fields. It is vital to encourage engagement from team members from multiple disciplines, including software development, infrastructure management, operations, and DevOps. This variety of viewpoints has the potential to find cost optimization solutions from various aspects and perspectives, which helps make effective decisions.

Only some engineering team members comprehensively understand the fundamentals behind cloud cost optimization. For this reason, educational resources or training sessions must be made available to acquaint team members with the foundations of CCM. With this newfound knowledge, they now have the tools to contribute to the conversation effectively.

Pro Tip   Make cost optimization a regular agenda item in engineering meetings. Simply talking about cloud costs more frequently keeps them at the top of everyone's mind. Have engineers present cost metrics, optimization wins, or new ideas each week. Encourage discussion and feedback. This continuous exposure through regular check-ins will organically raise awareness and make cost optimization feel like a shared team effort, not just an individual responsibility. Over time, it becomes ingrained in engineers' mindsets and part of everyday decision-making. Regular touchpoints are crucial to cultivating grassroots engagement and are critical to a sustainable cost optimization culture.

Set Clear Goals and Objectives

Outlining the specific aims and objectives of the conversations linked to costs is essential. You must determine your desired results, such as locating unnecessary spending, enhancing resource usage, or implementing cost-effective architectural patterns. Clearly stated goals make it easier to keep the talks on track and guarantee that the team remains on the same page throughout the process.

Before beginning the conversation, getting essential cost and usage statistics is vital. Using this data as a basis allows for identifying possible cost optimization opportunities. Analyze indicators such as resource consumption, instance types, storage usage, and network data transmission to see whether there are any inefficiencies or opportunities for improvement. The presentation of these statistics throughout the dialogue can generate conversation and encourage evidence-based decision-making.

Organizations can ensure that cost awareness becomes integral to engineers' responsibilities by aligning individual and team objectives with cost optimization targets. Review and discuss these metrics regularly with engineers, giving them feedback and direction on improving cost efficiency. The significance of cost awareness is emphasized when optimizing costs is made a quantitative and continuously evaluated component of engineering performance.

Identify Potential Areas for Cost Reduction and Optimization

During the discussion, you should urge team members to express their perspectives on potential opportunities to optimize costs. Some frequent topics investigated are rightsizing resources, utilizing reserved or spot instances, optimizing storage and database settings, utilizing serverless architectures, implementing cost-aware coding methods, and automating scaling procedures. Group brainstorming can encourage the whole team's participation in the idea-generation process, resulting in novel concepts.

Cost optimization is not a goal in and of itself; instead, it is one of several factors that must be weighed against one another, along with performance, dependability, and security. During the discussion, stress the importance of conducting a cost-benefit analysis before implementing cost-cutting initiatives. Encourage the team to conduct an impact analysis to determine how future modifications affect the system's performance, user experience, and security posture. A holistic strategy like this guarantees that efforts to reduce costs won't jeopardize the system's other equally important components.

Throughout the conversation, record the identified opportunities for cost optimization, the action items, and the team members responsible for them. This documentation guarantees that the conversation outcomes are documented accurately and can be monitored to determine how far along the implementation process you are. Project management or collaboration technologies are utilized to centralize action items, monitor progress, and facilitate accountability and visibility.

Pro Tip   Make it visual with dashboards. Interactive visualizations bring cost data to life better than spreadsheets. Leverage dashboard tools like Cloudability that connect to cloud billing data and display insightful metrics. Let engineers filter and explore the data, drill into details, and visualize usage and spending trends. Dashboards turn abstract numbers into compelling graphics, provoking curiosity and sparking cost conversations. They become a shared reference point and make cost impacts more tangible. Dashboards engage teams, focus discussions, and ground recommendations in data—critical for productive cross-functional cost collaboration.

Encourage the Pursuit of Continuous Improvement

Cost optimization should not be viewed as a one-time but a continuing process. Instruct the team to continually monitor established cost optimization strategies, measure their effectiveness, and iterate as necessary. Set aside time for regular follow-up talks to analyze the adjustments, evaluate the amount of money saved due to those changes, and look for new opportunities to optimize the situation. Using this iterative strategy helps ensure that cost optimization remains a priority and adapts to the ever-evolving system requirements.

Creating a collaborative environment, educating team members, defining clear goals, analyzing data, identifying opportunities, evaluating trade-offs, documenting action items, and cultivating a culture of continuous improvement are all necessary to facilitate cost-related discussions with cross-functional engineering teams to gather insights and perspectives on cloud cost optimization. In cloud-based systems, firms may successfully harness their engineering teams' collective expertise to optimize costs and drive efficiency if they incorporate these methods and put them into practice.

Ongoing Education to Cultivate a Culture of Cost Awareness

Educating engineering teams about cloud computing cost considerations is vital to cultivating a cost-conscious enterprise culture. This can be accomplished through various channels, including tech talks, lightning talks, summits, and office hours. Businesses can enable their engineering teams to make informed decisions that optimize cloud costs without losing functionality or performance if they provide targeted educational opportunities for their engineering teams.

Ideas for Education Sessions

- *Tech talks*: Tech talks are an excellent tool for increasing engineering knowledge on cloud infrastructure and its impact on cloud costs. They're formal presentations provided by industry professionals or seasoned practitioners on specific themes relating to cloud costs. These talks may cover various topics such as cost optimization strategies, best resource allocation practices, exploiting serverless architectures, optimizing data storage, or monitoring and managing spend. Tech talks offer engineers in-depth knowledge, insights, and practical examples, enabling them to understand the influence of their decisions on cloud costs and make more cost-effective design decisions.

- *Lightning talks*: Lightning talks are presentations that are often conducted in a rapid-fire fashion and are more concise than formal tech talks. During lightning talks, different presenters can discuss cloud cost issues and give quick ideas, case studies, or lessons learned in easy-to-consume sound bites. Lightning talks are efficient for covering various subjects in a condensed amount of time. This helps engineering teams obtain a wide variety of perspectives and ideas. They stimulate team members' involvement, engagement, and information sharing and blending.

- *Summits*: Summits are large-scale events that raise awareness and education about cloud computing costs. They connect technical teams from different departments or even several corporations so that they may learn from one another, share their experiences, and debate cloud computing difficulties and solutions. Summits often include various activities, such as keynote speakers, panel discussions, seminars, and interactive sessions. These activities cover a wide range of topics related to cloud cost optimization. They produce a cooperative atmosphere in which engineers may network with one another, share ideas, and gain a deeper understanding of cloud computing's financial implications.

- *#Piggy-Bank office hours*: #Piggy-Bank office hours are a more informal option for sharing ideas and discussions using the Slack/ Teams channel. During office hours, engineers can have one-to-one or small-group conversations with cloud cost specialists or representatives from the finance or operations teams. Engineers can seek help, pose questions, and receive individualized recommendations on optimizing cloud expenses for projects or use cases that are unique to them. Office hours encourage direct engagement, address specific concerns, and provide targeted support to assist engineers in effectively navigating the complexity of cost optimization.

Educational Tips

When creating educational initiatives, consider the challenges and requirements of the engineering teams they are targeted at. Adapt the subjects, examples, and case studies to align with their daily jobs and the use cases they encounter. Because of this relevance, engagement increases, and engineers are encouraged to apply the information they receive to their projects directly.

Invite subject matter experts from within the organization or people in related industries outside the firm to present tech lectures, lightning talks, or keynote speeches. These professionals should have hands-on experience in cloud cost optimization and offer real-world insights, best practices, and lessons learned from their work. Knowledgeable speakers lend legitimacy to educational endeavors and instill confidence in communicated content.

Include participatory activities in your event, such as question-and-answer sessions, roundtable discussions, or hands-on workshops, to inspire people to participate and engage actively. Engineers can ask specific questions, share their experiences, and partake in meaningful conversations around cloud pricing considerations when these formats are used. Participating in interactive sessions can benefit knowledge sharing, collaborative problem-solving, and peer learning.

Embed real-world examples and use cases to illustrate the impact of various cost optimization tactics. Engineers may identify real-world problems and better understand them, making applying the lessons they've learned to their projects more straightforward. Showcasing success stories of cost optimization projects and the results of those activities can motivate engineers and provide concrete evidence of cost optimization benefits.

Create a culture of lifelong education by making ongoing educational opportunities and resources available to the community. This may take the form of recurrent technical seminars, flash talks, or summits focusing on various cost factors related to cloud computing. In addition, they give engineers access to pertinent documents, blogs, articles, and online courses to learn quickly and in their own time. Continuous learning opportunities ensure engineers are continually updated on the latest and finest cloud cost optimization approaches and procedures.

Collecting feedback from engineering teams can help you evaluate educational programs' success and pinpoint areas that need improvement. Use post-event evaluations, feedback questionnaires, or surveys to understand the sessions' impact and collect suggestions for future themes or presentation styles. This feedback loop contributes to improving educational initiatives and helps guarantee that they cater to the requirements of engineering teams.

Organizations can educate their engineering teams on cloud cost considerations by employing tech lectures, lightning talks, summits, and office hours. This enables the engineering teams to make informed decisions and fosters a culture of cost awareness inside the firm. Engineers can acquire the information and skills to optimize cloud expenses while delivering efficient, scalable, and cost-effective solutions through these educational programs.

Reward Successes and Celebrate Wins

Acknowledging and rewarding employee success is vital for building a motivated workforce and fostering a culture of cloud cost awareness within the organization. Celebrating wins reinforces individual and team achievements and optimizes cloud usage and expenditures. It acknowledges their effort, ingenuity, and ability to solve problems. This boosts their morale and increases the level of job satisfaction they experience.

When companies celebrate and showcase the achievements of individuals or teams that have made substantial contributions to cost optimization, they not only show appreciation for the hard work they have put in, but they inspire others to follow in their footsteps and do the same. You can also foster team building with light-hearted competition to showcase cost-cutting measures and techniques.

Sharing success stories is an effective way to spread valuable insights and best practices throughout the entire organization. When staff are educated on the methods, procedures, or tools that led to cost reductions in specific projects, they can gain insights and find inspiration for their initiatives. Success stories demonstrate the viability and efficiency of various techniques to reduce costs and encourage others to investigate opportunities comparable to those in the success stories.

Employees can learn from their colleagues' experiences, inquire about cost optimization, and participate in related discussions. This stimulates information sharing between departments, fosters cross-departmental collaboration, and contributes to collective intelligence within the organization. This practice also enables employees to find new viewpoints, alternative ideas, and potential synergies across several teams or projects.

When cost savings successes are freely communicated, employees better understand the influence of cost optimization efforts on the organization's overall goals and objectives. This facilitates a deeper connection between cost-cutting measures and the business's overall mission by developing a sense of purpose shared by all organization members and aligning employees with the organization's financial goals.

A cycle of never-ending improvement and innovation can be fueled by publicly acknowledging and rewarding successful cost-cutting initiatives. Employees are encouraged to think creatively, explore new ideas, and submit innovative solutions to optimize costs by publicizing successful efforts. It creates a virtuous feedback cycle in which employees are given the impression that they have the authority to experiment, take risks, and discover creative ways to improve cost efficiency. This culture of continuous improvement has the potential to result in continual cost reductions and enhanced business outcomes over time.

The following are some techniques organizations should consider to celebrate wins and share success stories of cost-cutting initiatives properly:

- *Channels of constant and routine communication*: Establish dedicated communication channels to share success stories, such as internal newsletters, company-wide meetings, or specific Slack/Teams channels. All employees should be able to quickly and easily access these channels to keep current on recent accomplishments and gain knowledge from one another.

- *Narrative analysis and use of case studies*: Encourage individuals or teams that have realized significant cost savings to share their experiences in an organized fashion so that others can learn from them. These triumphant experiences can be retold as case studies, emphasizing the obstacles conquered, the methods utilized, the results obtained, and the knowledge gained. It may be helpful to add visual aids, such as graphs or charts, to explain the impact. This will make the story more attractive to the audience. It will also serve as a way of recognizing excellence in cost-controlling measures.

- *Programs of acknowledgement*: Establish recognition programs that honor employees or teams for exceptional project contributions to reduce costs. This could come in monetary incentives, certificates, public acknowledgment during company events, or mentions in internal company communications. Celebrating accomplishment in a way that is both visible and meaningful brings attention to the significance of optimizing costs. This motivates others to take an active role in the process.

- *Collaboration between different departments*: Organizing workshops, panel discussions, or internal conferences primarily focused on cost-cutting efforts is an excellent way to encourage collaboration and knowledge exchange between different departments or teams. Because of this, employees will have the opportunity to share their experiences, as well as the obstacles they faced and the successes they achieved, with a broader audience. In addition to this, it makes it easier for people of varying backgrounds to network with one another and share their thoughts.

Sharing successes is an effective strategy for motivating staff, promoting information sharing, enhancing collaboration, and driving continuous improvement. It's a critical part of creating a culture inside an organization that emphasizes cost-consciousness, stimulates innovation, and delivers long-term financial benefits.

Real-world Case Study: Identifying and Eliminating Unused Cloud Resources for Significant Cost Savings at Company A

This case study explores how Company A's cloud economics team achieved significant cost savings by identifying and eliminating unused or underutilized resources in their AWS DevTest and QA accounts.

Challenges

- *Hidden costs*: Company A's cloud economics team identified a significant amount of unused or underutilized resources in its AWS DevTest and QA accounts. These resources were likely not intentionally left behind but accumulated over time.

- *Cost pressure*: A recent cost increase prompted Company A to prioritize cost optimization efforts earlier than planned.

- *Scalability*: Manually identifying and removing unused resources was not feasible for long-term cost management.

Solution

- *Resource audit*: The cloud economics conducted a comprehensive audit of its AWS infrastructure resources, focusing on key metadata like name, key name, region, team name, tags, and utilization metrics.

- *Collaboration*: The team contacted individual users and teams to seek consent before removing unused resources like EC2 instances, EBS volumes, Redshift clusters, GuardDuty deployments, Elastic IPs, CloudWatch logs, etc.

- *Rightsizing*: The team collaborated with engineers to rightsize instances for underutilized resources, reducing their specifications based on actual needs.

- *Automation framework*: Company A planned to build an automation framework for identifying and removing untagged resources to address scalability challenges and prevent future accumulations of unused resources.

- *Education and best practices*: The team planned to conduct educational sessions to raise awareness about cost-saving practices such as:

  - Proper tagging of resources (service_name, service_owner, and Name tags)

  - Utilizing the latest and most efficient instance families

  - Rightsizing instances based on workload requirements

  - Turning off idle resources during non-business hours

  - Employing the remove_after_date tag for temporary infrastructure

Results

- *Cost savings*: Company A achieved substantial cost savings of approximately $3,130 per day by the last week of January through resource identification and optimization. This translates to over $1 million saved annually.

Impact

- *Improved cost efficiency*: Company A's proactive approach to cloud cost management has resulted in significant financial savings.

- *Scalable resource management*: The planned automation framework will ensure ongoing cost optimization and prevent the future buildup of unused resources.

- *Increased awareness*: Educational initiatives will equip developers and QA personnel with best practices for efficient cloud resource utilization.

This case study demonstrates the effectiveness of a collaborative and multipronged approach to cloud cost optimization. Company A achieved significant cost savings by combining resource audits, rightsizing, automation, and employee education and established a sustainable foundation for managing its cloud infrastructure efficiently.

Chapter Summary

This chapter delved into the critical topic of shifting left on cloud cost efficiency by cultivating a culture of cost awareness. Creating a cultural shift in your organization reaps long-term benefits for scaling your FinOps practice. This chapter covered these key concepts:

- *The #Piggy-Bank Framework*: A communication framework to provide better cost visibility and accountability across your FinOps and engineering teams

- *Effective collaboration*: Facilitating cross-functional collaboration between engineering, finance, and operations to foster more effective cost-savings

- *Education*: Providing ongoing opportunities to learn more about cost savings and performance

- *Celebrating success*: Encouraging teams to share their successes and be rewarded for finding innovative ways to reduce cloud costs

As you progress toward mastering FinOps/Cloud Economics, the next chapter will focus on another crucial aspect of CCM: cost optimization. We will explore advanced techniques, best practices, and innovative cost optimization approaches. This will ensure you get the most value from your investments without compromising performance or functionality. From rightsizing and reserved instances to spot instances and serverless architectures, we will uncover many cost optimization strategies to drive efficiency and maximize your cloud ROI. Get ready to unlock new possibilities and advance your FinOps journey.

References for Further Reading

https://granulate.io/blog/cloud-cost-management-complete-guide/

https://www.ciodive.com/news/cloud-cost-management/624229/

https://www.jamcracker.com/blogs/fundamentals-of-cloud-cost-management

https://eventura.com/cloud-services/cloud-cost-management-explained/

https://www.linkedin.com/advice/3/what-main-drivers-challenges-cloud-computing-cost

https://www.c-facts.com/cloud-cost-management/

https://www.nops.io/what-are-the-common-challenges-to-cloud-cost-management/

CHAPTER 6

Cloud Cost Optimization

Remember that dream house project we discussed earlier? Like any construction project, managing costs in the cloud is crucial for building a sustainable and efficient environment. Imagine not realizing that you're paying for multiple home insurance plans which you only need one or constantly leaving the lights turned on 24/7 when no one's home. In the cloud, this translates to unused resources, redundant services, and wasted money.

This chapter focuses on the toolbox essentials for cost optimization in your FinOps journey. It's like equipping yourself with the right tools and knowledge to ensure your dream house is built efficiently and doesn't break the bank.

As companies increasingly migrate their operations to the cloud, the promise of scalability, flexibility, and efficiency often overshadows the intricate landscape of cloud cost management. Yet, amidst the allure of these benefits, a significant challenge emerges: cloud cost optimization.

Cloud cost optimization ensures effective and sustainable operations in today's cloud computing landscape. Any company that uses cloud services might significantly impact its bottom line if it recognizes and takes advantage of potential cost optimization opportunities. The appropriate tools and approaches must be used for effective cost optimization.

This chapter examines a variety of strategies for locating cost optimization opportunities:

- *Methods for locating optimization opportunities*: Utilizing trusted advisor services from CSPs like AWS, following Azure and GCP cost recommendations, and optimizing containerized systems like Kubernetes

- *Prioritizing opportunities based on ROI*: Focusing on high ROI opportunities with minimal implementation effort to maximize resource utilization and cost savings

S. Kanumuri and M. Zeier, *Scaling Cloud FinOps*, https://doi.org/10.1007/979-8-8688-0388-8_6

- *Tactics for optimizing compute costs*: Avoiding EC2 instances, using efficient reservation purchasing, leveraging spot instances, and incorporating automation with technologies like Terraform

- *Storage cost optimization strategies*: Transitioning to cost-effective storage options, implementing lifecycle policies for Amazon S3, and utilizing autoscaling to reduce storage costs

- *Autoscaling for cost savings*: Autoscaling for non-container and container workloads, including integrating spot instances and leveraging KEDA for efficient scaling in containerized environments

- *Strategies for committed discounts*: Comparing savings plans and reserved instances, building a comprehensive cost optimization strategy, and emphasizing continual cost monitoring and optimization for long-term financial management

Organizations can get a competitive advantage by efficiently minimizing costs while creating and scaling their FinOps/cloud economics projects from the bottom up if they utilize the ideas and methodologies presented in this chapter and put them into practice.

Importance of Cloud Cost Optimization

Cloud cost optimization plays a pivotal role in the cloud computing world, where businesses employ cloud services to streamline operations, improve scalability, and achieve cost efficiency. Organizations that aggressively manage and optimize cloud computing costs have the potential to generate significant financial benefits and uncover a competitive edge in the digital world. In this section, we will investigate the significance of cost optimization in cloud economics in further detail.

Utilizing cloud services for application development and deployment allows businesses to pay for resources and services as needed, a significant benefit over the upfront investment required for on-premises hardware and software. On the other hand, firms need to implement adequate cost optimization procedures to avoid overspending or underutilizing cloud resources. Cloud cost optimization enables businesses to match cloud services spending to their actual consumption, ensuring that resources are utilized effectively and expenses are minimal to maximize ROI.

Cloud computing economics are inextricably linked to the capacity to scale infrastructure and resources quickly and effectively. However, scaling without considering costs might lead to budget overruns. Businesses can scale their cloud environments with cost optimization tools while monitoring their spending. Organizations can achieve seamless scaling without compromising their cost control if they identify potential for cost savings, rightsize their resources, leverage automation, and embrace cost-effective architectures.

Governance of Costs and Information Availability

Putting policies that optimize costs in place leads to improved cost governance and visibility. Organizations can acquire deep insights into their spending by establishing cost allocation and tracking methods, enabling them to discover cost drivers, spot inefficiencies, and make decisions based on accurate information. Because of this visibility, organizations can better comprehend the influence that certain services, projects, or departments have on total expenses, making it simpler to put specific optimization measures into effect.

Reduced Expenditures and Saving Gains

Saving money and cutting back on wasteful spending are two critical goals of cost optimization, which aims to achieve both. Utilizing reserved instances, spot instances, and autoscaling to match resource usage with demand dynamically are some of the numerous chances for cost reduction made available by cloud environments. Organizations can drastically cut their costs by proactively identifying and implementing these cost-saving methods, and they can then channel those savings toward innovation, growth, or other strategic goals.

Planning and Prediction of Financial Matters

Cost optimization is necessary for proper financial planning and forecasting in cloud economics. When businesses know current and expected costs, they can create more accurate budgets, effectively allocate resources, and estimate future expenditures. Because of this, firms can make decisions based on data, prioritize investments, and plan for long-term growth while maintaining financial stability and predictability.

Competitive Advantage

Cost optimization that is both effective and efficient can provide a substantial competitive edge in today's highly competitive corporate environment. Organizations that properly manage cloud computing costs can offer more competitive pricing to customers, strategically deploy resources, invest in innovation, and swiftly adapt to the market's needs. Businesses can keep ahead of the competition, give value to their consumers, and drive growth while preserving cost leadership when they have the agility and financial flexibility to do so.

Optimization of Resources and Environmental Responsibility

The pursuit of sustainability and resource optimization goes hand in hand with the cost optimization process in cloud economics. Organizations may lessen their environmental impact and contribute to a greener future by reducing resource waste, increasing energy efficiency, and adopting environmentally favorable practices. This alignment of cost optimization with sustainability goals benefits the environment, improves the firm's reputation, and appeals to ecologically sensitive customers.

Optimizing Cloud Compute Spend

In the ever-evolving realm of cloud computing, optimizing compute resources is a cornerstone for organizations striving to achieve operational excellence and financial efficiency. From sophisticated reservation mechanisms to dynamic autoscaling solutions, the landscape of compute optimization offers numerous opportunities for organizations to tailor their infrastructure to meet fluctuating demands while minimizing costs.

Let's explore the strategy for prioritizing savings opportunities and discuss the tools available to help your FinOps team optimize your cloud compute resources.

Identifying Savings Opportunities That Maximize ROI

An essential component of efficient cost optimization is locating opportunities that offer the greatest return on investment (ROI) with the fewest resources expended. It enables firms to target their efforts and resources at initiatives providing significant cost reductions with the minor investment required.

Let's dig deeper into the factors to consider and the approaches to identify cost-saving opportunities, outlined in Figure 6-1:

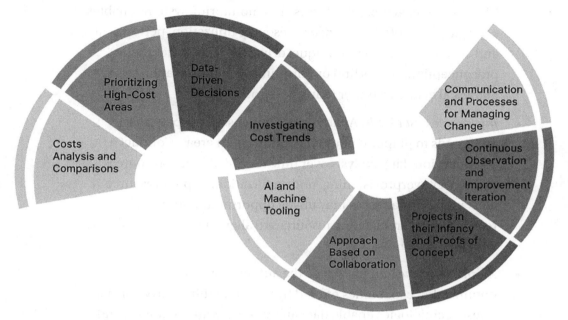

Figure 6-1. *Build vs. buy evaluation process*

- *Cost analysis and comparisons*: A detailed cost analysis and performance benchmarking exercise is imperative to locate potential optimization opportunities. This exercise analyzes current expenditure patterns, resource usage, and performance measures. By comparing an organization's costs to industry standards, best practices, and other comparable organizations, potential areas for improvement can be identified.

- *Prioritizing high-cost areas*: Direct your attention first to high-cost areas or resources significantly impacting the budget. By focusing initially on these areas, companies can realize considerable cost savings that affect their bottom line. This may involve analyzing expenses associated with computing resources, storage, networking, or services provided by third parties.

- *Data-driven decisions*: Utilize collected data and analytics as decision-making drivers. Leveraging the tools provided by the CSP, cost management platforms, and monitoring systems enables acquiring in-depth knowledge of resource utilization, performance, and cost patterns. This technique, driven by facts rather than preconceptions, helps find opportunities for optimization based on empirical evidence rather than guesswork.

- *Investigate cost trends*: Analyze previous cost usage patterns and trends to pinpoint potential optimization areas. Conduct a consumption data analysis over time for a given set of resources to uncover overprovisioning, underutilization, or poor resource allocation. This analysis may unveil opportunities for rightsizing, resizing, or re-architecting resources to align them more closely with workload demands.

- *AI and machine tooling*: Utilize the automation and cost optimization capabilities offered by CSPs and third-party partners. These technologies enable data analysis, recommendations, and automation of optimization processes. Trusted advisor tools, cost optimization frameworks, and machine learning systems can all assist in identifying opportunities with a high ROI and suggest steps to enhance cost efficiency.

- *Approach based on collaboration*: Incorporate cross-functional teams, including finance, operations, and information technology, in identifying cost optimization options. Each stakeholder may offer valuable insights and perspectives on areas where cost reductions can be achieved with minimal effort. Adopting a collaborative approach increases the likelihood of success and ensures that opportunities are thoroughly analyzed from various perspectives.

- *Projects in their infancy and proofs of concept*: Conduct proof-of-concept studies or pilot projects to evaluate the feasibility and potential impact of identified optimization opportunities. By testing optimization ideas in a controlled setting, organizations can assess the actual ROI and the effort required for execution.

This strategy helps mitigate potential risks and generates measurable outcomes before scaling optimization efforts across the organization.

- *Continuous observation and improvement iteration*: Optimizing costs requires firms to review and refine their tactics to achieve optimal results continuously. It is crucial to maintain a record of the effects of implemented optimizations and regularly reevaluate opportunities. As the cloud environment evolves and the organization's needs shift, new possibilities may arise, necessitating adjustments to existing optimizations to ensure continued effectiveness.

- *Communication and processes for managing change*: Effective communication and change management are essential when implementing cost optimization efforts. It is crucial to ensure that various stakeholders understand the benefits of highlighted opportunities and their reasons. Organizations can foster a more favorable acceptance of cost optimization measures by employing collaboration, education, and consistent updates.

Utilizing CSP Native Tools and Open Source Tools

In cloud economics, using tools provided by CSPs is one of the most essential aspects of cost optimization. CSPs offer various tools and services to assist businesses in monitoring, analyzing, and optimizing their cloud expenditures. These tools enable companies to make data-driven decisions and drive cost efficiency by providing essential insights, recommendations, and automation possibilities.

Utilizing cloud service providers' tools for cost optimization offers numerous financial advantages, including automated analysis, proactive recommendation-making, and centralized cost control. These technologies provide companies comprehensive visibility into cost usage patterns and potential savings opportunities. With this visibility, firms can identify cost drivers, monitor trends, and make data-driven decisions.

Additionally, optimizing resource allocation is crucial. Cloud service providers often suggest modifications such as rightsizing instances, utilizing reserved or spot instances, or adjusting configurations to ensure efficient resource distribution, thereby reducing costs and minimizing waste.

Moreover, automation plays a crucial role in cost optimization. Many CSP solutions offer automation capabilities, allowing businesses to automate resizing, scheduling, or provisioning according to demand. This ensures resources are active only when needed, maximizing cost efficiency.

Consistent cost-effectiveness is also achievable through constant monitoring and analysis provided by CSPs. By frequently assessing cost optimization recommendations and implementing necessary modifications, organizations can adapt to changing consumption patterns and optimize cost savings effectively.

Let's take a closer look at the tools available from the CSPs, along with the advantages and benefits of using them to optimize costs:

AWS Trusted Advisor

AWS Trusted Advisor is an all-encompassing cost optimization solution for AWS-hosted resources. It thoroughly analyzes an organization's AWS infrastructure and offers recommendations across various categories, including cost optimization. AWS Trusted Advisor scrutinizes underutilized instances, idle resources, and cost savings from reserved instances. It delivers actionable solutions for immediate implementation to reduce expenses, boost performance, and strengthen security. By leveraging AWS Trusted Advisor, organizations can identify opportunities to save money and implement adjustments to maximize their AWS cost efficiency.

AWS Compute Optimizer

AWS Compute Optimizer is a program that analyzes an organization's usage of Amazon Elastic Compute Cloud (EC2) instances and offers recommendations to improve costs and performance. AWS Compute Optimizer achieves this by employing machine learning techniques to analyze previous usage patterns. For instance, it suggests types and sizes that align with workload requirements while minimizing costs. AWS Compute Optimizer evaluates various characteristics, including CPU utilization, memory consumption, and network throughput, to identify rightsizing opportunities and potential cost savings. AWS Compute Optimizer facilitates cost savings and maximizes performance by enabling businesses to ensure that their EC2 instances are provisioned appropriately.

Azure Advisor Cost Recommendations

Microsoft Azure includes Azure Advisor Cost Recommendations as part of the Azure Cost Management and Billing service. This service employs sophisticated analytics to examine an organization's Azure consumption and expenditure habits. It identifies areas where cost optimization is feasible, such as underutilized virtual machines, wasted storage, or inappropriate resource configurations. Azure Advisor Cost Recommendations propose options to optimize costs, including downsizing or deallocating resources, leveraging reserved instances, or utilizing spot instances. This tool allows businesses to make educated decisions and optimize their Azure expenses.

Google Cloud Platform Active Assist

GCP provides users tools and services to optimize costs under the GCP Cost Management portfolio, including Active Assist. Active Assist is a portfolio of tools used in Google Cloud to generate recommendations and insights to help you optimize your Google Cloud projects, including cost optimization recommendations. Active Assist Cost Optimization Recommendations analyze a business's GCP usage and recommend optimizing expenses. Active Assist identifies potential cost reductions by rightsizing virtual machines, adjusting resource configurations, utilizing committed usage contracts, or using preemptible VMs. These recommendations assist businesses in identifying cost-saving opportunities and aligning their GCP resources with actual demand. These recommendations play a crucial role in optimizing cloud expenses.

OpenCost Recommendations Kubernetes/Containers Workloads

OpenCost, an open source software and community-driven initiative, offers cost visibility and optimization/rightsizing advice uniquely suited to Kubernetes and containerized workloads. These recommendations are in addition to cloud service providers' tools available to their customers. Technologies such as OpenCost provide insights into cost allocation, rightsizing, and resource optimization in Kubernetes clusters. They look at indicators such as the time spent using CPU, memory, and network resources to locate potential areas for cost optimization for organizations on their container workloads.

Pro Tip   Automate recommendations implementation. Tools identify optimization opportunities, but action is required to realize savings. Use APIs to execute recommendations at scale programmatically. For example, AWS Trusted Advisor and AWS Systems Manager can integrate to apply rightsizing and other advice automatically. Schedule regular scans and leverage automation to tune your environment—this bakes optimization into your workflows (versus one-off manual efforts). The combination of CSP analytics and infrastructure as code (IaC) allows you to turn insights into impact and sustainably maximize cost efficiency.

Deep Dive: Choosing Recommendations from AWS Compute Optimizer

As introduced in the previous section, AWS Compute Optimizer provides a robust method for optimizing the expenses and performance of EC2 instances in cloud environments. AWS Compute Optimizer uses machine learning algorithms to assess past usage patterns and provide recommendations for rightsizing instances, reducing costs, and improving resource utilization. Enhancing resource utilization, optimizing costs, and rightsizing instances can accomplish these goals.

AWS Compute Optimizer simplifies resource allocation by providing automated recommendations for EC2 instances. These recommendations are derived through machine learning algorithms, which continually examine past usage data. Automatic suggestions make it simpler for organizations to execute the proposed adjustments and improve their EC2 instances with less manual work required.

AWS Compute Optimizer's capabilities are enhanced due to its seamless integration with other AWS services, making it easier to use. It can be linked with AWS Systems Manager and AWS Auto Scaling, enabling businesses to automatically implement the recommendations and scale their resources according to demand. By utilizing these integrations, companies can ensure that their EC2 instances are continuously optimized and aligned with shifting workload requirements.

AWS Compute Optimizer provides continuous monitoring and recommendations for EC2 instances. It analyzes usage trends constantly and delivers up-to-date recommendations as the workload changes. This guarantees that businesses can continuously optimize their instances and react to evolving requirements, assuring cost efficiency and performance optimization over time.

AWS Compute Optimizer offers API integration and programmatic access, enabling businesses to incorporate its recommendations into their infrastructure workflows. This allows smooth interaction with existing automation frameworks, ensuring recommendations are automatically implemented and monitored.

Despite all of the advantages and valuable advice that AWS Compute Optimizer delivers, it is essential to note that companies should still thoroughly examine and validate the recommendations before implementing changes to ensure that they provide the best overall ROI and meet the needs of the applications and workloads in place.

Here are some critical considerations for deciding which recommendations to pursue, whether obtained from AWS Compute Optimizer or any of the CSPs' tools previously discussed.

Ranking Based on High ROI and Least Effort

A strategic approach that helps firms effectively prioritize their optimization efforts ranks cost optimization alternatives in order of high ROI and low effort. Organizations can maximize their effect while optimizing resource allocation by focusing on possibilities that provide significant cost savings with minimal effort. Let's go deeper into the advantages and factors to consider when evaluating things based on the highest ROI and the least amount of effort:

- *Obtaining the best possible savings*: When companies prioritize options for cost optimization based on high ROI, it guarantees that they target areas in which they can achieve the most significant cost savings. Organizations can spend resources and efforts where they will have the most significant impact on cost reduction if they identify possibilities that offer considerable ROI and then evaluate those prospects. This technique helps maximize the effectiveness of cost optimization programs and guarantees that resources are used in the most productive way possible.

- *Efficient resource allocation*: Ranking tasks according to their required work enables businesses to allocate resources effectively. Organizations can efficiently maximize their use of their time, budget, and human resources by concentrating their efforts on opportunities that can be implemented with a minimum of effort. This technique assures that firms can obtain quick wins and save time on laborious or time-consuming optimization efforts by preventing them from having to optimize.

- *Quick time to value*: When possibilities are prioritized based on their high ROI and low effort required, firms can realize cost savings more quickly. When firms focus on optimization opportunities that are relatively simple to implement, they can start learning the advantages of optimization much sooner. They can get a head start on saving money. This strategy shortens the time to realize benefits and improves cost-cutting efficiency.

- *Harmony with the objectives of the company*: A ranking considering the potential ROI and the amount of work involved helps guarantee that cost-cutting measures align with the organization's broader business objectives. Businesses can free up resources that can be invested in other crucial aspects of the company if they give the possibility of significant cost savings a higher priority. In addition, businesses may guarantee that activities aimed at cost optimization do not disrupt or detract from other strategic priorities by concentrating on possibilities that need low work and focusing on those prospects.

- *Consider both complexity and feasibility*: While it is beneficial to prioritize choices based on high ROI and low effort, it is also essential to examine the complexity and practicability of putting the opportunities that have been discovered into action. Some choices for optimization may offer a high ROI, but their implementation may be complex since they call for considerable technological or operational changes. Organizations must conduct a feasibility analysis of each possibility, considering various aspects such as the technical limitations, the availability of resources, and the potential influence on other systems or processes.

- *Evaluation and refinement on an ongoing basis*: The ranking is determined by high ROI; the least effort is more than a once-and-done activity. As the cloud environment continues to develop and businesses' requirements shift, new options for optimization may become available. It is essential to conduct ongoing assessments and perform iterations of the ranking to guarantee that efforts to optimize costs remain in sync with the organization's developing requirements. Regularly reevaluating things enables companies and organizations to adjust their objectives and seize new chances to cut costs.

- *Striking a balance between short-term effort and long-term impact*: While firms must evaluate opportunities based on the effort required, they should also consider the long-term impact of optimization possibilities. Although some projects involve more work upfront, they may save much money in the long run. Finding a happy medium between near-term benefits and long-term effects is essential to ensuring that cost optimization strategies are sustainable over time.

COST OPTIMIZATION RECOMMENDATIONS TEMPLATE

Here's a comprehensive cost optimization recommendations template for your organization:

Optimization Idea	Applicable Environment	Potential Savings	Risk	Execution Plan	Effort	Analysis Notes
What is the recommendation?	Production/ non-production	$ savings possible	Downtime/ business risks	When/how to execute it; consider automation	Rank from 1 to 5 (1 being easy and 5 being hard)	Additional notes

Rightsizing Compute Resources Based on Usage Metrics

In cloud economics, one of the most important aspects of cloud cost optimization is the utilization of rightsizing indicators. CPU utilization, memory consumption, and network throughput metrics provide valuable insights into programs and workload resource requirements. By examining these measures, businesses can precisely ascertain the size or capacity of their best cloud resources, ensuring effective resource allocation and cost savings.

Rightsizing Virtual Machines

When evaluating the suitable size or capacity of cloud resources like virtual machines or containers, metrics are vital. Monitoring metrics such as CPU utilization enable enterprises to find instances or containers that are routinely underutilized or overutilized, depending on the indicator. The process of altering the distribution of resources to correspond more closely to the amount of labor being done is called *rightsizing*. Organizations can avoid overprovisioning and underprovisioning by ensuring their resources' sizes align with requirements. This results in cost savings and enhanced performance.

Rightsizing a system based on usage measurements directly contributes to cost optimization, which is a goal of rightsizing. When organizations pay for capacity that isn't used, overprovisioned resources result in high costs for those businesses. Conversely, underprovisioning resources can result in performance concerns and higher operating expenses due to poor resource consumption. This can be avoided by precisely allocating resources. Utilizing metrics allows firms to find opportunities to resize resources to align with workload demands. This helps organizations effectively manage expenses and maximize the use of cloud resources.

Insights into the performance characteristics of applications and workloads can be gained through the use of performance improvement metrics. The utilization of CPUs, memory, and network throughput are three metrics that can help companies determine whether their resources are adequately sized to satisfy their performance requirements. Increases in application responsiveness, latency decreases, and overall user experience improvements can result from appropriately sizing resources according to performance criteria. Effective handling of peak workloads, eliminating performance bottlenecks, and guaranteeing optimal performance without the burden of excessive overhead are all possible when resources are distributed correctly.

When organizations use metrics for rightsizing, they scale their resources more efficiently and cost-effectively. Organizations can achieve the ability to determine the necessary capacity required during peak periods through the analysis of patterns of workload and fluctuations in demand. This makes it possible to scale dynamically, which means that resources can be supplied or deprovisioned according to real-time data and the directions of the business. Scalability and elasticity ensure that resources may be modified flexibly, eliminating the need for overprovisioning and enabling cost savings during periods of low demand. Scalability and elasticity are two aspects of elastic computing.

Using metrics creates a feedback loop that may be used continuously for continuous monitoring and optimization efforts. Companies can do all these things by regularly monitoring metrics, tracking resource consumption, identifying trends, and proactively adjusting resource sizes in response to shifting workload patterns. Continuous monitoring identifies potential bottlenecks, capacity difficulties, or resources that must be fully exploited promptly. An organization may ensure that its cloud environment continues to be efficient, cost-effective, and aligned with evolving business needs if it continually optimizes the sizes of its resources based on KPIs and does so continuously.

Considerations for Rightsizing

When making decisions regarding rightsizing, the granularity and accuracy of measurements must be considered. Granular measurements offer more accurate insights into how resources are utilized, enabling organizations to make decisions that align with reality. Ensuring precise metric collection and analysis is essential to prevent inappropriate choices regarding rightsizing, which may affect performance or lead to cost inefficiencies.

When determining a resource's optimal size, many metrics' dimensions should be considered, including CPU, memory, and network consumption. If a vital parameter is ignored in rightsizing a system, the results may not be optimal. The key to attaining optimal results is having a solid understanding of the dynamics at play among the various metrics and how those measures influence the overall resource requirements.

When utilizing metrics for workload rightsizing, companies should consider the variable nature of the workload. Different utilization patterns can be seen in workloads depending on factors such as the time of day, the cyclical nature of the work, or specific events. Considering the variable nature of the workload guarantees that the available resources will be adequate to meet peak demands without incurring excessive costs during times of low activity.

Automation and monitoring systems play a vital role when exploiting analytics for rightsizing. Implementing automated monitoring solutions that can gather and analyze metrics in real time provides timely insights that may be used to make intelligent decisions regarding rightsizing. These solutions can send out alarms, automate the provisioning or scaling of resources, and assure ongoing optimization in response to shifting workload patterns.

Pro Tip   Leverage autoscaling based on metrics' thresholds. Rather than relying on manual analysis, dynamic autoscaling can respond in real time to metric data. For example, scale out VMs when CPU usage exceeds 60% over 5 minutes. Scale in when under 40% for 10 minutes—set thresholds aligned to workload patterns and cost efficiency goals. Autoscaling ensures you have optimal capacity to handle demand spikes without overspending during lulls. The cloud elasticity adapts sizing continuously based on live metrics versus static manual oversight. Automated rightsizing is efficient, cost-effective, and responsive to workload fluctuations.

Upgrading to Current Generation Compute

As technology progresses, newer CPUs deliver better performance for less power and cooling, making these technologies more cost-effective than previous-generation CPUs. By upgrading to the latest EC2 instances, for example, enterprises can realize significant cost savings and optimize the performance of their cloud infrastructure beyond just rightsizing instances within the existing generation of compute options.

When managing and running applications in the cloud, AWS uses EC2 instances, virtual servers offering flexibility and scalability. EC2 instances, are available in a wide variety of types, sizes, and pricing models; each has unique performance characteristics and related costs. It is essential to have a solid understanding of the demands that your workload places on you and to determine whether or not EC2 instances are the most cost-efficient solution. Replacing older EC2 instances with new ones requires your team to analyze existing instances' efficiency in terms of performance and cost before considering alternative approaches.

To begin, conduct an in-depth analysis of the required amount of work and the expected level of performance. Determine the exact resource requirements, such as processing power, memory, and storage space, and consider the workload's requirements for scalability and variability. If you understand the peculiarities of your task, you can make educated selections regarding the infrastructure alternatives best suited to your workload.

The process of measuring the performance and cost of several infrastructure options is known as *benchmarking*. Benchmarking aims to determine which option will handle your workload most efficiently and cost-effectively. Businesses can discover the optimal solution that balances performance and cost by comparing the performance metrics and associated expenses of EC2 instances with those of alternative solutions such as serverless computing or containerization. This allows businesses to arrive at the best possible solution.

Once you've gathered information on your existing EC2 usage, you can decide whether to rightsize your existing compute (as previously discussed), update to the current generation of compute options, or pursue other alternative solutions. The business's needs will help determine which path to choose.

Alternatives to EC2

Investigating several solutions besides EC2 instances is necessary when optimizing costs. For example, serverless computing platforms such as AWS Lambda or containerization technologies such as Amazon Elastic Kubernetes Service (EKS) or AWS Fargate offer alternatives for applications with more flexible resource allocation and potentially reduced costs. When these options are evaluated, ways to cut costs and better use resources are possible but will require some investment in architecture updates.

Alternatively, CSPs provide various managed services that can reduce the operational overhead and expenses associated with maintaining infrastructure. For instance, Amazon Relational Database Service (Amazon RDS) offers a managed database solution that frees businesses from managing and maintaining their database infrastructure. By utilizing managed services, companies can offload maintenance responsibilities, lower operating expenses, and concentrate on their core business activities.

Assessing the Value of Managed Services

Some workloads have unique requirements or dependencies, which makes it challenging to remove EC2 instances altogether. In such situations, businesses can investigate cost-saving techniques such as savings plans and reserved cases to optimize costs while preserving the required performance and infrastructure levels.

Spot instances are another cost-effective pricing alternative, depending on the flexibility of your applications. Spot instances allow businesses to place bids on idle EC2 capacity that is in reserve. They are frequently offered at much cheaper costs than on-demand or reserved instances. Companies can realize significant cost savings by strategically employing spot instances and deploying workloads that usually function despite interruptions.

Capitalizing on Committed Spend Discounts

In today's dynamic cloud computing landscape, where agility, scalability, and cost efficiency are paramount, understanding and harnessing the potential of committed spend discounts is essential for organizations seeking to optimize their cloud expenditure. Committed spend discounts, offered by leading cloud service providers such as AWS, Azure, and GCP, present a strategic opportunity for businesses to achieve significant cost savings and financial predictability.

This section delves into the intricacies of committed spend discounts across various cloud providers, exploring their nuances, advantages, and challenges. By providing a comprehensive overview and actionable insights, we aim to empower you and your organization to leverage committed spend discounts effectively, enabling them to maximize their cloud investments while maintaining budgetary control and operational efficiency.

Understanding Savings Plans vs. Reserved Instances

Effective cost management and planning in cloud systems depend on understanding the distinctions between savings plans and reserved instances. These purchasing solutions offer significant cost savings compared to on-demand pricing but have different qualities and application scenarios. Let's take a closer look at savings plans and reserved instances:

Reserved Instances (RIs): These are ideal for predictable workloads with consistent resource requirements. RIs offer upfront discounts in exchange for a commitment to specific instance types, regions, and availability zones. RIs also provide a capacity reservation, ensuring access to chosen instances when needed.

Savings Plans: Offer greater flexibility for dynamic workloads or those requiring adaptability across instance types or services. Savings plans provide pay-as-you-go discounts based on your compute usage commitment, not specific instances. They don't offer capacity reservation but cover a wider range of resources, including EC2 instances, Fargate, and Lambda.

Reserved instances benefit CSPs, like AWS, by giving them advance notice of their customers' expected usage patterns. This allows them to forecast demand better and reduce costs. The CSP offers deep discounts for RI contracts to incentivize customers to commit to specific compute usage or capacity. Customers can enjoy lower expenses and long-term cost certainty by committing to a limited usage level.

Customers can reserve compute instances for a set period, usually one or three years, using reserved instances (RIs). When using RIs, customers commit to an instance type, location, and availability zone. When compared to on-demand pricing, reserved instances offer significant upfront cost savings. These savings are further reduced depending on the length of the commitment and the type of upfront payment (whole upfront, partial upfront, or no upfront).

Reservations for capacity are one of the critical features of reserved instances. This feature indicates that reserved instances are always accessible to the customer, regardless of usage. This may be advantageous for workloads with consistent or predictable use patterns. Customers could have to pay for unused resources if actual consumption exceeds the capacity reserved.

On the other hand, savings plans provide more flexible and comprehensive expense savings coverage. Savings plans are not restricted to availability zones or instance types. Instead, they offer a discount on consumption for various EC2 instances or other services the CSP provides. Compute Savings Plans, which apply to all EC2 instances, and EC2 Instance Savings Plans, which give even deeper reductions but necessitate a commitment to instance families and sizes, are the two alternatives offered by savings plans.

Savings plans and reserved instances differ in how flexible their usage options are. Savings plans give clients discounts on various instance kinds and services, which is especially helpful for workloads that demand flexibility and may require multiple instance types or services. Savings plans are a better choice for consumers with dynamic or changing workloads, due to their flexibility.

It's vital to remember that reserved instances and savings plans require rigorous planning and research to achieve the most significant cost savings. Evaluating past usage trends, workload requirements, and future estimates is critical to choosing the best purchase option. To assist clients in locating possible savings and selecting the most suitable pricing model, CSPs frequently offer cost analysis tools, such as AWS Cost Explorer.

Committed Spend Discounts by Cloud Provider

Having explored Savings Plans and Reserved Instances in AWS, let's delve into the offerings of other major cloud providers. While Azure and GCP offer committed spend discounts similar to AWS RIs, they differ in terminology and implementation.

Azure Reservations

Azure Reservations have the following characteristics:

- *Scope*: Azure offers reservations at both the Resource Group (similar to AWS RIs) and Subscription (similar to AWS savings plans) levels.

- *Flexibility*: Unlike AWS, Azure allows changing reservation scope within the contract period up to a specific spending limit. This provides some flexibility compared to AWS RIs.

- *Discount range*: Similar to AWS RIs, discounts are typically higher than savings plans but with stricter limitations.

- *Limitations*: Resource Group reservations apply only to the specific group and cannot be shared with other resources if unused. Additionally, Azure reservations are restricted to particular instance size groups, capacity priorities, and regions.

GCP Committed Use Discounts

GCP committed use discounts (CUDs) have the following characteristics:

- *Types*: Available by resource types (similar to AWS RIs) with two variants:

    - *Spend-based*: Discounted rate based on a committed minimum dollar amount per hour

    - *Resource-based*: Reduced rate based on a minimum level of Compute Engine resources in a specific region

- *Flexibility*: CUDs can be shared across projects within the billing account by enabling shared discounts. However, once purchased, they cannot be changed or canceled.

- *Discounts*: Up to 57% for resources and GPUs and 70% for memory-optimized machine types. Like AWS RIs, CUDs require upfront payment for the committed term (one or three years).

- *Sustained use discounts*: GCP offers an additional discount for continuous resource usage over time, automatically applied to VMs.

Choosing the Right Option

The best choice depends on your specific cloud environment:

- *Predictable workloads*: RIs (AWS, Azure) and CUDs (GCP) can offer significant savings. Consider flexibility needs when choosing between them.

- *Dynamic workloads*: Savings plans (AWS, Azure) offer greater flexibility for changing resource needs.

- *Upfront costs*: Savings plans (AWS, Azure) prevent upfront payments associated with RIs and CUDs.

By understanding the committed spend discount options offered by different cloud providers, you can choose the best fit for your needs and optimize your cloud costs. Consider factors like workload predictability, flexibility requirements, and upfront payment constraints. Additionally, explore other cost-saving strategies each provider offers, such as GCP's Sustained Use Discounts.

Challenges and Considerations of Committed Spend Discounts

Committed spend discounts, like savings plans or reserved instances, can significantly reduce cloud costs. However, organizations should be aware of some challenges and considerations, represented in Figure 6-2, that can be encountered before applying these cost-cutting measures. One of the main problems is ensuring the workload's characteristics match the committed spend discount. Committed spend discounts often require a commitment to specific types of instances, families, or services. It might be difficult to completely utilize the committed resources if the workload's requirements alter or develop over time, which could lead to instances being left unused or underutilized. Workload flexibility and future scalability must be carefully considered to get the most out of committed discounts.

Figure 6-2. *Challenges and considerations in committed spend discounts*

Committed discounts are a good fit for workloads with consistent and predictable use patterns. However, firms with highly dynamic workloads and frequent demand swings may need help to make the most of their commitments. Committed discounts may not be used to their full potential due to scaling needs, spike times, and unpredictable consumption. Companies must carefully assess if determined discounts are appropriate for unique workload patterns.

Foresight and planning are necessary to choose the right committed discount purchases. Organizations must examine past usage trends, identify recurring task demands, and precisely predict future needs. Understanding peak usage times, seasonality, and growth estimates is all part of this. Inaccurate usage forecasting can harm cost optimization goals by overprovisioning or underutilizing committed resources.

Committed savings usually require a commitment to a specific cloud service provider and its pricing structure. This may result in vendor lock-in, making switching to a different supplier or benefiting from new pricing alternatives complex. Businesses must analyze the long-term effects of vendor lock-in and the trade-offs between flexibility and cost savings in their cloud strategy. Typically, committed savings entail signing contracts with cloud service providers. Specific terms and conditions, such as payment schedules, commitment times, and cancellation rules, may apply to these agreements. Reviewing and comprehending these contractual duties is essential to maintain compliance and prevent unanticipated financial repercussions.

Constant monitoring and analysis are needed to ensure anticipated cost savings are realized after agreed discounts are implemented. Utilizing the tools provided by CSPs or third-party cost management systems, regular cost optimization evaluations are required to spot any disparities, assess usage trends, and make the necessary corrections to optimize costs continuously.

Companies using hybrid or multiple clouds may need help establishing committed discounts. Careful planning, coordination, and use of various discount models for each environment are required to coordinate and optimize determined discounts across various CSPs or on-premises infrastructure.

Best Practices for Optimizing Reservations

Reservation optimization is a cost optimization approach that enterprises can leverage to maximize the cost efficiency of their cloud resources, focusing primarily on reserved instances provided by CSPs like AWS, but also includes Azure Resource Group reservations and GCP CUDs. Organizations can save costs by efficiently managing and using reservations while maximizing performance and adaptability. Before signing a contract for spending commitments, your FinOps teams need in-depth knowledge of how they work and what workloads will benefit from them. While the following examples are AWS-centric, the theory behind them applies to all CSPs.

Understand Reservation Types and Services Offered

Standard Reserved Instances, Convertible Reserved Instances, and Scheduled Reserved Instances are just some of the many reserved instances cloud service providers make available. Each has its own price and flexibility options. Standard RIs offer significant savings but limited flexibility, while convertible RIs provide more flexibility but come at a slightly higher cost. Scheduled RIs are designed to reduce the on-demand spending of workloads that run during specific timeframes, such as the Black Friday sales event. They provide considerable cost savings for workloads with well-established consumption patterns. Understanding the many types of reservations enables you to select the choice most suited to your effort level.

Cloud service providers frequently offer RI exchanges or marketplaces for their customers, in which businesses can purchase, sell, or trade reservations with one another. Utilizing these platforms enables companies to maximize revenue from reservations by selling reservations that have been made but are not being used. In addition, companies can purchase new reservations at reduced prices. RI exchanges allow for greater flexibility in reservations and can further increase attempts to optimize costs.

The optimization of reservations across many CSPs must be considered by organizations operating in multi-cloud setups. Each service provider could have different reservation options and pricing structures. Analyzing each CSP's workload requirements, consumption trends, and price structures is necessary to optimize reservations across the multi-cloud environment.

Effective Commitment Planning and Analysis

Planning the purchase of reserved instances is essential to save cost. This entails researching past usage data, making projections about future resource requirements, and locating situations where reservations would benefit. Organizations can maximize cost savings and ensure reservations are efficiently utilized by linking purchases to anticipated workload demands. This aligns reservation purchases with expected workload demands.

Generally, reserved instances are linked to instance kinds, families, or sizes. To guarantee the most efficient use of reservations, it is essential to pair the workload that will be used with the type of instance used. Maintain a regular schedule to review the appropriateness of reserved instances for your workloads and make any necessary adjustments to ensure maximum cost savings.

Workloads with predictable and consistent utilization patterns are excellent candidates for use with reserved instances. This predictability allows the FinOps team to closely match the RI commitment to usage, maximizing savings without over- or underspending on RIs. On the other hand, workloads characterized by inconsistent or unpredictable usage could only benefit partially from RIs. The most appropriate reservation strategy can be determined by analyzing the most consistent workloads.

Finding the optimal proportion of Reserved Instances to on-demand instances is necessary in optimizing reservations. Workloads with variable or unexpected usage patterns may benefit from a combination of reservations for steady-state usage and on-demand instances for peak or burst periods. Reservations can cover steady-state consumption, while on-demand instances can cover peak or burst periods. This flexibility guarantees cost savings while preserving capacity and performance when needed.

Optimizing reservations requires instance-use analysis. Several CSPs offer software applications, such as AWS Trusted Advisor and Azure Cost Management, that generate utilization reports and make recommendations. These technologies help businesses optimize reservation purchases and cut expenses by identifying instances that could benefit from reservations based on past usage patterns. Organizations can maximize reservation purchases.

Purchase Reservations from the Root Account, Always

Regardless of your organization's many accounts or projects, purchasing them through the root account is the best way to optimize your reservation cost savings. Consolidating purchases at the root account level gives your FinOps team consolidated control and visibility over their cloud inventory, making invoicing and cost allocation easier to manage and giving the best visibility and control of reservation usage.

When you buy reservations from the root account, your business can distribute and utilize reservations among numerous teams or business units as efficiently as possible. This optimizes the reservation allocation for maximum cost savings.

Organizations gain additional flexibility in managing reservation inventory by purchasing reservations directly from the root account. Reservations can be bought, sold, or reallocated through reservation exchanges or markets, and organizations can leverage these options to trade within their organization or with others. This flexibility enables reservation allocations to align more closely with changing workload requirements, maximizing cost savings and resource utilization.

Centralizing reservation administration and conducting it from the root account enhances governance and compliance. This approach ensures consistent reservation procurement rules, standardization of terms, and adherence to compliance standards throughout the organization. By aligning reservation purchases with company norms, budgets, and compliance frameworks, possible risks are reduced, and regulatory standards are effectively met.

When considering scalability, the advantages of making reservation purchases through the root account become even more apparent for companies operating on a larger scale. Centralizing reservation administration simplifies overall cost optimization in scenarios where many accounts, regions, or workloads are involved. This approach streamlines the cost optimization process by eliminating the need for individual accounts to manage reservations independently and promotes efficiency throughout the organization.

Purchasing reservations from the root account gives purchasing teams better leverage for negotiations and contract management with the CSP. Purchasing teams can negotiate better terms for reserved instances' pricing and usage conditions by including a larger pool of resources in the contracts. These negotiations can lead to more favorable agreements that minimize costs and create long-term value.

When considering reservation management, purchasing reservations from the root account offers a consolidated and planned approach to the process. It enables centralized control and visibility, optimized use, flexible management of reservation inventory, improved governance and compliance, scalability, and negotiation options, among other advantages. This method allows businesses to optimize costs efficiently, streamline reservation management operations, and drive cost optimization activities throughout their cloud infrastructure.

Utilizing the Cheapest Spot Instances

As previously introduced, cloud service providers often have unused cloud compute capacity they decide to make available at deeply discounted prices, known as spot instances. Unlike on-demand instances or reserved instances, which are guaranteed for your use, spot instances are surplus computing resources made available by CSPs at a significant discount in exchange for accepting interruptions in their availability.

Spot instance pricing is almost always significantly lower than other instance pricing options, such as on-demand instances or RIs, often by as much as 90%. Because of this, spot instance are an appealing purchasing choice for workloads that are not time-sensitive and can take advantage of strategies such as workload scheduling and balancing. Spot instances are excellent for fault-tolerant applications, containerized workloads, batch processing, and stateless or distributed computing jobs. These workloads can withstand interruptions and be readily dispersed over several instances, enabling enterprises to use the spot instance market effectively.

However, it is essential to consider that spot instances follow the "spot market" pricing model, which means that prices are subject to change depending on the amount of supply and demand. Spot instances are only available on a best-effort basis and cannot be guaranteed. If the spot price exceeds the bid price, the CSP reserves the right to recover the instances without warning. As a result, businesses need to carefully design their applications and infrastructure to deal with the possibility of disruptions. This includes ensuring they have the necessary procedures to deal with spot instance termination gracefully.

Companies can take many different approaches to making the most of their use of spot instances. One option is to utilize spot instances as a component of an autoscaling group. Spot instances, on-demand instances, and reserved instances can be combined to produce cost-effective, dynamically scalable designs that automatically modify capacity based on workload demands. Businesses can create these architectures to take advantage of the cost savings that spot instances give while maintaining the required performance and availability level.

Another approach is to use a feature called Spot Fleet, which cloud service providers offer. This feature enables businesses and other organizations to construct fleets of compute resources by specifying a combination of spot instances, on-demand instances, and reserved instances. Spot Fleet is designed to keep the target capacity at a constant level automatically. It guarantees that the workload is continually operating at peak efficiency by utilizing the least expensive instances that are readily accessible.

Utilizing CSPs' tools and services is one option for companies looking to properly manage and optimize their spot instances. For instance, AWS offers services such as EC2 Spot Fleet, spot instance Advisor, and spot instance interruption notices. These services provide advice, insights, and notifications to help enterprises gracefully handle spot instance interruptions and make educated decisions.

Importance of Autoscaling in Cost Optimization

Cloud computing introduced the concept of autoscaling, enabling businesses to adjust infrastructure capacity dynamically in response to fluctuating workload demands. Autoscaling ensures that resources allocated to a service or application are dynamically scaled up or down to meet shifting performance needs, optimizing resource utilization and maximizing cost-effectiveness.

Autoscaling emerged to address challenges associated with conventional static infrastructure provisioning, where organizations manually estimated anticipated workloads and allocated resources accordingly. This approach frequently resulted in underprovisioning, causing performance bottlenecks and user discontent, or overprovisioning, resulting in excessive costs. Autoscaling evolved to automate resource capacity adjustment based on actual usage patterns, solving these challenges effectively.

To identify the current load on the system, autoscaling continuously monitors predefined measures, such as CPU utilization, network traffic, or request queue length. The addition or removal of resources, like virtual machines, containers, or storage, is triggered by autoscaling when the workload reaches or falls below predetermined criteria to maintain optimal performance.

Autoscaling's underlying technology depends on the CSP and the infrastructure used. For instance, in AWS, autoscaling is commonly accomplished via services like Application Auto Scaling or Auto Scaling Groups (ASG). ASG enables businesses to specify a collection of resources, like EC2 instances, and establish scaling rules based on measurements or predetermined events. Application Auto Scaling makes autoscaling more precise by extending this feature to other AWS services like DynamoDB, ECS, and Lambda.

Autoscaling can be used in multi-cloud or hybrid cloud systems and is not restricted to a single CSP. Thanks to centralized autoscaling features offered by some cloud management systems and tools, organizations may scale resources effortlessly regardless of the underlying infrastructure. These capabilities can be used across various clouds or infrastructure providers.

However, autoscaling does present some difficulties. Choosing the appropriate scaling strategies, including threshold values and scaling actions, requires thorough planning and comprehension of the application's behavior. Inadequate configuration could cause unstable scaling events frequently, increasing expenses. On the other hand, overly cautious practices could cause performance decline during peak times.

Additionally, autoscaling makes maintaining dispersed systems more complex. Architectural considerations and sophisticated monitoring tools are needed for proper load balancing across scaled resources. These tools guarantee data consistency and coordinate the scaling of multiple components.

Benefits of Autoscaling

Autoscaling offers numerous advantages, with one of the primary benefits being its ability to scale resources in real time based on actual demand, resulting in significant cost savings. Traditional static infrastructure provisioning often leads to overprovisioning, where firms allocate more resources than necessary to handle peak workloads. This practice wastes resources and drives up costs. However, autoscaling dynamically adds or removes resources in response to changes in workload, ensuring that the infrastructure is appropriately sized to meet current needs. Organizations can lower their infrastructure expenses by eliminating overprovisioning and spending only on the necessary resources.

Moreover, autoscaling enables businesses to leverage spot or on-demand instances at lower prices than dedicated instances. On-demand instances allow organizations to launch resources as needed and only pay for the time they use. Similarly, spot instances enable businesses to bid on available cloud capacity at significantly reduced costs, leading to further cost reductions. Organizations can optimize their infrastructure expenses and achieve significant savings by combining autoscaling with deploying these cost-effective instance types.

Additionally, autoscaling reduces operating overhead, providing another cost-saving advantage. With on-demand scaling, businesses must allocate time and resources to prepare for workload increases and adjust infrastructure as needed. Manual intervention increases the risk of errors and requires specialized staff to oversee and control the scaling process. In contrast, autoscaling automates this process, eliminating manual intervention and freeing up resources to focus on other critical activities. Improved operational efficiency resulting from careful resource allocation and reduced overhead leads to cost savings.

Furthermore, autoscaling enables businesses to adopt a "pay-as-you-go" business model, aligning expenses with actual consumption. Organizations can adjust to changing workloads without incurring additional costs during periods of low demand by dynamically scaling resources up or down. This flexibility ensures that resources are allocated efficiently, making them available when needed and reducing costs during periods of inactivity or low demand. Additionally, autoscaling allows businesses to respond swiftly to unexpected workload increases without manual intervention, mitigating potential performance issues and related expenses.

Lastly, autoscaling can save costs by enhancing application availability and reliability. By dynamically adjusting resource capacity based on workload demands, autoscaling ensures that applications have the resources to handle increasing traffic or demand. This proactive approach helps prevent performance degradation or system failures due to resource constraints. Improved application availability and reliability can reduce downtime, minimize revenue loss, and enhance customer satisfaction.

Combining Spot Instances with ASG

Adding spot instances to an Auto Scaling Group (ASG) for non-container workloads is a cost-cutting measure that can drastically lower infrastructure costs while preserving performance and availability. Spot instances are computing resources CSPs sell for far less than on-demand instances. Organizations can benefit from these inexpensive resources and reduce infrastructure costs by including spot instances in an ASG.

The first step in adding spot instances to an ASG is configuring a combination of spot and on-demand instances. The ASG establishes the desired number of instances, minimum and maximum capacity, and scaling strategies based on workload indicators. Organizations can manage the balance between cost savings and reliability by selecting a percentage or a precise number of spot instances inside the ASG setup.

The CSP offers the ASG when a spot instance becomes available based on the specified spot allocation strategy. The spot allocation strategy governs selecting and fulfilling instances from the available spot capacity. Low prices, various instance kinds, or capacity-optimized allocation are common tactics. Organizations can maximize their chances of receiving spot instances at the lowest cost by choosing the best technique.

Spot instances may be terminated if the spot price exceeds the highest acceptable bid price or the provider wants to reclaim capacity. To tackle spot instance interruptions, organizations can use tactics like combining on-demand and spot instances, implementing instance hibernation, or structuring applications to handle interruptions gracefully.

Beyond cost savings, adding spot instances to an ASG for non-container workloads has other advantages. First off, it makes the infrastructure more flexible and scalable. Organizations may quickly scale up their capacity with spot instances at times of solid demand without incurring significant fees. With this elasticity, applications may manage heavier workloads while using less infrastructure.

Second, spot instances can improve infrastructure fault tolerance and resilience. Organizations can reduce the chance of single-instance failures by varying instance types and distributing workloads among several spot instances. When a spot instance terminates, the ASG immediately replaces it with another spot instance or an on-demand instance to maintain the application's or service's continuous availability.

Additionally, by distributing resources, adding spot instances to an ASG for non-container applications encourages cloud cost efficiency. Organizations can develop a balanced resource mix that optimizes costs while maintaining performance by combining spot and on-demand instances. Spot instances can handle batch processing or nonessential workloads, whereas on-demand instances can be assigned to more urgent or vital jobs.

Organizations should closely monitor spot market prices and modify their bid prices to leverage spot instances in an ASG efficiently. By studying past spot prices and proactively setting bid prices, organizations can maximize cost savings while lowering the risk of delays caused by price changes.

Kubernetes Cost Optimization

Kubernetes (K8s) is a robust container orchestration platform that allows businesses to build, manage, and grow containerized applications effectively. However, the associated cloud expenditures will increase proportionately to your environment's growing number of containers and clusters. In a K8s context, cost optimization solutions aim to improve resource usage while minimizing waste and optimizing cloud costs.

Properly distributing resources according to their needs is essential to K8s cost optimization. Organizations can discover inefficiencies in resource use and modify resource allocation accordingly if they closely monitor container, pod, and node resource utilization. By analyzing indicators like CPU, memory, and network consumption, an organization can better determine the appropriate resource allocation for each job. This will reduce the likelihood of overprovisioning and improve cost efficiency.

K8s cost optimization includes efficient management of the resource's lifecycle. This involves shutting down or scaling down non-production environments during idleness and automatically increasing or decreasing resources based on the amount of work needed. By automatically altering the number of nodes or pods based on actual usage, businesses can dramatically cut expenses while minimizing wasted resources and maximizing efficiency.

Applying approaches to optimizing container density can also serve as an efficient strategy for reducing costs associated with K8s. Companies can obtain a higher container density by optimizing the placement of containers within nodes and adopting strategies such as vertical or horizontal pod autoscaling. This allows companies to reduce the number of nodes necessary. This consolidation not only enhances the usage of available resources but also has the potential to result in significant cost savings.

Additionally, organizations can optimize resource placement inside a K8s cluster by utilizing advanced scheduling algorithms and affinity criteria. Organizations can successfully control costs by making the best use of resources and taking advantage of choices that can help them save money if they assign pods to specific nodes based on criteria such as the requirements for those resources, the localization of the data, or even the availability of spot instances.

Using strategies for container lifecycle management is also essential for the cost optimization of K8s. Companies can free up resources and reduce expenses by automatically terminating or evicting containers or pods that either are no longer required or are not being used. Managing the lifecycle of containers and pods requires careful consideration of available options. Kubernetes Jobs offers automation capabilities, while custom scripts or controllers provide greater flexibility and control. Each approach has its benefits and drawbacks, so selecting the best fit for your specific needs is crucial.

In addition, businesses can reap benefits by using cost optimization tools unique to CSPs for K8s deployments. AWS, Azure, and GCP offer services such as AWS Cost Explorer, Azure Cost Management, and GCP Cost Optimization. These services provide insights, recommendations, and cost analyses targeted at K8's workloads. These tools can help firms identify opportunities to save money on K8s expenditures, optimize resource allocation, and efficiently manage those costs.

Cost Recommendations for Kubernetes/Containers

For businesses relying on containers for their deployments, cost optimization recommendations for Kubernetes and container workloads are essential to optimize cloud expenses. Tools like OpenCost utilize the work of the Kubernetes community to deliver advice, best practices, and insights tailored explicitly to the cost optimization process within Kubernetes clusters. Let's look deeper into the advantages and functions of open source cost management tools for containers:

- *Cost distribution and the availability of information*: The cost allocation features from container cost management tools like OpenCost allow businesses to understand better the cost split between the various components that make up their cluster. Because these technologies provide visibility into resource consumption, cost drivers, and expenditure patterns, they enable firms to identify areas in which cost optimization is essential. This enables enterprises to make educated judgments and properly prioritize their optimization efforts, attributing expenses to specific namespaces, deployments, or pods as necessary.

- *Appropriate allocation of resources*: Open source tools analyze the essential CPU, memory, and network consumption parameters to locate opportunities for rightsizing resources. These tools suggest improvements to ensure resources are utilized most effectively by recognizing containers that are either over- or underprovisioned. Containers that are the correct size lead to cost savings since they cut down on wasteful spending and maximize the exploitation of available resources.

- *Pod autoscaling and horizontal pod autoscaling (HPA)*: Organizations can improve resource allocation and reduce expenses by dynamically altering the number of replicas in response to changes in workload demand. Autoscaling guarantees that resources are supplied and deprovisioned as needed, which enables effective scaling while preventing overprovisioning during periods of low demand. Autoscaling also allows for the deprovisioning of resources when they are no longer required.

- *Locate instances and determine their node affinity*: Using node affinity rules, companies can deploy workloads or containers to spot instances, improving cost reductions without negatively impacting performance.

- *Automation to enforce shutting down of non-production workloads during non-business hours*: A viable strategy for businesses to decrease operational expenses is to shut down non-production container pods during off-peak business hours. By implementing planned shutdowns or automation frameworks, companies can effectively mitigate overages and successfully run non-production workloads during idle periods, leading to significant cost savings.

- *Integration with tools utilizing the IaC model*: Integration with IaC tools allows businesses to specify cost-optimized infrastructure and container resources as code. This opens the door to repeatability, scalability, and effective provisioning of resources. Organizations can continuously execute cost optimization strategies and automate the deployment and administration of cost-efficient resources when they adopt practices based on the IaC model.

- *Community-driven standards of excellence*: Cost recommendation tools that are open source benefit from community contributions and established standards. Because these initiatives are conducted collaboratively, businesses can benefit from the community's accumulated experience. They can also access cost optimization tactics, configurations, and guidelines validated through actual implementation. The fact that these tools are community-driven guarantees that they are always up to current with the latest advances in the Kubernetes and container ecosystems. As a result, they can provide businesses with recommendations for cost optimization that are both relevant and effective.

Terraform: Adding Instances List in K8s Instance Pool

Businesses extensively use the infrastructure as code tool known as Terraform because it automates the provisioning and management of cloud resources. Regarding Kubernetes instance pools, Terraform offers a declarative method that is versatile and efficient for adding instances to the collection. This method can be found under Add Instances in the Terraform UI. This strategy allows companies to grow their K8s clusters and optimize resource allocation following workload requirements.

Organizations can use K8s' unique features since Terraform can add instances to a K8s instance pool. The desired state of the infrastructure can be expressed in code using Terraform's declarative vocabulary, making it simple to manage and keep track of changes over time; because of this, consistency and reproducibility can be ensured, as the infrastructure can be provisioned in a predictable and reproducible way.

Organizations can define the appropriate Terraform configuration in a Terraform module, which allows them to add instances to a K8s instance pool. This module lets users specify instance kinds, sizes, networking setups, and other essential case factors. By simply giving businesses access to this configuration, they can quickly scale up or down their K8s clusters, altering the instance count in the Terraform module.

Terraform's connection with CSP APIs is one of the primary benefits of Terraform for managing K8s instance pools. Because Terraform is compatible with various CSPs, such as AWS, Azure, and GCP, businesses can create and manage instances seamlessly across numerous cloud environments. Because of this flexibility, companies can take advantage of various CSPs' most advantageous features and pricing alternatives.

Additionally, Terraform supports managing infrastructure lifecycles as part of its core functionality. This indicates that organizations can declare the intended state of the K8s instance pool, and Terraform will automatically collect the creation, modification, and deletion of instances to achieve that desired state. Application owners can add or remove instances from the pool according to workload demands. This ensures effective resource utilization and cost-effectiveness.

Terraform offers robust dependency management features. It allows organizations to create relationships and dependencies between different resources, which helps ensure that instances are introduced to the K8s instance pool in the correct order and without any conflicts. This both maintains consistency and eliminates any potential problems caused by allocating resources.

Additionally, Terraform supports more advanced features, such as remote state management, which enables businesses to save the current state of their infrastructure in a single, centralized location. This makes collaboration possible, simplifying the process of setting up versions of infrastructure and tracking changes. It also allows team members to discuss the state of the infrastructure, enabling seamless integration into a CI/CD pipeline. It also promotes the use of infrastructure as code best practices.

Storage Optimization

Effective storage optimization is not a complex task, but a practical approach that can be easily implemented. By migrating to cost-effective storage options, implementing lifecycle policies, and leveraging automation, organizations can significantly reduce their cloud storage costs while maintaining performance. Here are some critical strategies for optimizing cloud storage.

Migrating from Amazon EBS GP2 to GP3

Migrating from AWS EBS GP2 (General Purpose SSD) to GP3 (General Purpose SSD) is a valuable cost optimization option for enterprises aiming to optimize cloud storage expenses. GP3 is the latest generation of the GP series of SSDs. However, GP3 volumes offer increased performance at a reduced price, making them an attractive solution for many workloads. While GP2 volumes offer an appropriate mix of performance and cost, GP3 volumes provide improved performance at a reduced price.

Compared to GP2 volumes, GP3 volumes offer more excellent baseline performance. This is due to a maximum baseline performance of 3,000 IOPS (input/output operations per second) per volume. GP2 volumes do not provide this level of performance. Because of this improved baseline performance, businesses can improve their apps' performance without incurring additional costs. In addition, GP3 volumes enable enterprises to supply up to 16,000 IOPS and 1,000 MiB/s (megabytes per second) of throughput per volume, which provides flexibility for demanding workloads.

One of the most significant advantages of upgrading from GP2 to GP3 is saving money. Compared to GP2 volumes, GP3 volumes offer improved performance at a lower cost per gigabyte and lower overall prices. Because of this combination of increased performance and decreased pricing, businesses can achieve cost reductions without compromising performance. Migrating to GP3 allows enterprises to reduce their overall storage expenses while guaranteeing their applications operate at the needed speed levels.

The procedure for migrating from GP2 to GP3 is simple and may be carried out without interruptions to the apps' availability. AWS gives enterprises the necessary tools and documentation to complete the migration process. In most cases, this necessitates the creation of new GP3 volumes and the subsequent transfer of data from current GP2 volumes to the newly created GP3 volumes. Once the data has been appropriately moved, businesses may update their applications to use the new GP3 volumes, ensuring a smooth transition once it has been completed.

When planning the migration, it is necessary to analyze the performance requirements imposed by the workload. Identifying GP3 volume sizes and providing IOPS to satisfy those needs is essential. Before committing to the migration, businesses can analyze the performance of their workload on GP3 volumes using the AWS performance test function. This assists companies in ensuring that their applications perform up to their standards and expectations.

Organizations must consider various aspects during the migration, including the time required to transfer data and any potential impact on application performance. It is highly recommended to migrate during off-peak hours or take advantage of AWS services such as snapshots to reduce downtime and mitigate any effect on the apps or users.

After migration, enterprises must periodically analyze and optimize their GP3 volumes to save costs and improve efficiency. AWS offers monitoring tools, such as Amazon CloudWatch, that enable businesses to monitor GP3 volumes' performance parameters and make necessary adjustments to maximize performance or scale resources.

Pro Tip   Use AWS native tools like Elastic Volumes and Data Migration Service to automate and streamline the transition. These tools can replicate GP2 volumes to GP3 with minimal downtime. Schedule the migration during off-peak hours and redirect connections to new GP3 volumes. Ensure performance meets needs and terminate old volumes as soon as possible. Automating with native tools ensures a smooth, low-risk transition to realize GP3 savings. Implement ongoing post-migration monitoring to optimize volumes and maximize GP3 cost efficiency.

Slack Case Study: A Deeper Dive into Cost Optimization Success

Slack, a leading collaboration platform provider, achieved impressive cost optimization by strategically migrating to Amazon's general-purpose SSD (GP3) storage. This case study delves deeper than the headline figure of $600,000+ in annual savings, revealing the journey of meticulous planning, smooth execution, and ongoing optimization that can serve as a valuable blueprint for other organizations.

Planning the Path to Savings

Before embarking on the migration, Slack, a key player in the communication industry, meticulously mapped out its course. The Cloud Engineering team conducted a thorough workload assessment, analyzing the IOPS and throughput requirements of each application residing on GP2 volumes, which matched applications to the most appropriate GP3 tier, laying the groundwork for accurate cost projections. The team factored in existing GP2 storage costs, anticipated savings from GP3's lower per-gigabyte pricing, and the expected performance boost, resulting in a clear understanding of the return on investment. This meticulous planning ensured a smooth and cost-effective migration.

Streamlined Migration for Minimal Disruption

Slack prioritized minimizing disruption during the migration. The Cloud Engineering team opted for a phased approach, tackling smaller workloads first. This allowed them to test and refine the process, ironing out any issues before migrating their entire infrastructure. Automation played a vital role in this streamlined execution. Company A leveraged AWS native tools like Elastic Volumes and Data Migration Service to automate data replication and volume updates. This minimized manual intervention, reduced errors, and accelerated the entire process, ensuring a smooth transition with minimal impact on their platform and users.

Continuous Optimization for Long-Term Value

Company A's commitment to cost optimization extended beyond the initial migration. They implemented continuous monitoring with tools like Amazon CloudWatch, vigilantly scrutinizing their GP3 volumes for hidden cost inefficiencies. This proactive approach allowed them to identify and eliminate unused resources, dynamically

214

adjust IOPS allocation based on evolving demands, and scale volumes to match actual workload needs, ensuring they maximized the value of their storage investment. They extended automation by entrusting tasks like snapshot rotation and volume pruning to intelligent tools. This minimized manual intervention and potential errors, freeing IT resources for more strategic endeavors while ensuring long-term efficiency and cost control within their GP3 environment.

By following Slack's comprehensive approach, other organizations can unlock significant cost savings through strategic block storage optimization using GP3.

Amazon S3 Cost Optimization

Amazon Simple Storage Service (S3) is a popular object storage service provided by AWS. As businesses continue to store ever-increasing quantities of data in S3, optimizing S3 expenses to manage cloud expenditures is becoming increasingly important. When minimizing their costs on S3, businesses can use different tactics and recommended procedures.

Amazon S3 is a dependable and robust storage option. It provides a flexible and affordable storage infrastructure that meets the needs of different enterprises. Since it is built to provide durability of 99.999999999% (11 nines), data saved in S3 is exceedingly safe from corruption or loss.

Amazon S3's endurance is demonstrated using various methods. It disperses data among regional machines and facilities to ensure redundancy and fault tolerance. As a result of its automatic replication of data throughout a region, it is hugely resistant to hardware issues and disruptions in the data center. Further strengthening its endurance, Amazon S3 routinely uses checksums to verify data integrity.

Amazon S3's scalability and usability are additional benefits. S3 offers limitless storage space, allowing organizations to scale up their infrastructure without capacity planning.

Choosing the Right S3 Storage Class

One of the most critical aspects of S3 cost optimization is choosing the most suitable storage class for each object based on its use patterns and the level of durability required. S3 provides a variety of storage classes, such as Standard, Intelligent-Tiering, Standard-IA (Infrequent Access), One Zone-IA, Glacier, and Glacier Deep Archive. Standard is the default storage class. Organizations can select the storage class that will result in the lowest total cost if they investigate the number of times each object is accessed and the time needed to retrieve it. For instance, frequently accessed data may be kept in the Intelligent-Tiering or Standard classes. In contrast, data viewed less often or archived for longer could be saved in the Glacier or Glacier Deep Archive class.

Lifecycle Policies

Another efficient method of lowering expenses is to implement lifecycle policies and use S3's lifecycle management capability. These policies allow companies to automatically move things to different storage classes or expire objects based on rules that have been set. Organizations can minimize storage costs by transferring data to lower-cost storage classes or deleting unnecessary data if they define policies that fit the needs of how long data should be kept and how often it should be accessed.

Amazon S3 Intelligent-Tiering

The previously mentioned storage class called Amazon S3 Intelligent-Tiering automatically optimizes data storage expenses. Your objects are moved between two access tiers: the frequent access tier and the infrequent access tier. Using machine learning to assess their access patterns and automatically transferring data to the proper tier based on its usage patterns aids in cost savings. Intelligent-Tiering offers capabilities like automatic tiering and frequent access tier optimizations to further improve your applications' costs and performance.

Once you make the Intelligent-Tiering storage class the default, any new items uploaded to the bucket will automatically be stored in it. The bucket's current objects' storage classes remain unchanged, and the default storage class only applies to brand-new objects.

While Intelligent-Tiering has the same storage cost as the Standard storage class, cost reductions from automatically transferring data to the proper tier based on use patterns frequently balance the higher storage costs.

Data Compression and Deduplication

Data compression and deduplication are cost-effective ways to optimize storage. Compressing data before storing it in Amazon S3 reduces the storage footprint, which can lead to cost savings. Similarly, deduplicating data removes redundant copies of the same data, reducing data storage costs. By implementing these strategies, companies can maximize storage space and reduce overall costs.

Observing Data Transfer and API Calls

Monitoring and maximizing the efficiency of S3 data transmission expenses is also essential for cost optimization. AWS offers tools like Amazon CloudWatch and AWS Cost Explorer that allow enterprises to monitor and analyze data transfer costs. Organizations can decrease data transfer costs and optimize their overall S3 expenses if they identify data transfer patterns, optimize network setups, and use AWS Direct Connect or AWS DataSync capabilities.

Pro Tip   It is essential to efficiently implement access controls and manage permissions to prevent unwanted access and needless data transfer expenses. Companies should regularly audit their access permissions and make necessary adjustments to guarantee that only authorized users or apps can access S3 objects. Businesses can avoid unwanted data transfer or API usage by limiting access to only the appropriate parties, ultimately resulting in cost savings.

In addition, monitoring and analyzing usage data and billing information for S3 storage can provide helpful insights for optimizing costs. AWS allows enterprises to detect patterns, outliers, and possible areas for cost optimization by delivering comprehensive billing data and usage information. Businesses can proactively manage their Amazon S3 costs if they routinely monitor these KPIs and take the relevant measures, such as eliminating unwanted objects or optimizing storage allocation.

Advanced Cloud Storage Optimization Techniques

This section dives deeper into advanced strategies to maximize your cloud storage cost savings.

Contract Negotiation

Large organizations storing massive data volumes have significant leverage when negotiating cloud provider contracts. They can secure cost reductions through the following:

- *Volume discounts*: Negotiate significant per-gigabyte price reductions based on your projected storage needs.

- *Custom rate cards*: Tailor unique pricing structures reflecting your specific access patterns and data types.

Remember, successful negotiation requires in-depth analysis of your data usage and awareness of current market trends. However, the potential cost savings for enormous storage requirements can be substantial.

Data Compression and Deduplication

Compressing redundant data can dramatically shrink storage footprints, reducing storage costs and network transfer charges. Consider these techniques:

- *Data compression*: Utilize compression algorithms for archival data, achieving significant storage reduction (up to 80% in some cases). Implement different compression levels based on data types and access frequency for a flexible cost-benefit balance.

- *Inline data deduplication*: Eliminate duplicate data copies across your cloud storage, optimizing space and lowering costs.

Remember, compression and deduplication can impact performance. Weigh data accessibility needs against potential savings.

Efficient Data Migration with Transfer Devices

Large on-premises data migrations can incur high network transfer charges. Services like AWS Snowball and Azure Data Box offer alternative solutions:

- *Secure physical storage devices*: Ship vast data volumes offline at predictable costs, minimizing network bandwidth utilization.

- *Preconfigured and encrypted devices*: These devices ensure secure data transfer, simplifying migration.

- *Cost-effective for large datasets*: Using transfer devices avoids huge cloud egress charges and optimize transfer times for massive migrations.

Consider data volume, security needs, and network limitations when choosing between network transfers and physical device migration.

Backup Optimization Strategies

Backup optimization strategies significantly impact storage requirements and costs. Implement techniques like these:

- *Tiered backups*: Ensure robust protection for critical data by replicating it across a high-availability storage class, allowing cost-effective tiering for infrequently accessed files.

- *Deduplication for backups*: Eliminate duplicate data across backup versions, especially for repetitive snapshots.

- *Backup retention policies*: Define data retention periods based on regulations and business needs to avoid unnecessary backups.

Optimizing backup strategies ensures efficient storage utilization, avoids unnecessary retention costs, and maintains essential data protection.

Leveraging Cloud Storage Reservations

Predictable workloads present an opportunity for significant cost savings through cloud storage reservations. By committing to a specific storage capacity for a defined period, you unlock substantial discounts compared to on-demand pricing. Carefully assess your predictable storage needs and consider these solutions:

- *Azure Blob Storage Reservations*: Ideal for unstructured data like media files, backups, and logs. If your data volume remains consistent, substantial savings on capacity charges can be achieved.

- *Azure Managed Disks*: Ideal for mission-critical applications demanding consistent performance and high availability. Reserved instances for Premium SSD disks offer significant discounts compared to on-demand pricing for predictable workloads.

- *Azure Elastic File System*: Ideal for shared file storage accessed by multiple applications or virtual machines. EFS reservations offer cost savings if your EFS throughput and IOPS requirements are predictable.

Retention Policies for Cost Management

Retention policies dictate data retention periods based on regulatory requirements and business needs, preventing unnecessary accumulation of outdated information. This is achieved through:

- *Eliminating unnecessary data*: To avoid accumulating outdated information and associated storage costs, define data retention periods.

- *Reducing S3 charges*: Automate deleting irrelevant data to free up valuable storage space and lower S3 expenses.

- *Using tiered storage for historical data*: Move rarely accessed but valuable data to lower-cost storage tiers like S3 Glacier, ensuring future accessibility while minimizing costs.

- *Simplifying data management*: Utilize automated solutions to eliminate manual deletion and migration tasks, guaranteeing consistent and efficient data retention.

Embracing proactive retention policies and smart tiering empowers you to balance readily available essential data and efficient disposal of obsolete information, fostering optimization in cost, data governance, and overall cloud storage management.

Data Archival and Lifecycle Management

Conceptualizing your cloud storage as a dynamic ecosystem rather than a static repository unlocks significant optimization opportunities. Data archival and lifecycle management come into play here, automatically organizing and optimizing your data based on its usage and value. This dynamic movement ensures

- *Optimal performance*: Frequently accessed data remains readily accessible, enhancing application responsiveness and user experience.

- *Cost optimization*: Moving rarely used data to cheaper tiers significantly reduces S3 expenses without compromising accessibility when needed.

- *Improved data governance*: Automated lifecycle management guarantees consistent application of data retention policies, fostering compliance and simplifying data management.

Tools like Amazon CloudWatch and Azure Storage Insights provide granular data usage insights, empowering you to define customized lifecycle rules based on access patterns and data age. This data-driven approach ensures your storage resources align with your needs, maximizing performance and cost savings. By leveraging these advanced techniques, you can transform your cloud storage strategy from a static cost center to a dynamic and optimized asset that fuels business growth.

Optimizing Cloud Monitoring and Logging Spend

Effective cloud monitoring and logging expense management is crucial for maintaining a cost-efficient cloud infrastructure. Organizations can achieve comprehensive monitoring and auditing capabilities by optimizing tools such as AWS CloudTrail and Amazon CloudWatch without incurring unnecessary costs. Here are some strategies for optimizing cloud monitoring and logging spend.

CloudTrail Cost Optimization

CloudTrail is an event audit tool that AWS offers customers. It allows businesses to monitor and record events/actions within their AWS accounts for risk and compliance audits. Although CloudTrail is necessary for auditing, compliance, and security purposes, optimizing its usage to control expenditures is critical.

Configuring the logs to contain the relevant details is one of the most important aspects of reducing costs with CloudTrail. CloudTrail logs can record extensive information about API calls, such as the payloads of both requests and responses. However, keeping such a high degree of detail might lead to larger log files, which results in higher storage expenses. Organizations can determine the required level of specificity in the logs after assessing their unique compliance and auditing requirements. Adjusting the log parameters to record only essential information makes it possible to cut storage costs while maintaining visibility and compliance.

CloudTrail's log retention duration can also be more efficiently managed, which is another technique for reducing operational expenses. CloudTrail will keep a copy of your logs indefinitely by default, which may result in higher storage expenses than necessary. Compliance standards and functional requirements should be considered when determining an organization's appropriate log retention time. For instance, if compliance regulations require storing logs for a particular length of time, enterprises can define the retention term accordingly. Optimizing CloudTrail storage costs can be accomplished by performing routine maintenance on log retention settings, including reviewing and modifying them as necessary.

In addition, businesses may use S3 lifetime policies to reduce CloudTrail expenses further. After a predetermined amount of time, companies are granted the ability, through S3 lifecycle policies, to migrate CloudTrail logs to lower-cost storage classes such as Glacier or Glacier Deep Archive. Organizations can achieve considerable cost reductions while still meeting compliance and retention requirements by transferring logs to storage classes at reduced costs. However, retrieval times and associated costs must be considered when utilizing archival data storage, because accessing the logs may incur additional expenses.

Monitoring and analyzing CloudTrail usage and costs is essential in cost optimization. Organizations can monitor CloudTrail costs thanks to AWS cost allocation tags and thorough billing reports. By frequently analyzing these reports and recognizing any unexpected or odd consumption trends, organizations can take remedial actions to control expenditures successfully. This includes modifying log settings or optimizing storage allocation.

Integrating CloudTrail with Amazon CloudWatch allows enterprises to set up alarms and notifications based on certain log events, which assists these organizations in identifying and responding to crucial events in real time. This connection helps to optimize costs by enabling proactive monitoring of CloudTrail activities and decreasing the risk of needless log production or storage. It also allows proactive CloudTrail operations monitoring.

In addition, businesses can use AWS Trusted Advisor, which offers advice on improving the efficiency of AWS resources such as CloudTrail. Trusted Advisor recommends cost-effectively optimizing CloudTrail, such as locating redundant trails or unencrypted log files. By implementing these guidelines, businesses can reduce wasteful spending and improve CloudTrail utilization effectiveness.

CloudWatch Optimization

Amazon CloudWatch is a comprehensive monitoring and observation service that enables businesses to collect and analyze metrics, logs, and events from various AWS resources and applications. CloudWatch is a potent tool for monitoring and troubleshooting, but optimizing how it is used is essential to keep costs under control.

Choosing the correct level of metric granularity is an essential component in the whole process of CloudWatch cost optimization. CloudWatch collects metrics at different granularities, from one-minute to one-second intervals. CloudWatch gathers metrics at one-minute intervals by default; however, businesses can modify the data's granularity based on their operations' specific monitoring needs. When the granularity is increased to a higher frequency, the collected data points also grow, as can the associated expenses. Therefore, for companies to guarantee that they are gathering metrics at the appropriate level of granularity, they need to analyze the trade-off between real-time monitoring requirements and related expenses.

Efficiently managing log retention periods can be another technique for reducing CloudWatch costs. CloudWatch Logs allows companies to save and examine the logs produced by various AWS services and applications. CloudWatch will keep a copy of your records indefinitely by default, which may incur additional storage costs. Compliance standards, operational needs, and analysis requirements should all be considered when determining an organization's proper log retention duration. Optimizing the storage costs associated with CloudWatch Logs can be accomplished by performing periodic reviews and adjusting the log retention parameters.

Using the sophisticated capabilities CloudWatch provides, such as metric filtering and anomaly detection, can also minimize costs. An organization can extract specific data from log events and construct custom metrics through metric filters, enabling more targeted monitoring. Enterprises can avoid gathering extraneous data and cut costs by defining detailed filters and concentrating on the most critical metrics. CloudWatch's anomaly detection features enable the automatic identification of strange behavior in measurements, which can assist companies in detecting and reacting to significant occurrences. Anomaly detection allows firms to proactively monitor and troubleshoot problems, potentially cutting expenses associated with protracted events or downtime.

Consolidating and centralizing an organization's CloudWatch resources is another cost-cutting measure businesses should investigate. It may be more cost-effective to consolidate a user's CloudWatch resources into a single AWS account or region rather than creating individual CloudWatch resources for each AWS account or region. Some benefits of centralization are eliminating redundancies, increased visibility throughout the entire business, and better management of CloudWatch resources.

It is essential to the cost optimization process to conduct periodic reviews of CloudWatch utilization and associated expenditures. Organizations can monitor CloudWatch spending because of AWS's thorough billing reports and usage analytics, which are provided regularly. By analyzing these data, firms can recognize any unexpected or excessive usage patterns, enabling them to take remedial actions and maximize cost efficiency. It is essential to analyze and fine-tune the alarm configurations to avoid unwanted alarm triggers and the expenditures that come with them.

Integrating CloudWatch with other AWS services, such as AWS Budgets and Cost Explorer, increases visibility and control over AWS expenses. AWS Budgets enables businesses to establish cost thresholds and receive notifications when preset costs exceed those thresholds. This preventative approach enables companies to control CloudWatch expenditures quickly. AWS Cost Explorer offers enterprises the ability to obtain insights into cost patterns, find possibilities for cost savings, and make decisions based on accurate information by providing cost analysis and forecasting tools.

Optimizing Cloud Networking Spend

Although pay-as-you-go cloud networking offers unmatched scalability and flexibility, it can also result in unforeseen expenses. To optimize your cloud network spend, you need a multifaceted strategy centered on data transmission, traffic patterns, and resource use.

One significant cost contributor is data transfer between instances, regions, and the Internet. Using Amazon VPC Traffic Mirroring in this situation can be beneficial. By making a copy of your network traffic, you can discover opportunities for optimization and obtain meaningful insights into data flows. This may highlight possibilities for consolidating workloads inside the same Availability Zone (AZ) to reduce inter-AZ data transmission costs. To reduce egress costs further, consider utilizing AWS PrivateLink to link your VPC directly to AWS services rather than via the public Internet.

Scrutinizing traffic patterns is another key strategy. Analyze your network traffic to understand peak usage periods and identify unnecessary network activity. Bursting to larger instance types during peak hours can be more cost-effective than running constantly oversized instances. Similarly, consider reserved instances for predictable workloads—securing a fixed rate for a specific capacity over a defined timeframe. This can significantly reduce costs compared to on-demand pricing for consistent network traffic.

Finally, optimizing resource utilization plays a crucial role. Use CloudWatch network metrics to identify idle or underutilized resources like Internet and NAT gateways. Rightsizing your resources to align with usage can lead to substantial cost savings. Consider automated scaling solutions to adjust resources dynamically based on real-time network traffic demands.

By implementing these strategies and leveraging the insights from traffic analysis, you can transform your cloud network from a cost center to a cost-effective and optimized asset that supports your business needs.

Gamifying the Cloud Cost Challenge: Fostering Engagement and Collaboration

Traditionally, optimizing cloud costs can be a complex and potentially tedious undertaking. Here's where gamification steps in, transforming cost management into an engaging and collaborative experience. *Gamification* is the art of incorporating game-like elements into non-game contexts such as FinOps practices to make them more interactive and motivating. This approach fosters a positive cultural shift, encouraging teams across engineering, finance, and product departments to participate actively.

Why gamify FinOps? Gamification offers a multitude of benefits. It can educate teams on best practices and process improvements, driving collaboration and sparking healthy competition between departments. This playful approach not only motivates desired behaviors but also provides a fun alternative to traditional KPI tracking. By implementing gamified elements like leaderboards, short-term incentive programs, and team rewards, organizations can accelerate FinOps adoption, shorten the ROI timeline, and ultimately achieve significant cost savings. Remember, effective gamification hinges on well-designed incentives and a strategic timeline. Short, impactful rewards sustain engagement, while aligning the incentive structure with business objectives ensures impactful results. Find the right frequency that complements your overall goals and avoid overwhelming participants with constant incentives. By strategically incorporating gamification into your FinOps strategy, you can transform a potentially daunting task into a collaborative and rewarding journey toward cloud cost optimization.

The Sustainability Aspect

Investors' and consumers' interests are changing, giving environmental responsibility more weight. Companies are waking up to this change and looking for proactive measures to reduce their ecological footprint and become more sustainable.

Relationship Between Cost and Sustainability Optimization Under FinOps

Managing Cloud FinOps is essential to maximizing cloud utilization for environmental sustainability and cost-effectiveness. By managing cloud resources, businesses can decrease wasted energy and reduce their carbon footprint. This is advantageous for the environment and consistent with the increasing emphasis on corporate social responsibility.

225

Sustainability and Cloud Computing

The Environmental Benefits of Cloud Computing

Cloud computing can have a significantly lower environmental impact than on-premises IT infrastructure. The following are the benefits:

- *Economies of scale*: Cloud providers leverage economies of scale by operating massive, centralized data centers. This allows them to consolidate servers and implement energy-efficient cooling systems, significantly improving overall energy efficiency.

- *Adoption of renewable energy*: Cloud companies can switch to renewable energy sources like solar or wind power for their data centers, lowering their reliance on fossil fuels and cutting greenhouse gas emissions.

The Carbon Footprint of Inefficient Cloud Use

In optimizing cloud costs and resource utilization, it is essential to recognize the environmental impact of inefficient cloud use. Overprovisioned resources, idle instances, and unnecessary data storage lead to higher expenses and contribute significantly to energy consumption and greenhouse gas emissions. Understanding the carbon footprint associated with inefficient cloud use underscores the importance of adopting best practices for resource management and sustainability. By addressing these inefficiencies, organizations can reduce their environmental impact, align with corporate social responsibility goals, and contribute to a greener future.

The reason is as follows:

- *Wasted resources = wasted energy*: Inefficient cloud use, such as overprovisioned resources or idle instances, leads to wasted energy consumption. Cloud resources require constant power, and unnecessary resources contribute to greenhouse gas emissions even if the provider uses renewable energy sources.

- *Embodied emissions*: These are emissions produced by the construction, delivery, and utilization of tangible IT infrastructure. Even while cloud computing can lessen the requirement for hardware onsite, the cloud provider's data centers are nonetheless linked to embodied emissions.

Key takeaway: While cloud computing has environmental advantages, achieving those advantages necessitates optimal cloud resource utilization. By limiting resource waste, businesses can lower their carbon footprint related to energy use and embodied emissions.

Measuring and Reporting Cloud Sustainability

Key Sustainability Metrics

Evaluating your cloud footprint requires a data-driven approach. Here, we delve into critical sustainability metrics that tech experts should consider.

These are key metrics for energy efficiency:

- *Power Utilization Efficiency (PUE)*: Measures a data center's efficiency. It is computed by dividing the energy consumed for IT equipment by the facility's total energy consumption. A lower PUE indicates greater efficiency.

- *Energy Efficiency Ratio (EER)*: Quantifies a data center's ability to cool itself. It shows the cooling capacity (measured in watts) divided by the power input (measured in watts). Higher EER values correspond to more effective cooling.

- *Carbon Use Effectiveness (CUE)*: An extension of PUE, considers the carbon emissions related to the data center's overall energy use. A lower CUE indicates a lesser carbon footprint.

The following metrics inform you how the underlying infrastructure powering your cloud workloads affects the environment. By monitoring them, you may pinpoint areas for development and enhance the energy efficiency of your cloud environment.

- *Renewable Energy Usage*: Shows what proportion of the data center's power comes from renewable energy sources like solar, wind, or hydropower. A larger proportion denotes a more sustainable cloud environment. Knowing how dependent your cloud provider is on renewable energy sources can help you evaluate how your cloud usage affects the environment.

- *Carbon Intensity*: Shows how many grams of CO2 equivalent are released for every kWh of power consumed. A lower carbon intensity indicates a data center powered by a greener energy mix. You can calculate the overall carbon footprint related to your use of cloud resources by calculating carbon intensity.

Cloud Service Provider Sustainability Reporting

Cloud service providers frequently release sustainability reports to demonstrate their dedication to environmental responsibility. These reports are essential for helping companies assess how their cloud deployments affect the environment.

Sustainability reports typically contain information on the following:

- *Renewable energy utilized*: The CSP provides information about the percentage of renewable energy utilized to power data centers, provided by the source of renewable energy.

- *Energy efficiency initiatives*: The CSP details its use of technologies and strategies to increase the efficiency of data centers, such as server consolidation and the usage of water-cooling systems.

- *Efforts to reduce carbon footprint*: The CSP describes its measures to reduce its overall carbon footprint (e.g., investments in clean energy infrastructure, carbon offset programs).

- *Sustainability certifications*: The CSP lists third-party certifications (like LEED certification) that it has obtained that attest to its compliance with particular environmental requirements.

Tech professionals who analyze these reports attentively might choose cloud providers that support the sustainability objectives of their company.

Sustainable FinOps Practices

Sustainable FinOps goes beyond cost optimization; it emphasizes practices that minimize environmental impact alongside financial efficiency. Here, we explore key resource optimization techniques that directly reduce energy consumption and emissions.

Resource Optimization Techniques

The following resource optimization techniques reduce cloud costs and contribute significantly to a lower carbon footprint for your cloud operations:

- *Aligning Cloud Resources with Business Demands*: Ensure the amount of your cloud resources (such as virtual machines and containers) corresponds to your business's demands. Overprovisioning results in needless energy use and resource waste. Use tools like cloud provider monitoring services and cost management systems to find underutilized or idle resources for downsizing.

- *Taking advantage of automation and autoscaling*: Automate the provisioning and scaling of resources in response to variations in the workload in real time. Autoscaling ensures maximum resource use and minimizes energy loss from idle resources by automatically adjusting resources (up or down) depending on predefined thresholds.

- *Server consolidation and virtualization*: Workloads should be consolidated onto fewer physical servers, and virtualization technologies should be used to generate several VMs on a single physical server. This improves energy efficiency by lowering the number of physical servers that need to be powered and cooled.

- *Effective management of storage and data:* Adopt data lifecycle management techniques for efficient storage and data management. Archive dormant data to more affordable, low-power storage tiers. Regularly purge unnecessary or outdated data to reduce the space used up in storage and the energy it uses.

Selecting Green Cloud Service Providers

Numerous cloud service providers provide "green" cloud services fueled by hydro, wind, and solar energy. Choosing a green cloud provider is strongly related to a business's sustainability objectives. Businesses can drastically lessen the environmental effect of their cloud installations by selecting providers that measurably increase their use of renewable energy.

Significance of Sustainability

FinOps methods enable the integration of cloud economics and corporate social responsibility. A sustainable FinOps strategy can save businesses money and lessen their environmental impact. Optimizing cloud resource use decreases the embodied emissions related to data center infrastructure and reduces wasted energy consumption.

This dedication to sustainability extends beyond personal gain. Businesses that emphasize sustainable cloud operations stand to benefit. Investors and eco-aware consumers are increasingly drawn to companies that practice environmental responsibility. In today's market, sustainable FinOps practices can make a significant difference.

By adopting sustainable FinOps methods, tech professionals can guarantee that their cloud installations are financially sound and ecologically responsible, helping to create a greener future.

Pro Tip   Leverage cloud-based sustainability dashboards and carbon emissions reporting. Major CSPs like AWS, Azure, and GCP offer tools to estimate, monitor, and reduce your cloud carbon footprint. For example, the AWS Carbon Footprint Dashboard shows emission rates by service and region. Google Cloud Carbon Footprint Reporting details Scope 1, 2, and 3 emissions. Use these built-in sustainability insights to optimize workloads, rightsize resources, consolidate servers, and purchase carbon offsets when needed. CSPs have done the heavy lifting by providing carbon visibility—take advantage of it to make informed green decisions.

Chapter Summary

This chapter presented various cost optimization methods and tactics for the cloud economy.

Organizations can find opportunities to optimize their compute costs by

- Using tools provided by CSPs
- Leveraging cost optimization recommendations for Kubernetes/containers

- Rightsizing based on usage metrics

- Upgrading to the current generation compute

- Capitalizing on committed spend/usage discounts

- Utilizing the cheapest spot instances

- Autoscaling

Organizations can also find opportunities to optimize their storage costs by

- Migrating from AWS EBS GP2 to GP3

- Using S3 cost optimization

Organizations can also find opportunities to optimize cloud spending on monitoring and logging through

- CloudTrail optimization

- Cloud Watch optimization

We highlighted the importance of cost optimization in

- Enhancing operational effectiveness

- Driving financial viability

Organizations can learn about their spending habits and find savings by using tools like:

- AWS Trusted Advisor

- Azure Advisor Cost Recommendations

- GCP Active Assist Recommendations

- OpenCost recommendations for containers

AWS Compute Optimizer recommends optimal instance types/sizes by analyzing consumption patterns. This balances performance and cost.

We also discussed prioritizing opportunities with high return on investment and minimal effort, and the concept of gamifying cloud cost optimization to foster collaboration.

Finally, we discussed sustainability and its importance. Integrating cloud economics and sustainability can save a lot of energy and lessen their environmental impact by empowering engineers with sustainability. This allows organizations to maximize reductions and efficiently utilize resources.

In Chapter 7, we transition to the topic of *automation*, which is essential to achieving cost efficiency. Chapter 7 examines how automation can help to improve and streamline cost optimization operations. We'll detail how automating resource provisioning, scalability, and cost management operations may help businesses achieve continuous optimization and eliminate human inefficiencies.

References for Further Reading

https://www.crayon.com/us/resources/blogs/how-cloud-economics-is-paving-the-way-for-cost-optimization/

https://www.argonaut.dev/blog/kubernetes-cost-optimization-tools

https://modeone.io/blogs/five-tips-to-optimize-and-reduce-cloud-costs/

https://towardsaws.com/aws-cloud-cost-optimization-with-minimal-no-effort-ditch-your-old-gen-ec2s-benchmarking-info-a7edbe9e8a40

https://www.perfectscale.io/blog/kubernetes-cost-optimization-what-could-go-wrong

https://cloudfix.aurea.com/blog/migrate-gp2-to-gp3-better-performance-lower-costs/

https://devtron.ai/blog/introduction-to-kubernetes-event-driven-autoscaling-keda/

https://www.osam.io/post/comparison-between-savings-plans-and-reserved-instances

CHAPTER 7

Automation

Imagine your smart home packed with amazing features, but managing everything manually can be a chore. Implementing automation tools in your cloud environment is like installing smart features throughout your home to streamline processes and optimize energy usage (costs!).

Just like manually turning off lights or adjusting thermostats can be time-consuming and lead to wasted energy, relying solely on manual cloud resource management can be inefficient and expensive. Automation empowers your cloud environment to run more smoothly and cost-effectively.

This chapter explores how you can implement automation tools across various aspects of your FinOps strategy to create a truly "smart" cloud environment.

Automation Overview

In the fast-developing fields of cloud economics/FinOps, the ability to plan and scale operations effectively is necessary for businesses that want to make the most of their resources. Automation is a highly effective technique that makes this possible. Automating manual chores and implementing intelligent cloud cost management (CCM) technologies can streamline company operations, save time and money, and ensure a clean and optimized cloud environment.

It is impossible to overestimate the significance of automation in FinOps/cloud economics. Manually tackling tasks such as provisioning cloud resources and subsequent cleanup of resources no longer in use wastes valuable time and exposes engineers to the possibility of making costly mistakes. Automation provides a dependable and consistent method of handling these duties and frees up essential resources for more strategic activities.

© Sasi Kanumuri, Matthew Zeier 2024
S. Kanumuri and M. Zeier, *Scaling Cloud FinOps*, https://doi.org/10.1007/979-8-8688-0388-8_7

One of the most significant advantages of automation is that it reduces cloud expenses. By implementing automated cleaning systems, organizations can eliminate unused cloud resources that have gone unnoticed, resulting in excessive cloud charges. Automation enables developers to operate productively in settings that are not production-ready through intelligent guardrails and constraints, which also provide responsible resource management and ownership.

As an example of the waste and inefficiency of manual resource management and the subsequent cleanup procedures, consider the case of a hypergrowth security firm that collaborated with cross-functional teams consisting of over 100 engineers to clean up wasted cloud resources. Cleaning up only approximately 10% of the firm's unused cloud resources took over 45 days. This experience highlighted the difficulties and inefficiencies connected with resources provisioned manually and the urgent need for automated methods to perform cleanup.

Within the automation sphere, organizations can take specific steps to maximize cloud resource efficiency and reduce associated expenses. Organizations can clean their cloud infrastructure by deleting waste in regions where business operations are no longer active. Implementing scripts can target resources that have not been tagged or orphaned and halt instances that have been dormant for a lengthy period.

Another essential benefit of automation is that it optimizes and cuts cloud costs in ways that aren't possible via manual efforts. Businesses can significantly reduce cloud spending by shutting down non-production instances outside business hours and scaling down service pods to zero. In addition, actions such as automatically finding and eradicating obsolete images, database backups, and disk snapshots, as well as migrating S3 buckets to Glacier storage after a predetermined amount of time, all contribute further to efforts to optimize costs.

In addition to resource management and cost optimization, automation is essential in incident response to cost spikes. Relying on dashboards or scheduled reports to spot cost anomalies is neither scalable nor timely, and if cost spikes are not caught and addressed quickly, they could result in tens of thousands of dollars in excess cloud spending. It is vital to have an event management system that treats cost increases as occurrences that demand prompt attention and resolution.

This chapter investigates several automation dimensions within the FinOps/cloud economics framework. Automation enables businesses to construct and grow operations more effectively by streamlining various business processes. These processes include resource management and cleanup, cost optimization, and implementing incident response frameworks. Businesses have a better chance of succeeding in the ever-changing world of cloud computing if they invest in developing specialized automation tools and foster a culture emphasizing cost ownership and awareness.

Balancing Automation with Developer Flexibility

Organizations that want to improve their cloud operations have a complex and vital challenge: balancing the requirement for developer flexibility in non-production environments and the necessity for automated cleanup processes. On the one hand, developers working in pre-production environments need the liberty to experiment, create, and swiftly iterate to support agile development processes and encourage innovation. On the other hand, the absence of efficient automated cleanup processes can result in the spread of unused resources, increased expenses, and possible vulnerabilities to security.

The necessity of allowing developers some degree of freedom in pre-production settings may be traced back to several important considerations. Before new features, code updates, or configurations are introduced into production, they are tested in pre-production environments to ensure they function correctly. Developers rely on these environments to simulate production-like conditions, evaluate the impact of code modifications, and guarantee the program's reliability. Consequently, the capacity to quickly set up and take down resources is an essential component of productive development workflows.

On the other hand, automated cleanup methods are essential to keeping a cloud environment clean and optimal. Without these processes, resources that are no longer required or have been forgotten can be amassed, leading to "cloud waste." This waste involves unneeded funds on underused services, orphaned storage, and idle instances. Over time, the gradual accumulation of these resources can result in enormous expenditures, reducing the potential benefits of adopting the cloud.

The key to achieving the optimal balance lies in organizations implementing intelligent automation catering to developer needs and resource efficiency. Here are some effective automated approaches, represented in Figure 7-1, to efficiently manage cloud resources.

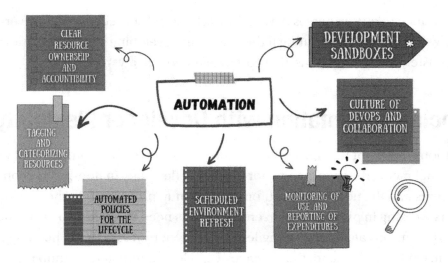

Figure 7-1. *Automation approaches for efficient cloud resource management*

- *Automated tagging and attribution*: Implementing a systematic tagging system and categorizing available resources can help gain visibility into resource consumption and ownership. When resources are tagged with the correct metadata, detecting unneeded resources and accepting automatic cleanup procedures is much simpler. As discussed in Chapter 2, tagging should be automated to tag all resources when provisioned for use automatically.

Pro Tip   Leverage "time to live" tags and lifecycle policies. Tag non-prod resources with a "TTL" key specifying days until automatic deletion. For example, ttl=3 would be deleted in 3 days—configure lifecycle policies to terminate resources past their TTL. Developers can spawn resources freely while automation cleans up stale ones based on time tags. This allows flexible self-service provisioning but limits sprawl. The TTL provides developers with clear expectations about resource lifespan. Start with a generous TTL, then tighten to balance flexibility and cost.

- *Automated resource ownership and accountability*: Clearly defining resource ownership and setting accountability for resource cleanup is one way to ensure that developers understand exactly what resources they are consuming. The "You build it, you clean it" approach encourages developers to constantly manage and clean up their resources by providing a financial incentive to their teams via automated spending reports and regular oversight reviews. While a necessary part of a strong FinOps practice, this approach should be combined with automation that finds and cleans up unused resources for the developers.

- *Automated policies for the lifecycle*: Businesses can enforce automated lifecycle policies using CSPs' technologies or develop automation scripts. Policy rules can be set up to schedule the deletion or shutdown of cloud resources after a certain amount of idle time (i.e., during which there has been no access to those resources). This helps to ensure that resources are not left running when they are not required to do so.

- *Automated scheduled environment refresh*: Organizations can schedule periodic refreshes/teardowns of cloud resources in sandbox accounts instead of operating them indefinitely. This reduces the risk of resource sprawl by ripping down the existing ecosystem and rebuilding it in a known, excellent state. This is easily automated using tools like Terraform to create new pre-production environments quickly.

- *Automated usage monitoring and cost reporting*: Automated cost reports and usage alerts give developers insights into their existing cloud resource usage and the impact of their actions on resource consumption in near real time. Automation takes this further by delivering reports at regular intervals or upon exceeding usage thresholds and integrating real-time cost dashboards directly into workflows. This transparency helps cultivate a sense of ownership and promotes prudent management of available resources.

- *Culture of DevOps and collaboration*: Fostering shared responsibility for resource management is made more accessible by promoting a culture of collaboration and communication among the DevOps community. Developers, operations teams, and other stakeholders can collaborate to optimally balance resource optimization and flexibility. Automated reporting, cleanup, and deployment tools provide the infrastructure for solid collaboration among teams.

- *Automated development workspace cleanup*: Reducing the disruption caused by shared non-production environments is possible by supplying developers with segregated sandboxes for experimentation and testing. Sandboxes may be subject to less stringent cleanup standards, while shared environments must adhere to more rigorous protocols.

Cost Optimization Through Automation

Automating cost-cutting processes is crucial for businesses that want to maximize resource consumption effectiveness while reducing cloud spending. Manual cost optimization techniques can be resource- and time-intensive depending on their complexity. Automation reduces manual intervention, resulting in more time and resource availability. It allows IT teams to concentrate on strategic initiatives and jobs with higher value rather than spending time on repetitive or mundane administrative cost management processes. Organizations can find opportunities to save money on costs, streamline operations, and obtain more control over cloud spending when they automate cost management activities.

Granular visibility into an organization's cloud resources and expenditure habits that can be gained through automation is a significant benefit. This feature allows real-time monitoring and tracking of resource utilization, cost allocation, and billing data. By utilizing automated tools and services for cost management, businesses can thoroughly understand their cloud-based expenditures and make decisions influenced by that understanding to achieve cost savings.

By continuously monitoring and analyzing resource utilization, automation makes it possible to take preventative measures that save money. Automated processes can detect underutilized resources, unused storage, idle instances, and wasteful load-balancing setups. Businesses can promptly improve resource allocation and cut unnecessary spending when these cost drivers are identified.

Automated cost optimization processes ensure that resources are provisioned and deprovisioned based on the level of demand currently being experienced. Companies can dynamically modify resource capacity by utilizing autoscaling techniques to match fluctuating workload levels. This elasticity helps resources be used to their full potential, reducing costs typically associated with over- or underprovisioning.

Automating governance processes helps businesses become more efficient at enforcing policies and meeting compliance standards. This improvement in efficiency is made possible by improved governance and compliance.

Pro Tip   Build a CI/CD pipeline for cost management. Treat FinOps like code by incorporating cost-efficiency sprints into your development lifecycle. Automate identification, surface savings opportunities, optimize self-service, and trigger policy enforcement. Schedule recurring cost scans—version control configurations and changes. With every build, you incrementally improve efficiency. Cost optimization becomes an automated, consistent practice rather than a one-off manual effort. CI/CD integrates governance, promotes collaboration, and sustains a culture of continuous cost improvement.

Best Practices for Minimizing Costs While Maximizing Automation Benefits

To help you automate your cloud cost savings, here are some best practices to consider:

- *Establish unambiguous objectives*: Clearly define your aims and goals to optimize your costs. Determining cost-saving targets, performance benchmarks, and critical metrics is crucial to measuring automation effectiveness. Align these goals with the broader business strategy and ensure key stakeholders are on board with the plan.

- *Implement cost management tools*: Utilize the cost management tools and services that CSPs provide that are unique to the cloud. These tools provide cost analysis, budgeting, allocation, and utilization analytics functions. Investigate whether or not the tools and services offered by third parties provide any additional functionalities or integrations suitable for the firm's needs.

- *Automate Monitoring and alerting*: Automated monitoring and alerting procedures are recommended to proactively discover cost anomalies or potential overspending. Establish benchmarks, warnings, and notifications if costs skyrocket, resources remain unused, or the spending limit is exceeded. Automated notifications allow quick action and help reduce the possibility of overruns.

- *Rightsize and optimize resources*: Employ automation techniques to examine resource utilization patterns and recommend rightsizing opportunities. Automated rightsizing examines the performance of the resources and makes recommendations concerning the instance types and configurations that are most suitable to meet the workload's needs while keeping costs to a minimum. Install automation processes to implement changes automatically.

- *Plans for reserved occurrences and financial savings*: Utilize automation to find opportunities to use Reserved Instances (RIs) or Savings Plans, then capitalize on those discoveries. Automated analysis can identify workloads with consistent demand patterns, allowing you to determine whether or not these workloads are candidates for cost reductions through upfront commitments. Purchases and renewals of reserved instances or savings plans should be automated to enable continual effective cost optimization.

- *Automated process of tagging and assigning costs*: Establish automated procedures to strictly regulate resource tagging and cost allocation. Correctly labeled resources make accurate cost attribution, tracking of cost centers, and improved visibility into cost drivers possible. Enforcing tagging policies and automating cost allocation processes can simplify chargebacks and increase cost accountability.

- *Review and make improvements at regular intervals*: The cost optimization process always continues. Review the cost optimization tactics regularly, evaluate automation efforts, and make necessary adjustments. Carry out regular audits, investigate cost trends, and assess the effect of automation on reducing costs and enhancing operational efficiency.

Challenges to Optimizing Costs Through Automation

Cloud environments can be complicated, often consisting of different services, regions, and accounts. Careful planning, integration of various tools and services, and resolution of interoperability difficulties are required to automate cost optimization across such environments.

Automated cost optimization systems need to consider the interdependencies and interactions of resources. When you modify one resource, it could affect other resources, disrupting essential services. Important things to consider when automating processes include ensuring your dependency mapping is accurate and handling potential adverse side effects.

Implementing automation tools, services, or bespoke scripts may involve one-time expenses; nevertheless, automation can result in cost savings over the long run. Companies must calculate their return on investment (ROI) and select cost-effective solutions tailored to their requirements and financial constraints.

Case Study: Improving Cost Savings by Moving from Manual to Automated Cleanup

In this case study, we explore the journey of a hypergrowth security firm transitioning from manual to automated cloud resource cleanup. This shift resulted in significant cost savings and enhanced operational efficiency and resource management. By addressing the limitations of manual cleanup and implementing robust automation strategies, the firm achieved sustainable cost reductions, improved visibility into resource utilization, and boosted overall productivity. The following sections detail the challenges faced, the solutions implemented, and the impressive outcomes of this transformative journey.

The Challenge: Manual Cleanup's Limitations

The security firm...

- *Rapid growth, untamed infrastructure*: We begin by examining the challenges faced by the security firm due to its rapid growth. This section will detail how manual resource provisioning led to a complex cloud environment with unoptimized resource utilization and "cloud waste."

- *Untagged resources, unclear costs*: This section will discuss the problems caused by untagged resources. The lack of a centralized tagging system made attributing costs to specific projects or teams difficult, requiring a significant manual effort from the FinOps team for cost attribution. Highlight the initial success of manual cleanup (e.g., $2 million saved) but emphasize its limitations for long-term scalability.

The Solution: Implementing Automated Cleanup Strategies

Recognizing the limitations of manual efforts, the security firm adopted an automated approach to resource cleanup by implementing the following strategies:

- *Policy framework for resource lifecycle*: Explain the establishment of a policy framework that defines clear rules for resource creation, tagging, and cleanup. Emphasize the importance of these policies in ensuring consistent practices and preventing resource sprawl.

- *Hierarchical tagging system*: Describe implementing a hierarchical tagging system for resource classification. Explain how this system facilitated easier identification and management of resources for cost attribution and automated cleanup.

- *Automation takes center stage*: Detail the investment in automation tools and custom scripts for resource cleanup. Explain how these tools identified unused resources based on tagging, activity levels, and predefined idle time limits. Describe the actions taken (deletion or archiving) to eliminate unnecessary storage usage and costs.

- *Education and open communication*: This section will highlight the importance of clear communication and collaboration during the transition. Explain the #Piggy-Bank Framework used to foster open communication about cloud costs. Describe the training workshops conducted to educate engineers about the new processes and the benefits of resource optimization. Mention the use of comprehensive documentation and transparent rules to empower developers regarding resource management.

The Results: Benefits of Automation

The transition to automated cleanup yielded the following significant advantages for the organization:

- *Sustainable cost savings*: Explain how the systematic identification and removal of redundant resources resulted in ongoing cost reductions, surpassing the initial manual cleanup efforts.

- *Enhanced visibility and cost attribution*: Describe the improved visibility gained by finance and operations teams into resource utilization and cost attribution. Highlight how this transparency enabled more accurate budgeting and financial planning.

- *Freed developers, boosted productivity*: Explain how automation lightened the workload for engineers by eliminating manual cleanup tasks. Emphasize how this freed-up time allowed developers to focus on core development activities, leading to increased productivity.

This case study demonstrates the power of automation in cloud resource management. By transitioning from manual to automated cleanup processes, the hypergrowth security firm achieved significant cost savings, improved visibility, and empowered its development teams. This case study highlights the importance of a well-defined policy framework, clear tagging structures, effective communication, and automation tools for achieving an optimized and cost-effective cloud environment.

Guidelines and Processes for Automated Cleanup

Automating any process is never as simple as *"create a script and turn it on."* There are always mitigating factors to consider to ensure the health of your environment and the continuity of your applications. Before leveraging any software automation to perform routine maintenance on cloud resources, your FinOps team needs to define the procedures and parameters for the tools or scripts that will automatically detect, eliminate, or optimize cloud resources that are active or idle.

The first challenge to be addressed is that accurately identifying idle or redundant resources can be difficult, especially in dynamic and complicated cloud systems. To guarantee resource identification and classification, dependable procedures for tagging and monitoring must be established, preferably by automating tagging as part of your CI/CD pipeline tooling.

When implementing automatic resource cleanup, organizations need to consider resource dependencies and interactions. If you delete a resource without considering how other services or systems use it, your production applications may be disrupted or have unforeseen repercussions. Organizations must construct accurate dependency mappings and perform cleanup procedures.

Finding the optimal balance between automated cleaning methods and conserving resources can be challenging. Organizations must define policies and controls to prevent removing vital resources or accidentally disrupting operational procedures. Granular control is necessary to guarantee that only resources no longer needed or used will be withdrawn.

Guidelines for the Most Effective Automated Cleanup Methods

The most effective automated cleanup methods include the following:

- *Define cleanup policies*: Consider the organization's requirements and create well-defined policies and procedures to clean up resources. Define the criteria to identify unused resources, such as inactive instances, detached volumes, or outdated snapshots. These policies should follow cost optimization and general resource management strategies.

- *Implement tagging and monitoring*: Put comprehensive and consistent resource-tagging procedures into action. Information about the owner, the objective, the project, or the expiration date ought to be included on tags. Utilize monitoring tools and services to keep track of resource utilization and locate any resources not being used to their full potential.

- *Utilize scripts and other automation tools*: Implement resource-cleansing procedures using automation programs, scripts, and cloud-native applications. Infrastructure as code (IaC), configuration management tools, and serverless functions can automate resource identification and deletion operations.

- *Maintain a routine of review and auditing*: Ensure that automatic cleansing operations are effective by conducting evaluations and audits regularly. Verify that the correct resources have been identified, evaluate how the cleanup operations have affected the environment, and modify any policies or scripts as necessary.

- *Considerations for backing up and restoring data*: Ensure adequate backup and recovery measures are in place before removing resources. It is essential to safeguard the availability and integrity of data by creating backups or snapshots of vital resources in case data is accidentally deleted or other unforeseen events occur.

- *Ensure collaboration and communication*: Participation from key stakeholders, including the development, operations, and finance teams, is essential to the success of automated cleanup procedures. Maintaining transparency by communicating the goals, policies, and status of the cleanup activities is critical to preventing any unintentional disruptions that may occur.

Automate Instance Type Restriction Enforcement

When deciding between performance and cost when provisioning compute resources, engineers often provision higher-performing (and more costly) resources than needed without controls to keep them in check. Usually, specific workloads or applications do not require or justify large instance types with terabytes of RAM or many GPUs. By automating the enforcement of instance types that can be provisioned, companies can ensure consistency across their cloud infrastructure and realize cost savings and cloud efficiencies.

Limiting large instance types offers significant performance benefits by preventing overprovisioning and promoting better alignment with workload requirements. By setting constraints, businesses can encourage the utilization of instance types that accurately match computing power, memory, and storage needs, thus avoiding unnecessary costs associated with excessive resource allocation. This approach optimizes workload performance and enhances cost-effectiveness by ensuring efficient resource utilization across various applications and workloads.

In addition to performance optimization, standardizing instance types contributes to consistency and cost efficiency within the infrastructure. Organizations can ensure uniform provisioning and simplify management processes by enforcing best practices and recommended instance types. Standardization facilitates easier monitoring and maintenance, reducing complexity and enabling more effective resource allocation. Furthermore, by limiting large instance types that deviate from established guidelines, organizations can leverage Reserved Instance Savings Plans and optimize cost savings through long-term commitments to specific instance types, ultimately enhancing return on investment in cloud infrastructure.

Implementing limitations on large instance types requires a systematic approach and careful consideration of many factors. To decide which instances are suitable for any use case, it is crucial to comprehensively analyze the workload requirements and performance expectations for the use case in question. Business stakeholders, application owners, and IT teams must collaborate to align resource allocation decisions with the business's objectives. A combination of policies, automated inspections, and governance frameworks can successfully implement these limits. In addition, cloud provider service control policies can be used to limit the utilization of significant instance types. Depending on the circumstances, these types may need to be improved for the organization's infrastructure requirements. This allows administrators to govern resource allocation and ensures only suitable and cost-effective instance types are used. Organizations can reduce waste and improve cloud resource efficiency by prohibiting deploying huge instance types irrelevant to the underlying architecture.

Monitoring and analyzing instance-type utilization is imperative to comply with constraints continuously. Workload requirements and resource demands may shift over time, necessitating adjustments to the restrictions placed on the instance type. Organizations can optimize their costs and resource allocation based on changing workload characteristics and business requirements if these limits are periodically reviewed and adjusted.

Pro Tip   While enforcement should not cause trouble in most cases, there might be edge cases that could hinder developer productivity; for instance, when the team is testing a disaster recovery (DR) solution in a new region with a business operation, or a database team is working on a load-testing use case and requires a large DB for testing purposes.

When a specific use case arises, one should approach the cloud infrastructure/platform/governance team and request an exception. Appropriate documentation must be provided when a developer wants to use large instance types or new regions.

Enforce Region-Based Provisioning with Control Policies

Cloud regions offer advantages such as proximity to users for reduced latency, enhanced disaster recovery capabilities through redundancy, and compliance with data sovereignty regulations. However, provisioning resources outside approved regions poses challenges, including noncompliance with regulations, increased latency affecting performance, and complexities in managing resources across disparate locations, leading to higher costs and operational difficulties.

Each CSP provides control policy tools that enable FinOps teams to limit the creation of infrastructure to the most efficient and cost-effective regions for the business. Control policies allow administrators to specify fine-grained guardrails for accounts belonging to their organization and provide a granular level of control over those accounts. By using control policies, businesses can enforce governance and compliance requirements, lower the risk of misconfiguration, and optimize costs by limiting the production of unneeded resources in regions not utilized. While each cloud vendor has different naming conventions for these policies, for the sake of simplicity, we'll use the AWS term SCP, or service control policy, in this section.

Setting and strictly enforcing region-based limits is a significant advantage of utilizing SCPs. Organizations often tend to use cloud resource in specific geographical areas (regions) where they operate and serve their customers. SCPs enable administrators to establish policies restricting the production of infrastructure resources in regions that are not utilized by the business, effectively minimizing the inadvertent provisioning of resources in unoccupied zones and reducing associated expenses.

Administrators can tailor SCPs to meet their business's requirements, such as limiting resource generation to regions relevant to the organization's operations. Administrators can effectively mitigate the risk of provisioning unnecessary resources by designating required regions and optimizing resource allocation.

Implementing SCPs is another way enterprises can maintain their security posture. Limiting the locations where resources can be provisioned can decrease the attack surface, minimizing the number of potential entry points that can be exploited. This strategy adheres to the principle of least privilege, which ensures that resources are made available only in situations in which they are needed. By reducing the number of regions used, organizations also reduce the complexity of their infrastructure, making it easier to monitor and secure.

The business, IT, and security teams must successfully collaborate to implement SCPs for region-based restrictions. It is crucial to pinpoint the geographical areas pertinent to the organization's operations and check that the policies align with the overall business strategy. Policies must be developed in close collaboration with the parties involved to achieve an optimal balance between control and flexibility.

In addition, the SCPs must undergo routine evaluations and updates. If the company decides to broaden its activities or make other adjustments, the regions in which new infrastructure must be built can shift. The SCPs should be evaluated regularly so that organizations can make any necessary adjustments to ensure that the policies appropriately reflect the changing requirements of the business.

Pro Tip   Leverage SCP condition keys like `aws:RequestedRegion` to restrict resource creation. This allows resources to be allocated to approved regions. Combine with identity and access management (IAM) permissions for robust, targeted control. Automate SCP deployment and updates using AWS Organizations APIs. Schedule periodic SCP reviews to align with business needs. Restrictive yet flexible SCPs prevent resource sprawl, improve governance, and optimize costs.

Case Study: Automating Cloud Cost Optimization Through Collaboration and Guardrails

This case study explores a successful cross-functional team effort to automate cloud cost optimization and implement guardrails. It highlights the challenges of manual cleanup and the benefits of collaboration between engineers, financial professionals, operations, and executives.

Challenges

As the company's cloud infrastructure rapidly grew, so did the associated costs, highlighting the need for improved financial management and efficient resource utilization.

- Rapid cloud infrastructure growth led to increased costs and a need for improved financial management.

- Determining who owned untagged and idle resources among over 50 engineers in different teams was laborious, time consuming, and not scalable.

Solutions

A cross-functional team was formed to address the escalating costs and inefficiencies, combining expertise from engineering, finance, operations, and management to tackle the problem comprehensively.

- *Cross-functional team*: A team consisting of individuals from engineering, finance, operations, and management was assembled to address the issue comprehensively.

- *Data analysis*: Examining cost allocation tags, trends, and over- or underprovisioned resource identification.

- *Phased cleanup*: Prioritizing high-impact areas and taking steps like removal, resizing, or rightsizing resources.

- *Guardrails with SCPs*: Limiting infrastructure deployment to relevant regions and restricting resource types to prevent overprovisioning.

- *Automation*: Developing scripts and workflows to automate resource identification and cleanup for ongoing optimization.

Results

The collaborative effort led to a significant cost reduction of approximately 10% within a month and a half, while establishing a foundation for sustainable cost management and resource optimization.

- Significant cost reduction (approximately 10%) achieved within a month and a half.

- Established a foundation for long-term cost management through guardrails and optimized resource utilization.

- Fostered a culture of accountability and ownership for cloud expenses.

Impact

This case study underscores the effectiveness of cross-departmental collaboration in cloud cost optimization, the scalability benefits of automation, and the importance of implementing guardrails to maintain long-term financial efficiency and responsible resource usage.

- Demonstrates the effectiveness of collaboration across various departments in cloud cost optimization.

- Highlights the value of automation in scaling cleanup efforts and reducing manual intervention.

- Shows how guardrails can prevent future cost increases and promote responsible resource usage.

This case study offers a useful road map for businesses looking to optimize cloud costs. Organizations may achieve substantial cost savings and create a solid foundation for cloud financial management by taking a cooperative approach, leveraging data analysis, implementing guardrails, and automating cleanup procedures.

Idle Resource Pruning Automation

The process of locating idle resources and taking corrective action is greatly aided by automation. Once firms have identified unused resources, they can implement automation measures to maximize resource utilization.

Automation Mechanisms for Efficient Resource Management

Implementing scheduling mechanisms, autoscaling, lifecycle policies, and DevOps principles can significantly reduce cloud waste and optimize resource utilization. By leveraging cost optimization tools and automation scripts, organizations can ensure that their cloud infrastructure operates efficiently and cost-effectively.

- *Scheduling and autoscaling*: One of the most effective ways to cut waste is to implement scheduling mechanisms that turn off or reallocate resources outside of regular business hours or during times of low demand. Autoscaling allows dynamic resource capacity adjustment in response to changes in workload. This method ensures that resources are scaled up when required and scaled back when not in use.

- *Lifecycle policies and resource expiry*: Defining lifecycle policies and expiry rules for resources, such as storage volumes or databases, can cause unused resources to be deleted or archived automatically after a predetermined time. This helps prevent unnecessary costs associated with resources no longer required, which is a benefit.

- *DevOps principles*: Adopting DevOps principles such as infrastructure as code (IaC) might make it easier to automate the process of provisioning and deprovisioning resources in response to changes in actual demand. Considering infrastructure as code enables tracking resource lifecycles, versioning, and automating those lifecycles.

- *Cost optimization tools and scripts*: Using cost optimization tools and scripts can automate identifying idle resources and taking corrective action about those resources. These tools can assess resource consumption patterns, make optimization recommendations, and even automatically implement optimization measures based on rules and regulations set.

251

Automated Optimization Ideas to Remove Waste

To effectively manage cloud resources and minimize waste, consider implementing the following automated optimization strategies:

- Ensure unattached disks are pruned regularly with automation, avoiding block storage waste. Write serverless functions to automate the process. Consider pruning these unattached disks by creating snapshots. This would enable engineering teams to build a volume from the snapshot if needed later.

- Prune older snapshots on disks, databases, and data warehouses according to your data retention policies, and ensure the process is automated to prevent snapshots from piling up.

- Ensure object storage has lifecycle policies turned on that move the data across storage classes automatically.

- Remove public IP addresses unattached to compute/network resources.

- Prune idle cloud resources in regions where business does not operate.

- Prune unused/idle load balancers and gateways.

- Identify unused compute and databases with no connections and usage. Confirm and communicate widely before you prune these, to have smoother flow with teams.

Pro Tip   Leverage cloud-native tools for optimizing resource utilization. Most CSPs offer services to help analyze usage patterns, detect idle resources, and even automate the scaling or shutdown of unused resources. For example, AWS offers Trusted Advisor to flag idle and underutilized resources. Azure has Advisor and Cost Management tools. Google Cloud has a Recommender. Leverage these built-in cloud optimization tools before looking at third-party solutions. They provide visibility into waste and easy remediation capabilities that integrate seamlessly with the provider's infrastructure. Combining native instruments with automation through IaC can optimize resource usage and significantly cut waste.

Automated Shutdown of Non-Production Resources During Off-Hours

In today's global environment, many organization's production applications are often in use 24×7 to service the needs of their global customer base. However, the same is not the case for non-production environments. Turning off resources not used in production when the engineers are not working is an efficient way to cut cloud costs and improve margins.

Strategies and Benefits of Automated Shutdown

Organizations can achieve significant cost savings by efficiently managing non-production resources, such as development, testing, staging, or sandbox environments, outside regular business hours. Cloud resources are typically priced based on usage, and leaving instances running during idle periods can incur unnecessary costs.

Organizations can prevent wasteful spending and optimize their cloud expenditures by configuring systems to automatically shut down these resources when they're not in use. This strategy cuts expenditures without sacrificing productivity and allows for better resource allocation.

Also, halting cloud resources when not in use contributes to sustainability and environmental preservation. Organizations can lessen their environmental impact by cutting power to unused resources and contributing to energy conservation. It conforms to the principles of responsible cloud usage, where resources should be distributed effectively to minimize waste.

Implementing this strategy requires automated scheduling procedures, which cannot be accomplished manually across a large organization. Cloud service providers provide the tools and services necessary to build automated workflows to control the stop and start of non-production cloud resources following defined schedules. For instance, Amazon Web Services offers AWS Lambda, AWS CloudWatch Events, and AWS Systems Manager Automation services. By using these tools, businesses can guarantee that non-production resources are reliably turned off outside of regular business hours.

Your FinOps team needs to carefully prepare schedules for starting and stopping your non-production resources, considering factors such as developers' different time zones in remote regions, the needs of the business, and users' accessibility. For instance, the schedule should ensure that all resources are activated well before business hours to provide enough time for the system to boot up and be ready for access. Collaborating with many stakeholders, such as the development teams and the business units, is necessary to align schedules with operations requirements.

However, there can be circumstances in which specific resources need to be kept active outside of the typical hours of corporate operation. When defining and implementing the shutdown schedule, work with the cross-functional team to locate and accommodate exceptions. Organizations can ensure that essential resources are shielded from automatically shutting down by establishing clear criteria and communication channels.

This cost optimization technique must incorporate consistent monitoring and evaluation to achieve its goals. Resource usage patterns must be monitored, business requirements analyzed, and schedules modified as needed. Organizations should perform regular effectiveness reviews of their shut-off strategies and make necessary improvements to optimize cost savings while satisfying operational requirements.

Create Cron Jobs to Schedule Resource Shutdown

Cron jobs are time-based schedulers used in operating systems similar to Unix. They allow administrators to set repeating tasks or scripts to run at predetermined intervals after scheduling. In cloud infrastructures, cron jobs can trigger scripts or commands that cease or terminate non-production resources during non-business hours or periods of low activity. This can be done during intense activity or when business hours are not in session.

When companies schedule cron jobs to stop non-production resources, ensuring these resources do not consume compute resources or incur costs when they are not actively employed. Cron jobs help automate the process and stop these resources during non-business hours. This practice allows for detecting redundant non-production resources in systems with uniform consumption patterns.

Proper planning and collaboration are required to implement cron jobs to terminate non-production resources automatically. Businesses must determine the most appropriate schedule for stopping and beginning the available resources based on the company's needs and typical consumption patterns. Collaborating with the development teams, the stakeholders, and the business units is necessary to ensure that the scheduled downtime matches the operational demands and reduces any interruption to the greatest extent possible.

When implementing cron jobs, it is essential to consider any potential dependencies or repercussions on other workflows or systems that may arise. For instance, if there are interdependencies between environments not used for production and settings used for production, organizations need to ensure that suspending non-production resources not used for does not harm production systems or result in data loss to reduce the likelihood of potential hazards or adverse effects, proper coordination and testing is necessary.

Automation and scripting play vital roles when deploying cron jobs to suspend non-production resources automatically. Organizations can write scripts or use automation products already on the market to perform the API calls and commands necessary to halt resources. The APIs and command-line tools offered by CSPs can interact with resources programmatically and begin or stop operations.

Monitoring and validating cron jobs is imperative to ensure their efficiency and dependability. Monitoring the execution of cron jobs, ensuring that the resources are appropriately stopped or terminated, and swiftly addressing any faults or errors should be standard operating procedures for organizations. Regular auditing and reporting can track cost reductions through auto-stopping and provide insights for further optimizing the process.

Automated Postmortem and Incident Response to Cost Spikes

To effectively manage cloud expenses and keep cost-effectiveness at a high level, automated postmortem and incident response to cost spikes play an essential role. Having a well-defined process in place for when cost spikes occur allows the FinOps team to quickly identify the fundamental cause of the cost spike, mitigate the impact of the cost spike, and prevent future cost spikes. If cost spikes are not addressed swiftly, they could have significant financial ramifications to your organization, causing tens of thousands of dollars in wasted cloud spend. Automated postmortem and incident response systems enable firms to identify cost spikes more quickly, allowing organizations to respond promptly. A prompt response reduces cost overruns and their financial impact.

When companies respond to unexpected expense increases, they build a culture of accountability and ownership of costs. Automated incident response systems assign specific roles to evaluate cost spikes, determine their underlying causes, and take corrective steps. This will benefit the organization as it encourages proactive cost optimization.

Automated postmortem analysis and incident response allow businesses to continuously improve by applying lessons learned from cost spike situations. Organizations can implement measures to prevent similar future cost spikes if they first investigate the underlying causes and discover patterns or trends. This strategy is iterative and fosters ongoing progress in cost minimization.

Challenges to Address for Automated Postmortem and Incident Response Systems

To automate cost increases, efficient monitoring and warning mechanisms must be set up. Organizations must establish thresholds and triggers that identify aberrant expense trends. Accurate and timely notifications are also necessary to respond to incidents effectively.

Cloud infrastructures and interdependencies across resources might make pinpointing the underlying causes of unexpectedly high costs difficult. Automated incident response procedures must be capable of performing extensive analyses considering various parameters, including resource use, configuration changes, workload variations, and integrations with third parties.

Effective incident response requires the various teams to coordinate their efforts. Examples of these teams include finance, operations, and development. Automated incident response procedures make collaboration easier, streamline communication channels, and supply a centralized platform for exchanging facts and keeping others up to date.

Best Practices for Automated Postmortem Analysis and Incident Response

Automating and addressing unexpected cost spikes in your cloud spend is one of the most important activities your FinOps teams should address. Here are some best practices to get you started:

- *Define incident management process*: Establish a clearly defined incident management approach to deal with expense surges. Define severity levels, escalation channels, and reaction timeframes based on the financial impact of cost spikes. Ensure that all incident responders, including the FinOps team, application teams, and cloud infrastructure people, clearly explain their roles and duties.

- *Automated alerting and monitoring*: Install automatic monitoring and alerting systems that keep track of crucial cost parameters and notify the appropriate stakeholders whenever data surges. Utilize cloud-native cost management tools, anomaly detection algorithms, and bespoke scripts to proactively identify aberrant expense patterns and set alarms.

- *Automated workflows for responding to incidents*: During incident response, you should develop automated workflows that assist responders through investigation and mitigation steps. These workflows may involve assessing cost breakdowns, reviewing resource use, comparing current data versus historical data, and determining potential opportunities for cost optimization. Automate any remediation activities that need to be taken, such as reducing the size of large instances, terminating them, or optimizing resource configurations.

- *Data-driven analysis and reporting*: Using automated data analysis and reporting capabilities facilitates root cause analysis and postmortem investigations. Create reports highlighting the incidents that caused cost spikes, their impacts, and the steps to mitigate them. Employ data visualization approaches to make cost patterns, outliers, and cost-cutting suggestions more easily understandable to stakeholders.

- *Continuous improvement through learning and adjustment*: Incident data analysis should be performed continuously to provide conclusions and optimize costs. Utilize past incident data to determine the reasons for common cost spikes, implement preventative measures, and update cost optimization methods. Share your organization's successes and failures and the lessons you've learned to foster a culture of continual learning and progress.

Case Study: Proactive Cost Management with #Piggy-Bank and Incident Management Integration

This case study explores how Company X leveraged the #Piggy-Bank Framework and incident management integration to achieve proactive cost management in its cloud environment. As discussed in Chapter 5, the #Piggy-Bank Framework is a cost monitoring and alerting system that triggers incident responses for unexpected cost fluctuations.

Background:

As Company X's cloud infrastructure grew, cost management became increasingly crucial. Company X implemented the #Piggy-Bank Framework to monitor cloud cost changes daily and weekly.

Solution:

The key innovation involved integrating the #Piggy-Bank Framework with the existing incident management system. Any cost change exceeding 10% triggered a high-severity ('SEV1') incident alert, which ensured rapid investigation and resolution of cost anomalies.

Here's the breakdown of the triggered incident response process, represented in Figure 7-2:

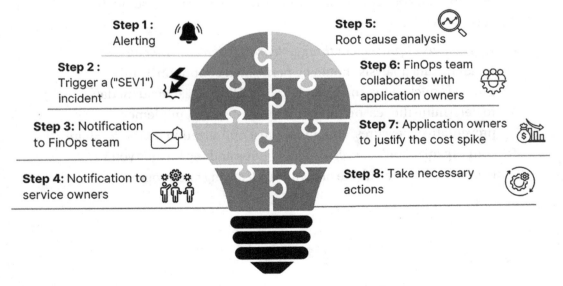

Step 1 : Alerting

Step 2 : Trigger a ("SEV1") incident

Step 3: Notification to FinOps team

Step 4: Notification to service owners

Step 5: Root cause analysis

Step 6: FinOps team collaborates with application owners

Step 7: Application owners to justify the cost spike

Step 8: Take necessary actions

Figure 7-2. *Incident response process for cost spike resolution*

1. Alerting. A cost change exceeding the threshold triggers an alert.

2. Trigger a ("SEV1") incident. The alert triggers a high-severity ("SEV1") incident within the incident management system.

3. Notification to the FinOps team. The incident management system automatically notifies the FinOps team of the cost anomaly.

4. Notification to service owners. The system also notifies the service owners (application owners) responsible for the resource experiencing the cost spike.

5. Root cause analysis. A collaborative investigation begins to identify the root cause of the cost fluctuation.

6. FinOps team collaborates with application owners. The FinOps team works with the application owners to diagnose the issue.

7. Application owners to justify the cost spike. The application owners investigate and explain the reason behind the cost increase.

8. Take necessary actions. Corrective actions are implemented based on the root cause to address the issue and prevent future occurrences.

Benefits:

- *Early detection*: Cost spikes or unexpected cost reductions were identified quickly, allowing for prompt investigation and corrective action.

- *Root cause analysis*: Incident alerts prompted engineers to identify the root cause of cost fluctuations. This could include

  - *Buggy code*: Escaped application bugs could lead to unexpected resource utilization and cost increases.

- *Misconfigurations*: Misconfigured autoscaling groups or Kubernetes deployments could cause inefficient resource allocation and higher costs.

- *Database inefficiency*: Inefficient SQL queries could lead to database overprovisioning and unnecessary scaling.

Results:

Integrating the #Piggy-Bank Framework and incident management system facilitated proactive cost management. This led to

- *Reduced cloud costs*: Early identification and mitigation of cost anomalies prevented unnecessary expenses.

- *Improved resource utilization*: Resource utilization was optimized by addressing the root causes of cost fluctuations.

- *Enhanced code quality*: Identifying buggy code led to code fixes and improved application performance.

This case study demonstrates the effectiveness of proactive cost management strategies. Company X achieved cost savings, improved resource utilization, and enhanced code quality within its cloud environment by integrating cost monitoring with incident management.

Slack Case Study: Automated Ad Hoc Cost Alerts into Slack Channels

Problem:

To monitor their cloud expenses, the engineering teams at Slack had to log into the CSP billing section manually and to view cloud costs and trends. This procedure was lengthy and opaque, making it challenging for teams to rapidly understand their spending patterns and pinpoint areas that could be optimized.

Solution:

A Slack application was developed to address this challenge and provide direct real-time cloud cost visibility within engineering team channels. This solution utilized tags assigned to cloud resources, allowing seamless linking between teams and associated costs.

Slack's App:

- *Integration*: The app integrates with the company's cloud billing data, retrieving cost information for specific teams based on resource tags.

- *Functionality*: Upon a user request through a simple command in their Slack channel, the app displays

    - Top-spending cloud services used by the team

    - Cost breakdown associated with relevant tags

    - Cost trends, including month-over-month (MoM), week-over-week (WoW), and quarter-over-quarter (QoQ) comparisons

- Benefits:

    - *Increased transparency*: Provides instant access to cost information within the familiar Slack interface

    - *Actionable insights*: Enables teams to identify cost drivers and optimize resource usage without navigating complex billing dashboards

    - *Improved collaboration*: Fosters discussions and shared understanding of cloud spending across teams

- *Results*: The Slack cost-monitoring bot has empowered engineering teams with real-time cost visibility:

    - *Reduced time spent*: Eliminates manual logins to the CSP billing portal, saving valuable engineering time

    - *Data-driven decisions*: Enables teams to make informed decisions regarding resource allocation and cost optimization strategies

- *Enhanced accountability*: Provides a clear picture of cloud spending, promoting cost awareness and responsible resource management

This case study demonstrates the effectiveness of Slack automation bots to simplify cloud cost visibility. By integrating seamlessly with existing communication channels and leveraging resource tagging, the Slack application empowers engineering teams with real-time insights, leading to more informed decision-making and improved cloud cost management.

Chapter Summary

This chapter focused on automation as an essential component of scaling your FinOps practices and ensuring your cloud spending and resources remain as cost-effective and efficient as possible. Key topics included the following:

- *Benefits of automation*: From reducing cloud spend and increasing cloud efficiency to increasing visibility and accountability of cloud resources, automating FinOps procedures helps your teams achieve their goals.

- *Best practices for automation*: This chapter provided a set of proven guidelines for creating automation procedures and policies for managing idle resources and addressing cost spikes.

- *Automated governance*: Leveraging automation to enforce compliance with provisioning policies ensures that developers stick to approved regions and resource types.

- *Real-world case studies*: The case studies demonstrated how companies have achieved their cost management goals through automation.

Automation frees your teams from manually tackling cloud management tasks. It provides a dependable and consistent method of handling cloud management duties so that your teams can focus on more strategic activities.

Next, Chapter 8 will discuss methods, best practices, and tools for efficiently managing software vendors and service providers. Specifically, we will focus on managing software suppliers. We will examine strategies for finding reliable vendors, articulating precise goals for working together, and sustaining robust partnerships. In addition, we will discuss contract management, performance monitoring, and the many strategies for resolving disagreements or problems that may crop up during the engagement with the vendor.

References for Further Reading

https://insights.daffodilsw.com/blog/automation-in-finops

https://www.cloudkeeper.ai/insights/blog/role-of-automation-in-finops

https://towardsthecloud.com/aws-scp-service-control-policies

https://aws-samples.github.io/aws-secure-environment-accelerator/v1.5.2/architectures/pbmm/auth/

https://www.globaldots.com/resources/blog/how-to-automate-your-cloud-resource-cleanup-for-good/

https://www.cncf.io/blog/2021/09/29/automation-is-the-future-of-cloud-cost-optimization/

https://alertops.com/incident-post-mortem/
#:~:text=Incident%20%E2%80%9CPost%2Dmortem%E2%80%9D%20
refers,downtime%2C%20outages%20and%20other%20incidents

CHAPTER 8

Vendor Management

Remember your dream house? When developing it, you will probably work with several contractors and services, including a landscaper, electrician, plumber, gutter cleaning service and possibly even a pool maintenance service, etc. Similar to cloud services, every vendor contributes a different set of abilities and knowledge.

However, what if you hired two electricians for the same job? Or unknowingly subscribed to two different lawn care services? In the world of FinOps, this translates to redundant Software as a Service (SaaS) subscriptions and potential overspending.

Effective vendor management in FinOps is like having a well-organized toolbox for your dream house project. It ensures you have the right tools (vendors) for the job at the right price and that everyone involved (engineering, procurement, etc.) works together seamlessly. This chapter explores the following key aspects of your FinOps vendor management toolbox:

- *Compare build vs. buy options*: Should you invest in building a feature in-house or leverage a readily available SaaS solution?

- *Evaluate vendor costs and overages*: Understand your true cloud spending and identify areas for potential savings.

- *Coordinate engineering and procurement*: Foster collaboration to ensure informed decisions and avoid duplicate services.

By building a comprehensive vendor management strategy, you can

- *Minimize costs*: Avoid unnecessary subscriptions and negotiate better terms with vendors.

- *Improve collaboration*: Break down silos between engineering and procurement for a unified approach.

- *Scale your FinOps projects*: Establish a solid foundation for optimizing your cloud costs as your business grows.

© Sasi Kanumuri, Matthew Zeier 2024
S. Kanumuri and M. Zeier, *Scaling Cloud FinOps*, https://doi.org/10.1007/979-8-8688-0388-8_8

Software as a Service is a sizable component of any organization's operational expenses (OpEx). Keeping track of software subscriptions across business units in large organizations can take time, leading to redundant purchases and lost opportunities to consolidate and improve costs. Effective vendor management solves this problem. The FinOps team can work with procurement to prevent onboarding redundant SaaS applications by ensuring all groups know the capabilities of currently deployed applications.

This chapter examines the crucial facets of vendor management in FinOps, such as comparing build and purchase options, evaluating vendor costs and overages, and coordinating the engineering and procurement teams. Organizations may minimize costs, improve collaboration, and scale their FinOps projects from the bottom up by building a comprehensive procedure for vendor intake requests, negotiating better terms, and preventing overages. So, grab your FinOps toolbox and start building a strong foundation for managing your cloud vendors!

The Importance of Vendor Management

Effective vendor management is paramount for organizations seeking to manage costs associated with SaaS and cloud services. With the increasing reliance on SaaS and cloud solutions, adept management of vendor relationships becomes crucial for optimizing OpEx. Poor vendor management practices can lead to inefficiencies, overspending, and challenges in tracking and controlling costs.

A significant challenge in vendor management arises from the proliferation of vendors, resulting in a complex vendor landscape that complicates negotiations and contract management. Managing numerous vendors can strain resources and make it difficult to ensure alignment with organizational goals. Furthermore, lacking visibility into all costs associated with SaaS products poses a significant problem, often leading to unexpected expenses and challenges in budgeting and forecasting. Consequently, establishing robust vendor management practices is imperative for organizations to mitigate risks and ensure the cost-effective utilization of SaaS and cloud services.

OpEx Impact of SaaS Subscription Costs

In today's digital environment, organizations increasingly rely on SaaS applications to streamline their processes, increase productivity, and deliver value to their customers. Relative to FinOps, these products offer analytics management, communication tools, project management, and customer relationship management. The cost of SaaS applications consumes a significant portion of many organizations' OpEx budget, so managing them effectively and efficiently is vital to ensure financial stability and optimize operating costs.

SaaS applications typically operate on a subscription-based pricing model, necessitating ongoing payments by businesses for software usage. These costs can escalate rapidly, particularly if multiple teams or departments within a company utilize numerous SaaS solutions. The scalability inherent in SaaS products allows businesses to adjust their subscription levels and usage according to their needs, facilitating expansion but potentially leading to increased expenses with rising usage and user numbers.

Moreover, the flexibility offered by SaaS packages enables swift adoption of cutting-edge tools and technologies, albeit with the risk of "SaaS sprawl"—the unchecked proliferation of multiple SaaS solutions within an organization. Each additional tool contributes to OpEx, potentially resulting in redundant functionality and elevated overall expenses if left unmanaged.

Switching to alternative solutions can be difficult for firms relying heavily on SaaS products because of the time requirement to move data, the existing investment in personnel training, and the complexity of integrations among deployed tools. These factors contribute to vendor lock-in, exposing businesses to price increases that impact OpEx as vendors look to increase their return on existing customers.

Another OpEx impact to consider when deploying new SaaS products is the time and money required to integrate them with current systems and data sources. These integration costs should be considered when calculating the overall OpEx to effectively calculate the total cost of using SaaS products.

Although SaaS product costs are part of OpEx, businesses can reduce them by managing vendors, negotiating pricing structures, discovering new technologies, and tracking usage patterns. By carefully evaluating the impact of expenses related to SaaS products within the context of OpEx, businesses can make informed decisions, improve cost efficiency, and allocate resources effectively to meet their financial objectives.

Increasing Visibility into Vendor Costs

Enterprises must prioritize increasing visibility into vendor costs and payments to effectively manage finances, reduce costs, and make informed decisions. This enhanced transparency is essential for addressing the complexities associated with vendor engagements.

Organizations can accurately assess their vendor relationships' financial impact by understanding vendor costs, including subscription fees, usage-based charges, and license prices. Limited visibility into vendor spending complicates tracking and management efforts, making allocating expenses accurately to relevant teams or projects challenging. Consequently, assessing vendor engagement's return on investment (ROI) becomes difficult, potentially hindering cost optimization efforts.

Furthermore, inadequate visibility into vendor costs can disadvantage organizations during contract negotiations. Understanding spending trends, usage analytics, and cost breakdowns enables organizations to negotiate advantageous pricing, discounts, or contract terms. Conversely, a lack of negotiating strength may increase costs and missed savings opportunities.

Moreover, inadequate visibility into vendor expenses and payments poses compliance and audit risks. Organizations rely on accurate tracking of vendor spending to fulfill financial requirements, licensing agreements, and contractual commitments. Ensuring compliance is crucial to avoid noncompliance issues, financial penalties, and damage to the organization's reputation.

Enhanced visibility into vendor costs also enables organizations to identify and capitalize on cost optimization opportunities. Comprehensive information about vendor costs, consumption trends, and alternative solutions facilitates the discovery of areas for consolidation, renegotiation, or elimination of redundant vendors. Organizations may overlook opportunities to reduce costs and enhance overall performance without this awareness.

Organizations should prioritize establishing reliable financial management systems and procedures to address vendor costs and payment visibility. This entails creating detailed records, tracking systems, and technologies offering insight into vendor costs. Organizations can improve financial management and governance by increasing openness and visibility, better contract negotiations, cost optimization, and decision-making.

Pro Tip   Centralize vendor spending data from disparate systems. Pull billing details, purchase orders, invoices, etc., into an expense analytics platform. Cleanse, categorize, and enrich data with advanced algorithms. This creates a unified view of vendor costs company-wide. Automate spend classification with AI and implement real-time expense tracking. Detailed reporting and data visualizations uncover granular insights. Partner with procurement when contracts are up for renegotiation and arm yourself with solid usage analytics. Enhanced visibility maximizes vendor engagement value.

Team Alignment and Collaboration

Effective vendor management requires seamless alignment across teams, encompassing executive leadership, FinOps, and procurement. This alignment ensures that organizational goals are met efficiently and cost-effectively.

Executive buy-in is crucial to provide direction and support for vendor management initiatives. It establishes a clear vision and commitment to prioritize vendor management as a strategic initiative. Without executive buy-in, efforts to optimize vendor relationships may lack the necessary resources and authority to enact meaningful changes.

Collaboration between FinOps and procurement is equally essential to optimizing costs, streamlining processes, and mitigating risks associated with vendor engagements. FinOps teams optimize cloud costs and resource utilization, while procurement teams manage vendor contracts and relationships. By working together, these teams can leverage their expertise to negotiate favorable terms, track expenses accurately, and identify opportunities for cost savings.

When teams are not aligned on vendor management goals, challenges such as fragmented decision-making, conflicting priorities, and missed cost-saving opportunities can arise, leading to increased expenses and reduced operational efficiency. Therefore, establishing alignment among all stakeholders is imperative to driving successful vendor management practices and effectively achieving organizational objectives.

Executive Leadership Alignment

Collaborating with senior leadership is crucial for efficient vendor management and favorable financial outcomes. Executive leadership, including the CFO, CIO, Head of Infrastructure, and other relevant executives, must actively support supplier management and make strategic, data-driven decisions with clear justifications.

First, executive leadership participation drives better vendor management initiatives. Their involvement ensures that all vendor decisions align with the organization's strategic goals and objectives. By collaborating with top executives, the vendor management team gains insights into the company's vision, financial priorities, and technological road map, facilitating informed decisions regarding vendor selection, contract negotiations, and overall vendor management strategy.

Executive leaders also possess in-depth knowledge of the company's financial landscape. The CFO, in particular, plays a crucial role in vendor management by guiding financial risk assessment, cost-saving strategies, and budgetary considerations. Their expertise ensures that vendor decisions are financially prudent, considering financial constraints, cost-benefit analyses, and long-term implications.

Furthermore, executive leaders often leverage valuable connections and networks. Drawing upon their contacts and knowledge, they can provide insights into vendor performance, market trends, and best practices. This information enables comparisons of vendor performance against industry benchmarks, identification of potential risks or opportunities, and access to valuable tools for assessing vendor capabilities and negotiating favorable contracts.

Engaging executive leadership is essential in critical decisions such as vendor selection, significant contract negotiations, and establishing extensive vendor relationships. By involving CEOs in these decisions, businesses can leverage their expertise, advice, and high-level perspective, ensuring that the organization benefits from their experience, subject-matter expertise, and understanding of organizational priorities.

Additionally, collaborating with executive leadership fosters an environment of transparency and accountability. Regular reporting to executives on vendor management activities, performance, and contract negotiations promotes shared responsibility, open communication, and early resolution of potential issues or challenges. This approach facilitates prompt decision-making and course corrections when necessary, ultimately contributing to the success of vendor management initiatives.

Pro Tip   Establish an executive steering committee that meets quarterly to align vendors with strategic objectives. Include leaders from procurement, finance, IT, and critical business units. Discuss upcoming deals, contract renewals, and vendor road maps. Facilitate cross-functional input into critical decisions. Executive committees lend governance, connect workstreams, and maintain visibility as vendor portfolios evolve. Making leadership a collaborative partner improves accountability, consensus, and unified direction for vendor relationships that move the needle.

FinOps and Procurement Collaboration

Effective vendor management depends on the interaction between FinOps and procurement. Together, these two roles can strengthen vendor selection, contract negotiation, cost-cutting, and vendor relationship management efforts by coordinating their efforts, utilizing their specialties, and achieving better results. The following main justifications underline the significance of collaboration between FinOps and procurement in vendor management:

- FinOps teams concentrate on cost research, optimization, and financial management. On the other hand, procurement teams are experts in contract negotiations, vendor evaluation, and sourcing. These teams can work together to coordinate operational and financial objectives. This will ensure vendor selection and management are consistent with the organization's strategic vision and financial goals.

- Vendors must be examined comprehensively for effective vendor management, considering their financial sustainability, product functioning, service level, and contract terms. FinOps teams can offer helpful insights into the effects of working with vendors on long-term costs and financial stability. Procurement teams evaluate vendors' talents, performance, and contractual requirements. Collaboration enables a more thorough assessment considering FinOps factors, improving vendor selection decisions.

- Collaboration between FinOps and procurement strengthens an organization's negotiating position when negotiating supplier contracts. FinOps teams can share information about past expenditure trends, cost structures, and financial limits. Teams in charge of procurement can use their knowledge of pricing structures, contract terms, and vendor relationships. By pooling their knowledge, they can negotiate more advantageous contracts, including price breaks, service level agreements (SLAs), and favorable terms and conditions.

- Collaboration facilitates cost optimization and risk mitigation. Based on data-driven insights, FinOps teams can pinpoint cost-saving areas, eliminate redundant providers, and optimize spending. Procurement teams can evaluate vendor performance, monitor contract compliance, and address possible concerns. FinOps and procurement can proactively spot cost-saving opportunities, reduce financial risks, and boost operational effectiveness.

- FinOps and procurement should cooperate to review vendor performance thoroughly. FinOps teams can provide financial data and analysis to evaluate vendor engagement value. Procurement teams can assess vendors' performance concerning contractual commitments, SLAs, and client satisfaction. Together, they can effectively monitor and evaluate vendor performance by pooling their knowledge, resulting in data-driven vendor replacement or retention decisions.

- Collaborative vendor management promotes continual improvement. Teams from FinOps and procurement can work together to monitor vendors regularly, analyze internal stakeholder comments, and pinpoint improvement opportunities. They can promote ongoing improvement in vendor selection, contract negotiation, cost-saving techniques, and overall vendor relationship management by exchanging ideas and lessons learned.

Team Education

Educating teams about the benefits of vendor products is essential for effective vendor management. Organizations can maximize their ROI and fully utilize their purchased tools by providing thorough knowledge and understanding of vendor solutions' capabilities and functionalities among team members.

First, by educating teams on vendor product features, they can make informed decisions about which products to use and how to use them efficiently. Teams can choose the best tools for their unique needs and requirements by understanding the range of capabilities. Preventing misuse or underutilization of vendor products ensures businesses extract the maximum value from their investments.

Additionally, providing teams with knowledge of vendor product features better equips them to take advantage of all functionalities. Vendor products offer various features and capacities that users need to understand or already know. Organizations can unlock the potential for innovation, process improvement, and increased productivity by educating their teams. Leveraging the sophisticated capabilities offered by vendor solutions, teams can learn new techniques for streamlining workflows, automating tasks, and optimizing work processes.

Educating teams on vendor product features also promotes collaboration and knowledge sharing within the company. When team members thoroughly understand vendor product capabilities, they can share best practices, insider information, and shortcuts. This encourages cross-functional collaboration and enables teams to gain information from one another's experiences, maximizing the organization's collective knowledge and skills pool.

Additionally, training teams on vendor product features ensures timely purchases and introduction of already available products. Teams can identify situations in which their needs can be met without additional tools or suppliers when they know the complete range of features provided by current vendors. Consequently, unnecessary expenses are reduced, the vendor landscape is simplified, and the challenges of maintaining many tools are minimized.

Educating teams about the features of vendor products increases their adoption and satisfaction with these products. When users are familiar with the features and functionalities offered, they can fully leverage the tools' benefits in their daily work, which boosts user engagement, reduces frustration, and improves satisfaction with vendor products. Engaged and satisfied users are likelier to use the tools efficiently, increasing productivity and improving the organization's results.

Pro Tip   Leverage vendor expertise with training and "office hours." Many vendors provide onboarding sessions, online courses, and technical training to support customers. But also have vendors host informal "Ask Me Anything" working sessions where teams can get personalized guidance. Let your teams drive the agenda based on their workflows and pain points. Hands-on training directly from vendor reps builds product expertise and unlocks use cases you may need to look into. Vendors want you to maximize the value of their solutions—take advantage of free training to build knowledge and optimize spending.

Build vs. Buy

Any discussion of vendor management should naturally include a discussion about build vs. buy because it addresses the fundamental decision-making process organizations face when acquiring new capabilities. Organizations must thoroughly evaluate whether to construct or purchase a solution to make an informed choice. This evaluation process, outlined in Figure 8-1, involves analyzing each option's advantages and disadvantages and matching them to the firm's requirements and strategic goals.

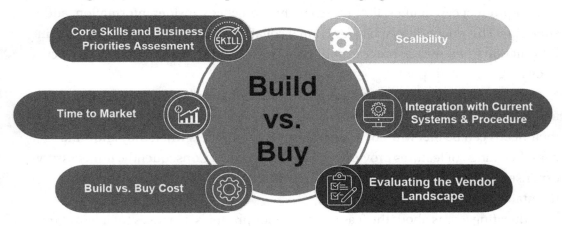

Figure 8-1. *Build vs. buy evaluation process*

Assessing an organization's core skills and business priorities is crucial to the evaluation process. Technical know-how, resources, and the capacity to support and maintain the system over time are needed to build a solution internally. It is possible to ascertain whether developing the solution aligns with the organization's priorities and satisfies the necessary development timetables and ongoing maintenance demands.

Solution development cycles are often longer because it takes time to gather requirements, design, build, test, and deploy a solution within an organization. On the other hand, purchasing a solution provides quicker installation because the product is already created and prepared for use. Companies must assess the urgency of their requirements to decide whether they can wait for an internal solution or whether time is essential.

Costs associated with development resources, infrastructure, upkeep, and continuing support are incurred when a solution is produced in-house. On the other hand, purchasing a solution entails up-front expenses, license costs, and sometimes recurring subscription costs. To choose the most cost-effective solution, organizations must assess the total cost of ownership throughout the system's anticipated lifespan and compare it to the available budget.

Organizations must evaluate their long-term growth goals and solution scalability requirements. When a solution is built in-house, more freedom and control over customization and scalability are available. Purchasing a product designed to address scalability issues might benefit you. Look for a product that has a successful track record in organizations or industries like yours.

Assessing how well the solution integrates with the organization's existing technology stack is vital. Building a solution internally gives you more control over integration, but ensuring seamless interoperability could take time. Purchasing a solution compatible with current systems can simplify integration and lower the likelihood of technical difficulties.

Organizations should assess potential providers' standing, record, and stability before purchasing a solution. Extensive vendor research, customer evaluations, and due diligence can ensure that the chosen solution is supported by a trustworthy vendor with a track record of delivering high-quality products and first-rate customer care.

Eliminating Redundant Vendor Products

Avoiding duplicate vendor goods is critical, especially in cloud cost management. Duplicating vendor products leads to unnecessary cost duplication, which encompasses additional vendor license fees, subscription rates, and maintenance expenses.

Such redundancy escalates operational costs and complicates compatibility and integration efforts, as disparate vendors often employ proprietary software platforms and data formats. Consequently, integrating multiple vendor products may result in inefficiencies, higher maintenance expenses, and increased demand for IT support.

Redundant vendor products pose challenges to collaboration and productivity within the organization. With each vendor's product featuring a unique user interface, feature set, and learning curve, the proliferation of similar functionalities can confuse and divide teams, preventing the development of consistent processes and decreasing productivity. This challenge is further exacerbated when employees switch between various systems, leading to inefficiencies and data management issues.

Furthermore, redundant vendor goods often stem from vendor management and governance issues, necessitating extensive efforts in establishing and managing relationships, contracts, and service level agreements with each vendor. Such complexities detract from strategic vendor partnerships and incur additional administrative burdens and ongoing performance monitoring costs.

By avoiding redundant vendor products, organizations can simplify their vendor management procedures, consolidate spending, and streamline their portfolio, ultimately fostering better negotiation leverage, enhanced customer service, and effective teamwork with fewer vendors.

Comprehensive Intake Forms for Procurement Teams

In any organization, the procurement team is the final gatekeeper for onboarding new vendors and managing negotiations. However, they need information from the engineering teams about the vendor, the product, and why it must be effective. The first step in optimizing the procurement process and ensuring that all necessary data is gathered up front is to create an intake form for engineering teams to complete before a new vendor purchase.

The intake form acts as a standardized template to assist engineering teams in providing pertinent information and needs, facilitating a robust and manageable procurement process. The intake form should include questions that motivate engineering teams to think about various aspects of the purchase decision and act as a liaison to facilitate leadership conversations and alignment. Table 8-1 provides key questions to include in the intake form to help thoroughly analyze the tooling possibilities and guarantee that the procurement choice aligns with the organization's requirements, spending limit, and strategic goals.

Table 8-1. *Intake Form Key Questions*

Question	Explanation
Why do we need the vendor product?	Identify the problems and inefficiencies with the current state and explain how the vendor product can bridge the gap(s). Think of this as an executive blurb explaining why we need the product.
How does this tool align with company goals?	Justify the business objectives and articulate the product's value-add. This avoids nice-to-have purchases and guides teams to quantify impacts on metrics like productivity, quality, or time to market. Demonstrate the contribution to strategic goals to justify the investment and measure ROI.
Alternate tools evaluated?	Identify any other tools that have been evaluated to solve the business need. This ensures that engineering teams have explored other options to determine if better tools are available to meet their needs. Before selecting a vendor, you can compare various devices' features, pricing, and capabilities.
Tooling trade-offs?	Describe the tools assessed and their trade-offs (pros and cons). This information fosters improved collaboration and knowledge sharing across business units and shows that teams have researched products and finalized the best-suited products for their needs. When considering comparable tooling alternatives, teams can draw on the results, pricing structure, and lessons from earlier evaluations.
Number of licenses needed?	Specify the number of licenses required for the tool. Knowing licensing requirements allows organizations to estimate licensing expenses effectively and arrange appropriate distribution. It also ensures that enough licenses are acquired to meet the needs of the engineering teams while preventing pointless costs.
Pricing model?	What's the pricing model for the vendor product/ service? Financial factors are significant in procurement, and the vendor pricing model significantly impacts costs. Organizations can evaluate a product's viability financially and determine whether it is compatible with their budgetary constraints by understanding its pricing structure. Contracts may range widely from per-license to utilization-based models. Pricing information can help make better decisions because it ensures procurement is within budget.

(*continued*)

Table 8-1. (*continued*)

Question	Explanation
Finance blessed?	Has this new software/ hardware been budgeted for? Organizations can ensure procurement follows financial policies and processes by asking whether budget permission has been received. It guarantees that the appropriate financial resources are available to procure the desired tool and prevents potential budgetary challenges or delays.
Leadership approval obtained?	Is the leadership aware of this procurement? The key to successful procurement is leadership alignment. This ensures that key stakeholders are on board and supportive before purchasing. It assists in averting future disputes or difficulties and guarantees that the procurement choice is consistent with organizational strategy.

Organizations can acquire crucial data to direct the procurement process by including these critical questions in the intake form. Making procurement an objective-setting exercise improves spending decisions, ensures investments have a significant impact, and drives data-driven decisions across the organization.

Vendor Deal Strategy and Contract Negotiation

In the quest for cloud optimization, selecting the right vendor and negotiating a favorable contract is crucial. This section delves deeper into crafting a successful vendor deal strategy, the steps will equip you to secure a win-win outcome for your organization.

Building an Effective Strategic Deal Strategy

Crafting a strategic deal strategy involves a comprehensive approach to understanding your organization's needs, researching the market, and ensuring executive alignment.

1. Needs Assessment and Goal Setting

Effective deal strategies begin with thoroughly assessing your organization's requirements and objectives.

- *Align with stakeholders*: Work with engineering and finance executives to comprehend the particular requirements and objectives the vendor's product should fulfill.

- *Describe your success*: Clearly state the goals you hope to achieve, be they lower costs, more functionality, or higher service standards. This shapes the deal strategy to align with your objectives.

2. Market Research and Benchmarking

Conducting detailed market research and benchmarking helps ensure your negotiations are based on solid data and industry standards.

- *Competitive landscape*: Research industry pricing for comparable vendor solutions. Network with peers to understand market rates and benchmark the proposed contract's fairness.

- *Pricing models*: Get acquainted with typical pricing schemes such as usage-based, subscription-based, or tiered models. Examine the vendor's capacity to scale, adjust, and transparently price its offerings to meet changing demands and future expansion.

3. Executive Involvement

Involving critical executives in the negotiation process ensures the deal aligns with your organization's strategic vision.

- *Strategic alignment*: Ensure the chosen vendor aligns with your organization's broader strategic vision. Involve key executives (CFO, CIO, Head of Infrastructure) to review contract terms, negotiated savings, and engineering requirements.

Negotiating for Optimal Value

Negotiating vendor agreements ensures you achieve the best possible value for your organization while maintaining a strong vendor relationship.

Understanding Pricing Structures

Grasping the intricacies of pricing models and leveraging your organization's strengths can significantly enhance your negotiation outcomes.

- *Negotiate the best deal*: Leverage your organization's buying power, market research on pricing models, and network insights to negotiate favorable pricing, discounts, or additional perks. Strike a balance between securing good terms and fostering a positive vendor relationship.

Pro Tip   Leverage the following negotiation tactics:

- *Volume discounts*: Negotiate volume discounts for increased purchases.

- *Migration assistance*: Secure vendor assistance with migrating to their platform.

- *Training and development*: Request training or professional development credits for your team.

- *Longer contract terms*: Consider committing to a longer-term contract in exchange for steeper discounts.

Contract Analysis and Negotiation

Partner with your legal team to meticulously review contract terms encompassing the following key contractual elements:

- Pricing and licensing

- Support and maintenance

- Service level agreements (SLAs)

- Termination provisions

- Intellectual property (IP) rights

> **Pro Tip**   Future-proof the contract by addressing missing features, if applicable. If the vendor promises future feature additions, specify them with deadlines in the contract. Include a clause allowing deal termination if these features are not delivered on time.

Protecting Your Interests

Ensuring your interests are safeguarded when working with vendors is paramount to maintaining a successful and risk-managed partnership.

Exit Strategies and Risk Mitigations

Implementing clear exit strategies and risk mitigation measures is essential for scenarios where the vendor fails to meet expectations. Consider potential vendor lock-in and plan for easy termination if necessary.

- *Termination clauses*: The contract should include clear exit strategies for scenarios where the vendor fails to meet expectations. Consider potential vendor lock-in and plan for easy termination if necessary.

- *Managing overages*: Anticipate potential overages or unforeseen situations during negotiations. Secure additional consumption buckets or user seats within the contract, if applicable.

> **Pro Tip**   Negotiate client responsibility clauses by addressing the following:
>
> - *Hidden costs*: Scrutinize client responsibility clauses to avoid hidden costs. Collaborate with procurement, legal, and compliance teams to negotiate these clauses upfront to ensure clarity for both parties.
>
> - *Renewal rates*: Carefully review rate clauses for potential automatic price increases in subsequent years. Negotiate a reasonable and predictable pricing structure.

Communication Is Key

Effective communication with your vendor is crucial for achieving successful and mutually beneficial outcomes.

- *Transparency and collaboration*: Foster open and honest communication with the vendor. Be transparent about your budget constraints and desired outcomes.

- *Partnering with the vendor*: Engage the vendor account manager and communicate your financial limitations. Explore possibilities for additional discounts or incentives to expedite the deal closure.

Beyond the Basics

This chapter serves as a foundation for effective vendor management. To further enhance your expertise, consider exploring these additional aspects:

- *Common pricing structures*: Learn more about tiered, pay-as-you-go (PAYG), and subscription pricing structures and how they affect cloud budgeting.

- *Negotiation strategies*: To obtain power and negotiate the finest terms for your company, become knowledgeable about successful negotiating techniques. Examine strategies such as mirroring, bracketing, and anchoring.

- *Proofs of concept (PoCs)*: Utilize PoCs to thoroughly evaluate vendor products before full-scale deployment. PoCs allow you to assess functionality, performance, and integration capabilities in a controlled environment.

- *Evaluating support/additional contracts*: Carefully analyze support contracts, considering response times, resolution timeframes, and available support channels. Ensure the support offering aligns with your organization's needs.

Adopting these strategies and continuously refining your vendor management practices can create successful partnerships that deliver optimal value and accelerate your cloud journey.

Negotiating CSP Enterprise Discounts

Finding the right level of commitment is the primary concern during the talks on the CSP contract regarding enterprise discount programs. It's crucial to approach negotiation creatively and create a situation where both parties, CSP and your organization are benefitting from the contract terms. There is no one-size-fits-all answer to the budget you commit to, but there are a few critical factors to consider.

It's important to remember that any CSP prefers commitment and revenue growth. This motivates them to give you a discount, resulting in a win-win situation. Therefore, showing your company's growth trajectory is crucial during the negotiation. You can demonstrate your potential for growth and influence the negotiation's conclusion by pointing to factors like finance team alignment, new region growth, expansion into other industries, client base growth, growth rate estimates, new feature additions, and acquisitions.

Additionally, feel free to ask the CSP representative for recommendations. They frequently offer support and direction throughout the negotiation process, drawing on their knowledge to help you get advantageous terms.

It is essential to be conservative while approaching the commitment amount. If you feel confident about committing $X annually, consider starting the CSP contract discussion at a commitment of $0.7X. With this strategy, you can agree to increase the commitment to the CSP and request additional discount points. Being cautious at first allows bargaining and might result in better terms. For instance, suppose you're confident that your company requires $1 million worth of cloud services annually. By proposing a $700,000 commitment initially, you demonstrate your commitment to the CSP while leaving room for negotiation. The CSP might counter with a proposal to increase your commitment to $800,000 in exchange for a 15% discount on your total spending. This translates to annual savings of $150,000, effectively exceeding the initial $1 million budget estimate while securing a significant discount.

A different tactic to consider is aiming for special pricing discounts, especially if you frequently purchase a service. In these circumstances, you can ask about rate cards or exceptional pricing choices, which offers more significant discounts for high usage cloud services than a traditional CSP Enterprise contract. Determine the most expensive services and contact CSPs to see whether they provide rate cards for specific services, such as storage or data transfer. It's vital to remember that when a rate card is used to purchase a service, a CSP contract cannot be available because the rate card's discount is often more significant.

Choosing between a 3-year plan and a 5-year plan demands careful consideration of the commitment duration. In addition to the higher commitment to CSP, the longer the commitment, the more favorable the CSP contract conditions will be. However, unless there is considerable reliance on the CSP and no plans for significant changes soon, a 5-year commitment may not be advised for startups and companies with fast-changing demands. Consultation with the platform, cloud, and SRE (site reliability engineering) engineering teams can help evaluate strategies for supporting additional CSPs and choose a suitable commitment period. Businesses and growth-stage startups rely heavily on CSP infrastructure, have no ambitions for multi-cloud environments, and could consider a 5-year commitment to take advantage of CSP contract reductions.

Consider negotiating for migration credits during the contract negotiation process, especially if you're planning to migrate workloads from other CSPs or on-premises environments to the new provider. These credits can significantly reduce the cost associated with workload migration. They might cover fees for services such as the following:

- *Data transfer*: CSPs often charge egress fees for transferring data from their cloud environment. Migration credits can help offset these costs.

- *Professional services*: Some CSPs offer migration support services like workload assessment, planning, and execution. Negotiation credits can be applied to these services.

- *Training*: Migration can require training your team on the new cloud platform. Migration credits can help cover the cost of training courses or certifications.

By securing migration credits, you can significantly reduce the upfront costs and complexities associated with workload migration.

The CSP Marketplace is another option to consider when increasing your commitment to cloud spending. Up to 25% of the overall CSP contract commitment, all purchases made on the marketplace contribute 100% toward CSP contract spending. For instance, if your total contract commitment spend is 1 million, anything less than or equal to 250,000 in CSP marketplace spending contributes towards fulfilling the contract. Reaching the appropriate commitment levels and accessing the associated savings can be significantly aided by the CSP Marketplace.

You can secure favorable pricing, optimize cloud spending, and ensure a smooth transition to the new cloud environment by effectively negotiating your CSP commitment contract.

Avoiding and Managing Contract Overages

Avoiding and effectively managing contract overages is paramount for organizations to maintain financial health and adherence to budgetary constraints. Contract overages occur when the organization exceeds vendor limits, usage, or fiscal thresholds. Organizations must implement proactive strategies and measures to mitigate overage risks. By identifying potential overage risks early and taking appropriate actions, organizations can minimize financial losses and ensure optimal utilization of resources.

Clear Usage Policies and Guidelines

Clear usage policies and guidelines for vendor products and services should be defined, communicated to all relevant stakeholders (including engineering teams and end users), and specify acceptable usage thresholds, limits, or quotas for each vendor's product or service. This ensures everyone understands the expectations and constraints of using vendor products effectively. Such clarity promotes accountability and helps prevent misuse or excessive usage that could lead to overages or other issues.

Tailoring Policies by Pricing Structure

It's crucial to tailor usage policies to your specific cloud pricing structure. For example:

- PAYG policies might focus on setting spending alerts and establishing approval workflows for exceeding certain resource usage thresholds.

- RI policies might optimize instance utilization and ensure efficient workload scheduling to avoid underutilization charges.

Monitoring and Tracking Mechanisms

Organizations must implement robust monitoring and tracking mechanisms to manage contract overages to monitor vendor product usage and consumption continuously. By leveraging monitoring tools and analytics, organizations can gain valuable visibility into usage patterns and identify potential overage risks or anomalies. Regularly reviewing usage data enables organizations to proactively identify trends, anticipate potential overages, and take preventative actions to mitigate risks before they escalate. This proactive approach ensures organizations can control their contracts and avoid unexpected financial liabilities.

Cloud pricing structures can significantly impact how you monitor for potential overages. Here's a brief overview of how to monitor common pricing structures:

- *PAYG*: Monitor resource usage metrics (e.g., compute hours and storage consumed) to identify potential overages. Utilize cost monitoring tools and set spending alerts to proactively address approaching usage limits.

- *Reserved instances (RIs)*: Monitor the utilization rates of your reserved instances. Identify idle instances and optimize their usage to avoid underutilization charges. Leverage tools to analyze usage patterns and schedule workloads efficiently.

- *Subscription-based pricing:* Monitor usage trends within the subscribed tier limits. Analyze usage patterns to anticipate potential upgrades to higher tiers before exceeding limits. Consider setting up alerts to approach tier limits to facilitate timely decision-making.

- Monitoring responsibility can vary depending on your organization's structure. A dedicated cloud cost management team or relevant departments like finance and engineering might be involved.

- Foster close collaboration between the vendor management team, finance department, and procurement team to manage contract overages effectively. This collaboration ensures that all relevant stakeholders are aligned and equipped to address overage situations promptly and efficiently. By working with the finance department, organizations can establish a clear process for flagging and addressing overages, enabling proactive management of financial risks. Additionally, ensuring that procurement teams know usage trends empowers them to negotiate favorable terms, including overage provisions, in vendor contracts, thereby mitigating the impact of potential overages on the organization's budget.

- Maintain open communication channels with vendors to address contract overages promptly and effectively. Organizations can gain valuable insights into the reasons behind excess usage by discussing overage situations with vendor representatives, facilitating informed decision-making. Exploring opportunities for exemption or resolution, such as negotiating waivers or adjusting overage charges based on the vendor's policies and the organization's relationship with the vendor, helps mitigate the financial impact of overages and maintains positive vendor relationships.

- Conduct regular usage reviews to assess the necessity and efficiency of vendor products or services. Organizations can reduce the risk of overages and improve cost control by identifying areas where usage can be optimized or consolidated. Working closely with engineering teams and end users to evaluate alternative solutions or approaches ensures that needs are met without incurring additional costs and fosters more efficient resource allocation.

- Establish robust approval processes for requests that incur additional costs or potential overages. Before approving such requests, it's essential to understand the financial impact and budgetary implications involved clearly. Involving finance and procurement teams in the approval process ensures thorough evaluation of feasibility and the economic impact of accommodating the request, contributing to better cost management and budget adherence.

- Periodically review vendor contracts to ensure alignment with the organization's evolving needs and objectives. Evaluating whether the current contract terms and pricing structure adequately address overage risks and provide flexibility is crucial for effective contract management. If necessary, consider renegotiating contracts to include provisions that better manage and mitigate overage situations, ensuring better cost control and budget management.

- Continuously offer education and awareness programs to engineering teams and end users concerning usage policies, budgetary constraints, and avoiding overages. Cultivating a culture of cost consciousness and responsible use across the organization is essential for effective cost management. Additionally, explore technology solutions and automation tools to monitor and control usage, provide real-time alerts on potential overages, and streamline vendor management processes for better efficiency.

- Following an overage incident, conduct a comprehensive analysis to pinpoint the root causes and identify areas for improvement. Utilize the insights from the analysis to refine processes, update usage policies, and enhance future vendor management practices. Implementing these strategies and actions enables organizations to minimize overage occurrences, effectively manage them, and ensure better cost control and budget management within their vendor relationships.

- Automation tools can streamline cost monitoring across different pricing structures. Explore these tools to enhance efficiency.

Automating Efficient License Management

Automating licensing management is essential to maximizing cost efficiency and using available resources within an organization. Tracking and maintaining software licenses, subscriptions, and access permissions for various tools, apps, and services is all part of the process of licensing management. By automating this process, organizations can verify license compliance, cut costs connected with unused licenses, and speed up provisioning and deprovisioning authorizations. Let's discuss the positives and negatives of automated license management and the most effective strategies.

Automated license management can ensure compliance with software licensing agreements and regulations. It allows companies to monitor license expirations, monitor how often licenses are used, and avoid noncompliance problems. By automating license administration, businesses can avoid legal repercussions and financial penalties associated with license infractions.

Enterprises can optimize software license costs by automating license management. This effectively tracks license use and identifies licenses that need to be used or used more effectively. Companies can cut costs on redundant licenses and avoid overspending by reclaiming or reallocating licenses, saving money on licenses that need to be actively used.

When license management is automated, the amount of manual labor required for supplying and deprovisioning licenses is significantly reduced. Due to this feature, granting access to authorized users and canceling access for users who no longer need licenses is streamlined. This results in an increase in resource efficiency, a reduction in the load of administrative work, and the elimination of manual errors in license provision.

Automated license management can provide a more detailed view of license inventory, usage patterns, and renewal deadlines. It allows businesses to generate reports and analytics on license consumption, expenditures, and compliance status. Because of this visibility, decision-makers can make informed choices regarding acquiring, renewing, and optimizing licenses.

Automation makes provisioning and deprovisioning licenses easier. When new users join an organization, automated workflows can facilitate the timely provisioning of licenses based on specified roles or user profiles. This can make it easier for the business to meet its compliance obligations. Similarly, automated deprovisioning guarantees that licenses are immediately recovered whenever users quit their positions or switch roles. This prevents unwanted expenses from occurring.

Pro Tip   Integrate your identity and access management (IAM) system with license management tools. Tie user provisioning/deprovisioning workflows to license assignment and revocation. When an new hire is onboarded in the IAM system, a license is automatically assigned from the available pool. When an employee is offboarded, the license is automatically revoked. Scheduling regular IAM license syncs ensures alignment and quickly reclaims unused permits. This linking of identities to licenses through automation provides visibility, optimizes costs, and maintains compliance as your workforce changes.

Because of the wide variety of licensing models used by different software manufacturers and applications, license management is a complex process. Every type of licensing could call for a different set of integration methods and APIs for automation. Organizations need to understand the licensing models of various software tools to automate license management and adapt to those models effectively.

It can be challenging to integrate license management systems with other IT systems, such as user directories, asset management tools, and procurement systems. Integration must be frictionless to achieve correct user provisioning, license tracking, and reporting through automation. Organizations need to anticipate integration difficulties and develop effective integration frameworks.

It might be challenging to keep track of license utilization in dynamic and dispersed environments. Some licenses may be related to specific people or devices, while others may be based on concurrent users. Organizations must develop the necessary tracking systems to accurately track license consumption across various apps, platforms, and environments.

The Most Effective Methods for Automated License Administration

Effective license administration is crucial for maintaining compliance and optimizing software costs. Implementing automated processes can significantly enhance the efficiency of managing software licenses. Figure 8-2 outlines the critical steps for an effective automated license administration system.

Figure 8-2. *Steps for effective license administration system*

- *Central repository for software licenses*: Maintain a centralized repository to keep license information organized and controlled. This repository should include specifics such as license kinds, entitlements, expiration dates, and users or devices associated with those licenses. A centralized repository makes tracking licenses easier, helps identify usage trends, and automates procedures.

- *Provisioning automated workflows*: Install automated workflows to manage license provisioning better. Automation workflows can be set up to automatically initiate license provisioning based on established user profiles or roles whenever an additional user is added to the organization. This eliminates manual intervention and guarantees rapid access to the necessary licenses.

- *Regular license audits*: Perform frequent audits of your licenses to look for ones that must be used to their full potential. Reports identifying licenses not regularly utilized can be generated more easily with automation. After that, companies can reclaim or reallocate these licenses, cutting unnecessary costs.

- *Notifications regarding license renewal*: Notifications of license renewal should be automated to guarantee on-time license renewals. Ensure license administrators know upcoming expiration dates by programming automated notifications and reminders well in advance. This prevents licenses from expiring unintentionally and saves money by avoiding additional fees associated with late renewals.

- *Integration with the asset management system*: Integrating license management with asset management systems is the best way to track and report licenses. Because of the automated connectivity between these systems, businesses can track licenses and their hardware and software assets. This provides them with comprehensive visibility into the whole licensing lifetime.

- *Continuous analysis of licensing procedures*: Maintaining a consistent review and update schedule for licensing policies ensures they align with evolving software licensing models and the organization's requirements. Maintain awareness of vendor license terms and conditions changes and adjust automated procedures as necessary.

Chapter Summary

Vendors should be treated like partners in building and scaling FinOps/cloud economics from the ground up. The success of any organization's vendor management initiatives depends on developing trusting relationships, being open to dialogue, and having a shared understanding of what is beneficial for both parties. Organizations may successfully traverse vendor management difficulties and produce significant results by encouraging collaboration and transparency.

In this chapter, we covered the following key vendor management topics:

- *Importance of vendor management*: Effective vendor management and enhanced visibility into vendor costs are essential for optimizing operational expenses associated with SaaS and cloud services, facilitating cost optimization, and informed decision-making.

- *Team alignment and collaboration*: Effective vendor management relies on seamless alignment among executive leadership, FinOps, and procurement, fostering collaboration to optimize costs, strengthen negotiating positions, and ensure efficient attainment of organizational goals, supported by thorough team education on vendor product features to maximize utilization and return on investment.

- *Negotiation strategies*: Crafting a successful vendor deal strategy and negotiating contracts requires thorough preparation, effective communication, and skillful negotiation tactics to ensure alignment with organizational goals, fair pricing, executive involvement, legal comprehension, expectation protection, and fostering open communication with vendors for mutual benefit.

Taking a strategic approach to vendor management creates value and mutually beneficial partnerships.

Evaluating and improving vendor management processes is essential as the Cloud FinOps journey progresses. Conducting regular contract reviews, investing in ongoing training, and utilizing technology and automation can further increase the efficiency of vendor management operations.

Organizations can benefit from the knowledge, resources, and innovation that vendors bring by adopting a collaborative approach. By engaging vendors as partners, organizations can open new doors for growth, cost reduction, and operational excellence in their FinOps/cloud economics activities.

References for Further Reading

https://www.calqulate.io/blog/operating-expenses

https://www.icontroldata.net/blog/benefits-of-cloud-vendor-management-payment-solutions

https://www.tonkean.com/blog/benefits-aligning-procurement-finops

https://coresignal.com/blog/data-redundancy/

https://www.cflowapps.com/complete-guide-to-vendor-management-definition-benefits-challenges-process/

https://help.sap.com/docs/strategic-sourcing/supplier-management-setup-and-administration/082b37ccf5254be08fb370f2671de249.html

https://www.sweetprocess.com/intake-process/

https://www.gartner.com/smarterwithgartner/best-practices-for-cloud-negotiation

https://www.financierworldwide.com/negotiating-cloud-contracts

https://upperedge.com/cloud/3-keys-negotiating-successful-cloud-agreements-2/

https://www.cio.com/article/220137/vendor-management-the-key-to-productive-partnerships.html

https://www.withum.com/resources/why-do-most-executives-love-cloud-based-collaboration-tools/

CHAPTER 9

Reviewing Your FinOps Toolbox

Imagine you've built a wonderful new house (your cloud environment). It has all the necessary features and flexibility with smart home technology (scalability, elasticity, etc.). But just like any house, it needs ongoing maintenance and care to ensure it runs smoothly and efficiently (cloud cost management).

At first, you may concentrate on just keeping the lights on and preventing significant leaks to save money. While this is an excellent place to start, your new dream house has yet to be fully used, so you need a comprehensive home improvement plan.

We will discuss the following topics in this chapter:

- The 6-Factor FinOps Formula: Understanding the Flow from Start to Finish

- The #Piggy-Bank Framework: Building Cost Awareness

- Real-World FinOps Success Story: Leveraging the 6-Factor FinOps Formula

- Best Practices for Cloud Cost Management

- Beyond Cost Reduction: The Comprehensive Scope of FinOps

- Building Sustainable Value: Securing Executive Buy-In for FinOps

- The Road Ahead

© Sasi Kanumuri, Matthew Zeier 2024
S. Kanumuri and M. Zeier, *Scaling Cloud FinOps*, https://doi.org/10.1007/979-8-8688-0388-8_9

The 6-Factor FinOps Formula: Understanding the Flow from Start to Finish

The 6-Factor FinOps Formula introduced in Chapter 1 acts like a comprehensive house maintenance plan. It considers

- *Cloud Cost Visibility*: Having clear visibility into how each room (cloud resource) is being used through *smart home technology analogous to cost visibility dashboards*.

- *Cloud Cost Insights*: Understanding how much energy each appliance (service) consumes (analyzing usage patterns).

- *Cloud Cost Optimization*: Adjusting to improve efficiency, like switching to LED bulbs (rightsizing and efficient resource usage), adding solar equipment to use renewable energy (autoscaling), and limiting carbon footprint (sustainability).

- *Automation*: Setting up smart systems to adjust settings (automated cost alerts and guardrails).

- *Cloud Cost Governance*: Establishing house rules to ensure responsible use of utilities (chargeback models).

- *Vendor Management*: Negotiating better rates with your utility providers (negotiating with cloud service providers).

By following this plan, you can not only save money on utilities (cloud costs) but also

- *Improve overall comfort*: By ensuring all rooms function optimally (optimized cloud performance)

- *Increase the value of your house*: Through responsible management and potential upgrades (demonstrating the ROI of cloud investments)

- *Live more sustainably*: By reducing energy waste (optimizing resource utilization for environmental benefits)

Your cloud environment is a continual investment, just like your home. By taking a strategic approach, you can ensure that cloud cost management (FinOps) meets your demands and adds value over time.

As you conclude this investigation into cloud cost management (CCM), you must establish a thorough strategy to succeed in the long run. The 6-Factor FinOps Formula is a robust framework for establishing a sustainable and optimized cloud financial landscape. The following subsections review the six factors of the 6-Factor FinOps Formula and cross-reference the corresponding chapters in which they are covered.

Cloud Cost Visibility: The Foundation for Informed Decisions

The cornerstone of effective cloud cost management lies in cloud cost visibility. This factor emphasizes the need for robust tools and processes to gain granular insights into cloud spending across various services and resources. Envision an intricate dashboard providing up-to-date data on resource usage and associated costs. This level of transparency allows you to make educated decisions, understand potential overspending, and monitor spending trends over time. (Chapter 2 provides an in-depth and detailed understanding of cloud cost visibility.)

Cloud Cost Insights: Transforming Data into Actionable Intelligence

Data without analysis is merely information overload. The 6-Factor FinOps Formula highlights the importance of cloud cost insights. This component explores the potential of data analytics and visualization methods to glean valuable conclusions from your cloud cost information. You may identify areas for optimization and make data-driven decisions that promote continuous improvement in your cloud financial management by examining trends, patterns, and anomalies. (Chapter 3 dives deep into cloud cost insights.)

Cloud Cost Governance: Aligning Cloud Spending with Business Priorities

Effective cloud financial management necessitates a framework for control and accountability. Cost governance addresses this need by outlining the implementation of governance mechanisms. This factor focuses on establishing budgeting frameworks, enforcing cost controls, and allocating costs effectively. You ensure responsible resource utilization and financial discipline by aligning your cloud spending with your broader organizational priorities and policies. (Detailed information on cost governance and policies can be found in Chapter 4.)

Cloud Cost Optimization: Balancing Cost and Performance

Achieving a balance between performance and cost-effectiveness is crucial. The 6-Factor FinOps Formula includes cloud cost optimization, which stresses creating plans and techniques to minimize your cloud expenses without compromising essential features like performance or scalability. This involves identifying areas of overspending, rightsizing resources to eliminate waste, and leveraging pricing models and discounts offered by CSPs. (Chapter 6 elaborates on cost optimization techniques.)

Vendor Management: Building Strategic Partnerships for Mutual Benefit

Cloud vendors play a significant role in your cloud journey. Vendor management within the 6-Factor FinOps Formula underscores the importance of establishing solid relationships with CSPs. Through proficient contract administration, license optimization, and tactical bargaining, you can unlock financial benefits and obtain entry into beneficial services provided by your CSPs. With its deep dive into the nuances of vendor management, Chapter 8 arms you with the information needed to craft winning deal strategies and negotiate successfully.

Automation Framework: Streamlining for Efficiency and Scalability

Imagine automating repetitive tasks associated with cloud cost management. The 6-Factor FinOps Formula emphasizes the significance of an automation framework. By leveraging automation and infrastructure-as-code practices, you can streamline cost management processes. This factor highlights the automation of resource allocation, cost-saving policy implementation, and swift responses to evolving business needs. This focus on automation is covered in depth in Chapter 7 but also interwoven throughout the book, recognizing its crucial role in scaling your FinOps practice effectively.

Road Map for Sustainable Cloud Financial Management

By embracing the 6-Factor FinOps Formula, you have a comprehensive road map for sustainable cloud cost management. This framework transcends mere cost reduction, fostering a culture of continuous optimization, informed decision-making, and collaboration. Remember, FinOps is a journey, not a destination. The 6-Factor FinOps Formula provides the guiding principles to navigate your FinOps journey, no matter which stage—crawl, walk, or run—your organization is in.

The #Piggy-Bank Framework: Building Cost Awareness

As cloud usage proliferates across enterprises, a lack of cost awareness often leads to overprovisioned environments, unused resources, and mounting bills. The #Piggy-Bank Framework provides a structured approach to cultivate a cloud cost consciousness culture across the organization. From driving visibility into cloud usage to educating engineers across the organization, this framework is your guide to successful cloud cost management.

What does the #Piggy-Bank Framework entail?

The #Piggy-Bank Framework aims to institutionalize consideration of cloud costs into technology decision-making. It is built on four tenets:

- *Visibility*: Access to granular data on cloud usage and spending
- *Literacy*: Education on reading usage reports and optimization techniques
- *Shared responsibility*: Collective ownership of cloud costs across teams to reduce waste through peer accountability
- *Thrift*: Regular reviews to incrementally improve efficiency

By ingraining these behaviors across the organization, cloud cost accountability becomes second nature rather than an afterthought.

- **Driving Visibility into Cloud Usage**

The first tenant of the #piggy-bank framework is providing engineers with visibility into the infrastructure costs they directly influence through their choices—instance types, resource sizing, new service adoption, etc. By seeing monthly expenditures broken down at a granular level, they gain perspective on how decisions translate to dollars.

- **Building Literacy Around Cloud Finances**

Making sense of cloud usage reports and drilling into specifics requires basic literacy on cloud pricing models, billing concepts, and optimizing configurations for cost. Training helps contextualize cloud expenses within engineering workflows. Engineers learn how tweaks in provisioning and resource sizing affect the monthly bill.

- **Encouraging Shared Responsibility to Curb Waste**

Peer accountability by shifting the focus from individual blame to a collaborative approach where everyone shares the responsibility for optimizing cloud costs fosters a sense of ownership and encourages different teams to work together toward reducing waste and cost efficiency.

- **Institutionalizing Thrift As a Practice**

Resource optimizations and cost reviews must become a regular ritual. Teams set aside time to analyze usage trends, identify savings opportunities, shut down unused resources, and rightsize instances. Making thrift a habit helps drive down costs.

- **FinOps Teams Drive Adoption**

Dedicated FinOps teams provide tools, training, and frameworks like #Piggy-Bank to instill financial accountability. They lead the culture shift, ensuring cloud costs are no longer an invisible downstream expense.

- **Educating Your Engineers About Cloud Costs**

Rising cloud adoption puts engineers at the forefront of cloud spending decisions. While good for agility, a lack of cost awareness can balloon cloud bills. Educating engineers is crucial.

Engineers influence costs through instance selection, architecture choices, and scaling decisions. However, they often prioritize speed over cost, leading to overprovisioning and waste. Bridging the gap between developers and finance requires making engineers partners in cost management. This can be achieved through training on cloud finances, implementing a collaborative FinOps model, giving engineers cost visibility tools, and fostering a cost-conscious culture through incentives and ongoing optimization practices. With the right knowledge and tools, empowered engineers can become champions of cloud cost optimization.

The #Piggy-Bank Framework provides a proven blueprint for organizations to build cost consciousness at scale. FinOps teams can create a grassroots culture shift that maximizes cloud ROI by driving visibility, education, accountability, and thrift.

Real-World FinOps Success Story: Leveraging the 6-Factor FinOps Formula

Company A, a large organization with over 1,000 cloud accounts and hundreds of millions of dollars in annual cloud spend, faced significant cloud cost challenges: a lack of centralized cloud cost governance and spend tracking. This resulted in limited visibility into overall spending and the potential for waste. The cloud infrastructure team, primarily responsible for ensuring cloud functionality, needed more resources to manage the financial side.

Embracing the 6-Factor FinOps Formula

Company A recognized the need for a strategic approach to cloud cost management and embarked on a FinOps transformation journey. Here's how the Cloud FinOps team part of the Cloud Infrastructure org, leveraged the 6-Factor FinOps Formula to achieve success.

Cloud Cost Visibility: Shining a Light on Spending

The initial hurdle was the sheer number of accounts. To gain control, the FinOps team focused on the top ten spending accounts. Cost dashboards were developed, providing executive and technical teams with deep insight into resource utilization and spending patterns. This newfound visibility helped identify high-cost services and resource allocation across production and non-production environments.

Cloud Cost Insights: Uncovering Hidden Opportunities

The focus on the top ten spenders yielded immediate results. A non-production account containing idle resources from a forgotten POC was discovered. Left unchecked, this account was hemorrhaging money. Company A saved a staggering $1.8 million annually by terminating these resources.

Further analysis revealed another optimization opportunity: unattached volumes not connected to any virtual machines. These "orphaned" resources (cloud waste) cost the company $0.5 million annually. Company A achieved additional cost savings by identifying and optimizing these idle volumes.

Cloud Cost Governance: Shifting Accountability

Previously, the cloud infrastructure team shouldered the burden of all cloud costs. Company A implemented a chargeback model to foster cost awareness and accountability across the organization. This shifted funding responsibility for cloud resources to the individual teams utilizing them.

Initially, chargebacks were handled manually, ensuring every aspect of cloud spend was tracked and allocated. As the program matured, the process was automated, streamlining cost allocation across all accounts.

Cloud Cost Optimization: Continuous Improvement

Despite the initial focus on top spenders yielding significant savings, their costs continued to crawl to the preoptimized state in a few months. To address this, Company A implemented automated guardrails and policies. These included automatically deleting unattached volumes after 30 days, with snapshots created for recovery. This enforced lifecycle management and prevented resource sprawl, ensuring ongoing cost optimization.

Automation: Efficiency Through Technology

Manual chargebacks were time-consuming and prone to error. Recognizing this, the FinOps team in collaboration with the SRE team, automated the chargeback process as the program matured. This ensured consistent and efficient cost tracking and allocation across all accounts. Additionally, Company A developed automation tools for lifecycle management tasks, like automatically deleting idle volumes with backups.

Vendor Management: Leveraging Usage Data for Better Deals

Initially, Company A lacked leverage when negotiating with cloud vendors. However, the comprehensive cost analysis provided by the FinOps efforts yielded valuable insights. Armed with usage data, the company could identify areas for potential discounts. This resulted in a significant win: a 20% discount on a specific storage service, further reducing cloud spend.

Results: A Transformation Achieved

Through the strategic implementation of the 6-Factor FinOps Formula, Company A achieved impressive results:

- *10% reduction in total cloud spend*: A significant cost saving directly impacting the bottom line.

- *Automated chargebacks for efficient cost allocation*: Ensures accurate cost visibility and accountability across teams.

- *Improved cloud cost monitoring with alerts*: Enables proactive cost management and avoids surprises.

- *Implementing automated guardrails for cost optimization*: Enforces best practices and prevents resource sprawl.

- *Reducing cloud waste from 30% to less than 5%*: Optimizes resource utilization and maximizes the value of cloud investments.

Company A's success story demonstrates the power of the 6-Factor FinOps Formula. Organizations of all sizes can achieve significant cost savings and optimize their cloud journey by adopting a data-driven approach and fostering collaboration across teams.

Best Practices for Cloud Cost Management

Mastering cloud cost management unlocks the full potential of your organization's cloud investment. This section summarises strategies for gaining crystal-clear cost visibility, extracting actionable insights, fostering a culture of cost awareness, streamlining cost optimization tasks through automation, and managing cloud vendors effectively. From prioritizing high-impact opportunities to integrating sustainability, this section is a summary of all the tools and techniques to maximize ROI and ensure long-term cost efficiency.

Cloud Cost Visibility

- A well-defined tagging strategy with the following five key components is crucial to optimize cloud cost analysis and allocation:
    - Define a standardized taxonomy relevant to your business.
    - Communicate this framework clearly with all stakeholders.
    - Regularly review and refine tags based on feedback and cost trends.
    - Leverage CSPs and infrastructure as code (IaC) automation tools to ensure consistent tagging during resource provisioning.
    - Enforce tagging compliance through governance tools and automation to prevent untagged resource creation.

    While establishing a tagging strategy requires initial effort, the resulting cost visibility and optimized resource management will deliver significant cost savings in the long run.

- To enhance cost visibility, establish a multidimensional cloud cost hierarchy. This can reflect organizational structure (business hierarchy), development vs. production (resource type hierarchy), or delegation of workload in a top-down approach from the VP to the director to the manager and then the team lead (leadership hierarchy). Leverage tagging to categorize costs and provide top-down visibility for leadership while fostering accountability across teams. This flexible approach allows customization based on your specific needs.

- Leverage cost trend analysis to manage cloud expenses proactively. Analyze costs over various timeframes (MoM, WoW, DoD) to identify spikes, anomalies, and optimization opportunities. Build reports and dashboards with multilevel cost breakdowns for deeper visibility, informed decision-making, and optimized resource allocation.

- Implement executive summary dashboards for high-level financial oversight. These condense key cost metrics into reports and graphs, showcasing overall cloud spend, cost trends, and departmental/

service/account allocations. This allows executives to quickly grasp the financial health of the cloud environment and make informed strategic decisions.

- Leverage technical/team deep-dive dashboards for granular cost analysis. Restrict visibility to relevant teams and tailor reports to actionable insights. Focus on identifying expensive workloads, underutilized resources, and rightsizing opportunities for cost optimization.

- Leverage existing vendor offerings instead of building your own CCM tool when the FinOps team is lean. Evaluate these tools based on VIA criteria: Visibility (cloud services, tags, hierarchies, drill-down, trends), Insights (unit economics, resource utilization, budgeting, forecasting, dashboards, alerting), and Actions (automation, integrations, collaboration tools, training/support, advanced features). Choosing a CCM tool based on VIA ensures you get the visibility, insights, and actions needed to optimize cloud costs and maximize ROI.

- Leverage a shared service cost allocation model to attribute costs fairly across internal departments. Cost transparency through "showback" methods fosters departmental accountability and encourages cost-optimization behaviors even if not directly charged back.

- Proportional cost allocation assigns shared service costs based on each team's overall cloud spend percentage. This simple method assumes higher resource usage translates to a larger share of shared service expenses.

Cloud Cost Insights

- For proactive cloud cost management, leverage cost anomaly detection. This identifies unexpected spending patterns, resource inefficiencies, and unit cost variations. Analyze historical data to establish baselines and compare current costs. Deviations beyond thresholds or statistical significance indicate anomalies. Investigate these to optimize resource allocation and provisioning and implement automated cost controls. This ensures long-term cost efficiency. Ensure you look at all the cloud services you consume and monitor their spend.

- Leverage unit economics to gain a deeper understanding of your cloud spending. Collaborate with your data and application teams to identify key unit metrics relevant to your business, such as cost per gigabyte stored, cost per million API requests, or cost per monthly active user (MAU). Don't be afraid to start with a basic approach using multiple metrics if a single metric isn't readily available. This initial analysis will provide valuable insights, and you can refine your unit economics model as you gather more data. By tracking costs per unit resource (e.g., VM hour, GB storage), you can pinpoint areas for optimization, compare pricing models to find the most cost-effective options, and allocate costs for better departmental or project visibility. Ultimately, this data-driven approach empowers you to make informed decisions on resource selection, configuration, and pricing, ensuring you maximize the value of your cloud investment.

- Continuously identify and eliminate cloud waste to optimize spending. Cloud waste can reach 30%, so ongoing vigilance is crucial. Implement guardrails like automation and quotas to prevent waste from creeping back in after initial cost savings. This ensures long-term cost efficiency.

- Use cloud waste as one of your FinOps success KPIs. It should stay flat or trend downwards over time. Otherwise, you have an immediate problem to address.

- Turn off your non-prod workloads during non-business hours and maintain a calendar of long weekends/holidays during which you can take advantage of additional days of savings.

Cloud Cost Governance and Culture

- Leverage technical program management (TPM) principles to integrate cost awareness throughout the project lifecycle. This can be achieved using intake forms that capture detailed cost breakdowns alongside Jira integration for task tracking and cost discussions. By fostering early consideration of cost factors, teams can make informed decisions and optimize costs throughout development using data-driven insights. In case your company does not have a dedicated TPM department, the person primarily dealing with Cloud FinOps can fulfill the tasks of a technical program manager and work across teams to foster a culture of cloud cost awareness.

- Promote the #Piggy-Bank Framework to cultivate a culture of cloud cost awareness. This collaborative approach uses a Slack/Teams channel to foster open communication and shared responsibility between engineering, finance, and procurement. Regular data visibility, educational programs, and team discussions empower informed decisions and cost-saving strategies. Recognition and evaluations based on cost optimization efforts further incentivize participation. The #Piggy-Bank Framework establishes cloud cost awareness as a core principle by fostering visibility, literacy, accountability, and continuous improvement.

- Cultivate a culture of cost awareness from the beginning of the development lifecycle by integrating a "shift left" approach and ongoing educational programs. "Shift left" empowers engineers to make cost-effective decisions early on by incorporating cost estimation, optimization techniques, and cost-conscious design patterns (e.g., autoscaling) during planning and design. Complement this with regular internal meetups or educational sessions like tech talks, lightning talks, or office hours. These sessions can equip engineers with the knowledge to understand cloud cost implications and best practices, like rightsizing resources and optimizing data storage. By combining early-stage cost considerations with ongoing education, you ensure engineers have the tools and knowledge to make informed decisions that optimize cloud costs without sacrificing performance or functionality.

Cloud Automation

- Treat significant cost spikes as critical incidents. Define thresholds and leverage anomaly detection to identify them promptly. Automate workflows to investigate root causes, including resource usage and configuration changes. Implement automated actions like rightsizing instances or cost optimization. Data-driven analysis helps identify trends and prevent future spikes. This fosters cost accountability, reduces financial impact, and promotes continuous improvement.

- Prioritize automation for cost optimization tasks across communication channels. This minimizes manual effort and ensures consistent cost visibility across engineering, finance, and procurement teams.

- Overcommunication is better than undercommunication. Communicate widely before automating or enforcing a policy. Communication ensures alignment and enables easier troubleshooting when issues arise.

Cloud Cost Optimization

- Focus on high-impact, low-effort cost optimization opportunities. Prioritize initiatives based on a cost-benefit analysis, prioritizing those with significant cost savings and minimal implementation effort. Execute these high-ROI opportunities first to maximize cost savings with minimal resource allocation.

- Go beyond tactical things. Observe resource utilization, query execution times, and other metrics that better depict your workload observability. These metrics can provide insights into where systems can be improved using techniques like autoscaling, auto-stopping, serverless, commit discounts, spot instances, and many more.

- Integrate sustainability into your cloud cost management strategy. Prioritize resource optimization (rightsizing, autoscaling), leverage renewable energy sources offered by cloud providers, and utilize cloud-based sustainability dashboards to minimize your cloud's environmental footprint and associated carbon emissions. This promotes environmental responsibility and can be a competitive differentiator.

Cloud Vendor Management

- Leverage a standardized intake form during cloud resource procurement to justify business needs, ensure budget alignment, and promote collaboration across engineering, finance, and leadership. This streamlines the process, gathers vital data upfront, and fosters cost-effective decision-making.

- The FinOps team must partner with procurement and finance to review every engineering decision with a build vs. buy evaluation, the consequences of operating without the vendor product, and the company goals alignment to ensure that every product procured adds value to the organization.

- Meticulously review vendor contracts to identify potential cost pitfalls, such as overage fees and high renewal costs. Negotiate these terms before signing the contract to optimize long-term spending and avoid overages.

Beyond Cost Reduction: The Comprehensive Scope of FinOps

The rise of FinOps highlights a fundamental shift—cloud financial management can no longer be an afterthought. Organizations are recognizing the need for proactive strategies to maximize cloud value. While cost optimization drives initial FinOps adoption, its scope is much broader.

FinOps establishes organization-wide disciplines for managing cloud spending efficiently by breaking down silos between technology, finance, and business teams. Beyond cost cutting, FinOps enables data-driven cloud investment decisions aligned to business priorities.

Moving Past Cost Reduction

For most organizations, reducing cloud costs is the gateway to FinOps. As cloud bills mount, they implement tools and practices to eliminate waste, improve efficiency, and save money.

But the FinOps journey doesn't end there. Cost is just one, albeit significant, variable. Once organizations have a robust handle on cloud expenses through monitoring, governance, and automation, the focus shifts to linking cloud investments to business value.

The FinOps Journey Begins with Costs

For most organizations, FinOps starts with controlling cloud bills and reducing waste. But over time, they realize it is an enabler of data-driven cloud strategies and decision-making.

FinOps elevates cloud financial management from tactical upkeep to a strategic function, delivering long-term value. It provides the financial guardrails enterprises need to become cloud-smart.

Boosting Visibility and Accountability

FinOps empowers organizations to view cloud spending not as a cost center but as a value center. Granular cloud cost visibility and insights enable finance and engineering teams to have informed discussions on managing budgets.

When business units and product teams own cloud expenses through chargeback/showback models, they are incentivized to optimize resources and become judicious about spending. Accountability leads to more intelligent decisions about cloud initiatives.

Informing Strategic Decisions

By enabling data-driven assessments of cloud spending, FinOps provides the foundation for critical strategic decisions:

- Which workloads should move to the cloud for maximum ROI?

- How can we optimize existing cloud resources to deliver more excellent business value?

- Which technologies, architectures, and providers best align with business goals?

- Are our cloud investments aligned with organizational priorities?

- How do we most effectively distribute cloud budgets between business units?

The insights from FinOps help shape your cloud strategy and technology transformation road map based on sound financial analysis.

Continuous Management Is the Key

Rather than a one-time exercise, organizations must embrace FinOps as an adaptive and iterative competency. Continuous monitoring, automation, and collaboration between finance and engineering teams help drive cost efficiency as a regular discipline.

FinOps matures cloud financial management through improved forecasting, budgeting, accountability, and agility. Monitoring and optimizing cloud costs empowers innovation by making more resources available for development.

Building Sustainable Value: Securing Executive Buy-In for FinOps

Unmanaged and uncontrolled cloud expenses can significantly hamper your company's financial health. Getting executive buy-in is the first step toward building a FinOps team, which has the potential to transform the game.

This road map empowers you to achieve executive buy-in through a collaborative approach:

- Partner with a cross-functional team to identify and quantify high-impact cost reduction opportunities.

- Foster a culture of cost awareness by implementing the #Piggy-Bank Framework and establishing shared communication channels.

- Present a compelling narrative showcasing achieved cost savings and the established culture of cost awareness.

- Develop a scalable plan for a dedicated FinOps team, outlining its mission, vision, and charter.

By demonstrating success and presenting a clear path forward, you can secure executive sponsorship to scale cloud cost optimization across the organization and maximize your cloud ROI.

Beyond Cost Savings: A Holistic Approach to FinOps Value

Often, a FinOps team's first step in winning over executives is highlighting cost savings. However, concentrating only on cost can ignore FinOps's broader value proposition. Here's why a more comprehensive approach is key:

- *Limited view*: A narrow focus on cost reductions can paint FinOps as a cost center, neglecting its strategic role in optimizing cloud ROI. In addition to saving money, FinOps enhances cloud security, promotes agility, and enables informed decision-making.

- *Neglecting systemic change*: FinOps isn't just about immediate cost reductions and driving lasting cultural and behavioral shifts. By promoting collaboration and best practices, FinOps fosters a culture of cloud cost awareness throughout the organization.

- *Siloed ownership*: Focusing solely on cost savings might position FinOps as a finance-driven initiative, limiting its effectiveness. Departmental cooperation (engineering, finance, procurement) is necessary for effective FinOps. FinOps encourages shared accountability for cloud expenditures and uses a variety of expertise to achieve the best outcomes by encouraging cross-functional collaboration.

The 6-Factor FinOps Formula: A Holistic Vision

The 6-Factor FinOps Formula provides a comprehensive road map encompassing visibility, insights, optimization, automation, governance, and vendor collaboration. By mapping FinOps initiatives to these factors, the narrative transcends mere cost reduction and highlights its broad organizational impact.

Selling the Big Picture

- *Cloud Cost Visibility*: Establishes the foundational need for financial transparency before cost optimization efforts.

- *Cloud Cost Insights*: Underscores the importance of data-driven analytics in informing strategic decision-making.

- *Cloud Cost Optimization*: Conveys continuous improvement, not a one-time cost reduction exercise.

- *Automation*: Demonstrates how FinOps elevates cloud financial management beyond manual processes.

- *Cloud Cost Governance*: Highlights the alignment of cloud strategies with broader business objectives.

- *Vendor Management*: Signifies an integrated approach with cloud service providers for optimal value extraction.

This narrative shifts the focus from short-term cost savings to building long-term financial competencies around the cloud. It positions FinOps as an institutionalized strategic initiative rather than a series of tactical cost-cutting projects.

FinOps: A Strategic Imperative

By leveraging the 6-Factor FinOps Formula, FinOps can be positioned as a strategic cloud imperative, not merely a technical exercise. Executives will recognize its value beyond the finance department, enabling

- *Data-driven decisions*: Investment in cloud initiatives guided by priorities and aligned with financial goals.

- *Widespread accountability*: Shared ownership of cloud spending across business units, fostering financial responsibility.

- *Enhanced financial acumen*: Developing organization-wide cloud financial literacy and expertise.

- *Risk mitigation*: Establish actionable insights into utilization, spending, and forecasting inform risk reduction strategies.

- *Demonstrable ROI*: Aligning cloud spending with business outcomes for measurable returns.

- *Dynamic planning*: Implement accurate budgeting facilitates agile planning and efficient resource allocation.

By emphasizing these long-term benefits, the 6-Factor FinOps Formula establishes FinOps as a vital business initiative worthy of executive sponsorship. While cost savings offer an initial selling point, the 6-Factor FinOps Formula unlocks a compelling value narrative that resonates with executives, fostering sustainable FinOps adoption. This framework empowers companies to embark on the FinOps journey with a clear road map and unwavering executive confidence.

The Road Ahead

Cloud computing has fundamentally transformed modern organizations' operations, offering immense opportunities for innovation, agility, and cost efficiency. However, to fully realize the cloud's promise, organizations must master the art and science of CCM and optimization.

In this comprehensive guide to Scaling Cloud FinOps, we explored the emerging discipline of FinOps and delved into practical strategies, frameworks, and tools to effectively manage cloud costs at scale. Through the journey across critical topics like cost visibility, governance, insights, automation and vendor management, key lessons, and best practices, we have emerged to pave the way to accelerate cloud financial success.

As emerging technologies proliferate and cloud adoption accelerates, the economic principles of the cloud will only grow in significance. The insights and frameworks contained in this guide provide the blueprint to build robust FinOps practices. While the destination is clear, the road may yet take unpredictable turns.

New services and pricing models will emerge, requiring organizations to adapt and evolve their approaches. Domains like cloud security, sustainability, and industry regulations will intersect with cost management in novel ways. Against this dynamic backdrop, fostering a culture of experimentation, knowledge sharing, and continuous learning becomes critical.

Cloud cost optimization is a journey of minor incremental improvements that compound over time. Each 1% of efficiency gained through an improved process or technology innovation adds to the vision of operational excellence. For visionary organizations, FinOps presents an opportunity to gain a strategic advantage—by optimally harnessing the economic potential of the cloud.

The principles and strategies covered in this guide reflect proven approaches that pave the path to scalable and sustainable CCM. While the specific tactics and tools may change over time, the core tenets of cross-functional collaboration, automation, and a culture of ownership will endure. By instilling these timeless lessons, businesses can confidently navigate the road ahead.

The possibilities of the cloud remain largely uncharted. As cloud technologies continue their relentless march forward, so must FinOps practices to keep pace. With the rapid rate of change, no one can anticipate what the cloud landscape will look like years from now. However, the principles of visibility, optimization, and governance will form the guiding light to help organizations unlock future innovations in a financially responsible way.

CCM calls for equal parts strategic vision and meticulous execution. With the frameworks and recommendations contained herein, practitioners now have an authoritative guidebook to advance their FinOps journey. As the cloud transforms industries in ways we cannot yet fathom, scalable cost management capabilities will be the critical differentiator between industry leaders and laggards.

Immense value is waiting to be unlocked from cloud deployments through further optimization. Organizations will realize the cloud's full economic potential by staying vigilant and striving for continuous improvement. The principles covered in this guide represent today's best practices and emerging trends in CCM.

With these lessons and a vision for the future, organizations now have a road map to build world-class FinOps practice and fully harness the power of the cloud. Though the destination seems distant, the next step forward is directly before you. So, contemplating the road ahead, take that step confidently, cognizant that this journey requires persistence but promises sizable rewards.

Index

Y, Z

Printed in the United States
by Baker & Taylor Publisher Services